THE
LAST
STAND
OF THE
RAVEN
CLAN

A STORY OF IMPERIAL AMBITION, NATIVE RESISTANCE, AND HOW THE TLINGIT-RUSSIAN WAR SHAPED A CONTINENT

GERALD EASTER
AND MARA VORHEES

PEGASUS BOOKS
NEW YORK LONDON

THE LAST STAND OF THE RAVEN CLAN

Pegasus Books, Ltd.
148 West 37th Street, 13th Floor
New York, NY 10018

Copyright © 2024 by Gerald Easter and Mara Vorhees

First Pegasus Books cloth edition November 2024

Interior design by Maria Fernandez

Alexander Archipelago / SE Alaska map on page xiii and Refuge Rock map
on page 66 courtesy of Julie Witmer Maps.

Endpapers map of Arctic Sea and Eastern Ocean from the Naval Ministry
of the Russian Federation 1844, courtesy of US Library of Congress.

All rights reserved. No part of this book may be reproduced in whole or in part
without written permission from the publisher, except by reviewers who may quote
brief excerpts in connection with a review in a newspaper, magazine, or electronic
publication; nor may any part of this book be reproduced, stored in a retrieval system,
or transmitted in any form or by any means electronic, mechanical, photocopying,
recording, or other, without written permission from the publisher.

Library of Congress Cataloging-in-Publication Data is available.

ISBN: 978-1-63936-736-8

10 9 8 7 6 5 4 3 2 1

Printed in the United States of America
Distributed by Simon & Schuster
www.pegasusbooks.com

For our intrepid travel companions,
Shay Lydon and Van Vorhees

There is not one Lingít person, from the most modern corporate executive to the most unsophisticated villager, from the oldest great-grandparent whose dim eyes can see only memories to the youngest child who has just learned to form the words, who will not say "This is our land, for we still belong to it. We belong to Lingít Aaní."

—Ernestine Hayes, *Blonde Indian*

Contents

Glossary

Aleut: Russian term referring to the Unangan and Alutiiq people of southwestern and south central Alaska.

Alutiiq (pl. Alutiit): Indigenous groups that traditionally inhabited the central coast of Alaska, including the outer Kenai Peninsula, Prince William Sound, Kodiak Island, and the Alaska Peninsula, also called the Sugpiaq.

Anóoshi: Tlingit name for Russians.

at.óow: Tlingit word for sacred clan-owned items that cannot be claimed by an individual. Might refer to names, houses, stories, songs, land, images of animals or the supernatural, and objects made with the images of those things.

baidarka: Lightweight kayak made from a driftwood frame with a taut sea lion skin cover, used by Indigenous groups in the Aleutian Islands.

Chaatlk'aanoow: Tlingit settlement and fort site at Point Craven at the southern tip of Chichagof Island, built and abandoned by Angoon clans, and later temporarily inhabited by the Sitka Kiks.ádi, after the Battle of 1804 and the Survival March.

Chugach: A branch of Alutiiq (Sugpiaq) peoples inhabiting Prince William Sound and the Kenai coast.

Gájaa Héen: Tlingit fishing grounds, site of the first Russian fort (Fort Saint Michael) near Sitka, now known as "Old Sitka."

Haida: Indigenous group who originally inhabited Haida Gwaii, an archipelago off the coast of present-day British Columbia.

hít: Tlingit for house, a social unit and the structure where an extended family lived.

Hoh: Indigenous people who originally inhabited the coastal areas in present-day Washington State, today considered a branch of the Quileute.

Kashaya Pomo: Indigenous group in Northern California that originally inhabited the coastal area in what is now Sonoma County, also known as the Kashia Band of Pomo Indians.

Kolosh: Russian name for the Tlingit, from *kolyozh*, the Chugach word for "alien."

kwáan: A people's ancestral place or traditional territory. There are twenty-one recorded traditional territories of the Tlingit, and these are at the heart of the way that Tlingit associates the relationship between peoples, clans, and lands.

Lingít: Tlingit

naa káani: Member of opposite clan commissioned to conduct a ku.éex', or potlatch. The naa káani helps to invite the other guests, and serves as "master of ceremonies" at the ceremony.

New Archangel (Novoarkhangel'sk): Russian name for their settlement at Sitka.

New Russia (Novorossiya): Russian name for their settlement at Yakutat.

Noow Tlein: Original Tlingit village and fortification in Sitka on the site later called Castle Hill by the Russians.

potlatch (ku.éex'): A traditional celebration common among the Tlingit, Haida, and other Indigenous groups in the Pacific Northwest. A Tlingit potlatch is often hosted by a clan or clans of the same moiety, with the guests being of the opposite moiety.

promyshlennik (pl. promyshlenniki): Russian hunter, fur trader, and/or mercenary in Siberia and Alaska.

Quileute: Indigenous people who originally inhabited the coastal areas of Washington State.

Saint Paul Harbor: Russian settlement established by Baranov on Kodiak Island, now called Kodiak.

Shís'gi Noow: "Fortress of the Saplings," the Kiks.ádi stronghold during the Battle of 1804.

Three Saints Harbor: Russian settlement established by Shelikhov on Kodiak Island, now called Old Harbor.

Tsimshian: Indigenous people who were the original inhabitants of the coastal area of British Columbia.

Unangan: Original inhabitants of the Aleutian Islands, called Aleuts by the Russians.

Xutsnoowú: "Fortress of the Bears," Tlingit fort and village at Angoon.

Tlingit Names and Places

The Tlingit language (Lingít) was first written down by Russian Orthodox missionaries, who used Cyrillic script to record and translate. Throughout the nineteenth and much of the twentieth centuries, anthropologists and explorers used ad hoc phonetic transcriptions, resulting in great inconsistency in the spelling of names and places. In more recent years, American and Canadian scholars have established more accurate and consistent phonetic orthographies. In this volume, we have used the modern American orthography which is the preference of the Tlingit speaking community in Southeast Alaska. Diacritical markings are used extensively to indicate pronunciation, including differences in tone (high versus low) and where the sound originates (lips versus tongue versus throat), all of which can impact meaning.

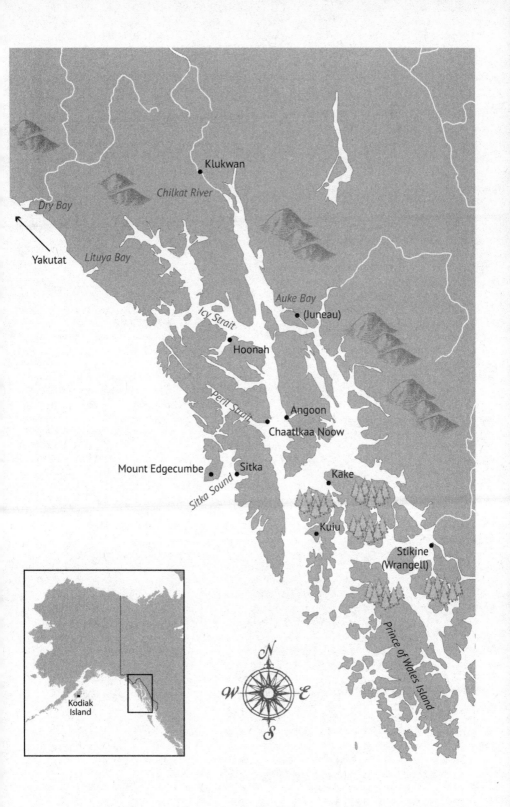

Klukwan

Chilkat River

Dry Bay

Yakutat

Lituya Bay

Icy Strait

Auke Bay

(Juneau)

Hoonah

Peril Strait

Angoon

Chaatlkaa Noow

Mount Edgecumbe

Sitka

Sitka Sound

Kake

Kuiu

Stikine
(Wrangell)

Prince of Wales Island

Kodiak
Island

N

W   E

S

Raising the Past

With an indignant croak, a glossy raven took flight from its canopy perch as a heavy dugout canoe splashed into the Indian River below. Concealed in the mist, the craft skimmed along the shore to a spot where a crowd had gathered. The crew issued a startling cry as the high-pointed prow cut through the gray curtain. The amassing spectators on land spun in unison to see the cloaked figures on the water raising their paddles skyward. It was, in fact, a friendly gesture. Recognizing the traditional Tlingit request for an invitation, the Raven clan hosts on shore beckoned the Eagle clan guests at sea to join the celebration. It was late September 1999, in Sitka, Alaska, and the occasion was a totem pole raising.

More than two thousand rain-soaked enthusiasts convened at Totem Park on the south side of Sitka to dedicate the city's latest carved creation—a memorial pole in honor of the Tlingit warrior K'alyáan and the Battle of Sitka of 1804. Beyond southeast Alaska, neither K'alyáan nor the Battle of Sitka feature prominently in Native American history. Yet the man and the conflict profoundly shaped the destiny of North America. Today, the geo-political configuration of the continent is defined by the colonial descendants of the Spanish, the British, and the French. But not the Russians. It did not have to be this way. Just as a Spanish inheritance defines the southern end of the continent and a French inheritance defines a sizable section of the eastern middle of the continent, a Russian inheritance of some kind, if not Russia itself, might have permanently occupied the northwestern flank of North America.

XVI   PROLOGUE: RAISING THE PAST

By the onset of the nineteenth century, the Russian Empire already reached across the Bering Sea and Aleutian Islands to the Alaskan mainland. The objective of this expansionist project was to corner the lucrative North Pacific fur trade and colonize the American coastline down to Northern California. The audacious scheme was moving apace until the tsar's plunderers were finally confronted and stalled in Sitka. In response, Russia launched its first and only military assault on the American mainland. Ultimately, it was neither Old World superpowers Spain and Britain nor New World upstart the United States who thwarted Russia's grand ambitions, but a defiant band of Tlingit warriors, led by the Kiks.ádi leader K'alyáan.

A caravan of six yellow buses pulled up to the park entrance, spilling out the student body of Mt. Edgecumbe High School. The crowd swelled, the rain picked up, the mood was cheery. The site chosen for the K'alyáan pole was a snug clearing amid a hundred-acre stand of spruce and hemlock. To the local Tlingit community, this forest glade was hallowed ground, where ancestral blood had been spilled nearly two hundred years earlier. It marked the former location of Shís'gi Noow—Fortress of the Saplings—an ingeniously designed rainforest stronghold, where the culminating battle in the Tlingit-Russian war took place. And while the land straddling the Indian River was set aside by the US federal government in 1890, making it Alaska's oldest national park, it was not until this day that the epic struggle would receive official recognition, Tlingit-style.

"Ever since I became leader of the Kiks.ádi, the K'alyáan pole has been in my mind," said clan head Al Perkins, a descendant from the line of K'alyáan himself. All of Tlingit society is divided into two lineage groups, represented by the Raven and the Eagle. The Sitka-based Kiks.ádi belong to the Raven side.* When it was Perkins's turn to assume leadership, the

---

* Clans are the main economic, social, and political unit in Tlingit society. Traditionally, local clans hosted ceremonies, engaged in trade, organized hunting parties, cooperated or fought with other clans, and controlled territories and resources. All clans belong to one

elders tutored the young man on Tlingit oral history and entrusted him to preserve and pass on the story of the Battle of Sitka. "Al, you will never forget our ancestors, our way of life, and the way our people lived," Perkins was told. It was a formidable challenge.

Throughout the nineteenth century, the sons and daughters of Tlingit-Russian war veterans gathered annually to mourn at the site of Shís'gi Noow, but by the middle of the twentieth century, memories of the battle had begun to fade. During World War II, the US Army took control of the park, closing off access to the public and converting the grounds into an ammunition depot. After the war, the neglected and overgrown site became the local lover's lane. Then, in the 1980s, a minor civic event galvanized Kiks.ádi leader Al Perkins.

In 1989 local businessman Lloyd Hames gifted the town a statue of Alexander Baranov, touting the founding governor of Russian Alaska as an icon of commerce. To the Tlingit community, Baranov was better known as the harbinger of destruction, who had led the Russian assault on their homeland. The celebration of their antagonist in a prominent public space infuriated Al Perkins. "When the statue commemorating Baranov went up, I knew that a memorial for K'alyáan must rise as well," he said. Perkins convened a meeting of clan leaders, whose ancestors had fought at the Battle of Sitka. "This kind of project entails a lot of community support," he observed. The Kiks.ádi leader persuaded fellow clan elders to pool resources, eventually raising $50,000 to finance a memorial pole.

Next, he needed to find someone who could bring his vision into reality. He approached Tommy Joseph, a Tlingit artist and master carver of the Eagle-descended Kaagwaantaan clan. Because the K'alyáan pole was the inspiration of Raven-affiliated clan elders, it was Eagle clan members who

---

of two lineage groups, or moieties, identified as Raven or Eagle. Traditionally, the society is exogamous and matrilineal, which means individuals marry someone from the opposite moiety, and children are born into their mother's clan. Tlingit culture displays a strong emphasis on social balance between moieties.

organized the ceremony. Tlingit custom has long dictated that family and friends from the opposite group, Raven or Eagle, are expected to take responsibility for managing important life observances—such as weddings, funerals, and housewarmings—for their clan counterparts. For centuries, totem pole raisings were among the most momentous occasions for Tlingit households. But the practice had fallen out of favor during the US government's forced assimilation campaigns. The ancient art form was nearly lost, save for a handful of master carvers, who discreetly kept the old knowledge alive for a later generation to utilize.

At thirty-five-years old, Tommy Joseph was particularly young to be a master carver. Short in years but long in experience, Tommy had been hooked on woodcrafts since elementary school in his hometown of Ketchikan, studying the city's rich collection of nineteenth-century Tlingit and Haida totem poles and apprenticing with the last remaining traditional carvers. He was a virtuoso in form line art, the distinctive northwest drawing style of curvilinear animated figures. Tommy later said that the commission from Al Perkins was "the biggest pole that I had ever worked on."

Tommy sketched numerous drafts of the pole in accordance with the wishes of clan elders. Each Tlingit clan has its own crest, inspired from nature, conveying a legend about their origins and history. His task was to incorporate these crest images in a nimbly balanced and continuously flowing design concept. For a year and half, Tommy could be found daily in the carving shed of the Indian Cultural Center at the national park, along with assistant carver Tim Beltran. With long black hair and a flannel shirt, he patiently worked the handheld adze, rasps, and traditional tools to turn the rough-grained cedar trunk into a visual epic. The sculpted clan crests were made vivid with red, turquoise, black, and white paints.

Tommy did not just carve the K'alyáan pole, but acted as maestro on the day it was erected. It would be a traditional Tlingit pole raising—"the way things were done in the old days"—by hand, using the strength of the community to lift the monument skyward.

The rain fell harder. Tommy coaxed a path through the crowd and strode to the center of the clearing. The pole rested horizontally, its base lined up over a deep hole and its middle propped up on a crossbeam, cradled by two tripods, which Tommy had fashioned out of tree limbs. Six anaconda-thick ropes were tied around the midsection. Tommy made a final check of the rigging and the crossbeams, then delivered instructions to the six teams of volunteers. He looked to Al Perkins for a cue. *Ready*. The Kiks.ádi leader had envisioned this moment for more than a decade. *Pull*. A resounding grunt went through the clearing.

Lifting a thirty-five-foot pole by hand requires brawn and balance. If the top weight gets too far out from the center of gravity, the pole can easily snap. The six lines were secured two in front, one on each side, and two behind. Teams of more than a dozen volunteers gripped each of the ropes. The Eagle-descended Kaagwaantaan clan manned the frontline teams, providing the brute strength to lift the massive log off the ground. The morning showers had softened the grass, which turned to mud under the trampling rope teams. The frontline haulers slipped on the soggy turf and fell on their knees. The heavy shaft wobbled, then lurched dangerously sideways toward the spectators. Looking the part of orchestra conductor, Tommy stood intently focused in the center and coordinated the multiple players all around him. He waved his arms furiously and barked orders—right, right, left, forward, steady. And the pole was vertical again.

While looking upward to gauge its position, Tommy sighted a bald eagle and black raven swirling above the treetops, monitoring the commotion below. It was an auspicious sign. The great pole teetered upright. The crossbeams bracketed the weight over the freshly dug hole. More volunteers rushed to the base to secure the monument in place. Cheers rang out. Tears were shed. The rain fell.

The spectators beheld the vibrant stacked figures, depicting the story of the Battle of Sitka. Eyes fixed on the raven head at the base. Contrary to popular notion, the rank order of a totem pole starts at the bottom, not the top. "Ignorance of Native culture has resulted in the misleading figure of speech about the low man on the totem pole," Tommy Joseph said. "The most important figure is the lowest on the pole." At the base was a carved homage to K'alyáan. It was a likeness of the raven war helmet worn by the Kiks.ádi war commander in battle against the Russians. With a realistic black beak and feathered raven's head, the war bonnet is among the most sacred relics to the Tlingit, no less so than the Liberty Bell is to Americans. Tommy re-created the helmet in eerie detail, down to the raven's gleaming copper eyes.

The pole pays tribute to the Tlingit bands that joined forces in the Battle of Sitka. Moving up the pole, K'alyáan's war helmet is embraced by an upright frog, representing the Kiks.ádi, the Sitka clan that led the effort against the Russians. Next up is a beaver, the crest of the Deisheetaan clan, close allies of the Kiks.ádi, who played a crucial role in the final outcome.

Three more crest images were carved one on top of the other—a dog salmon, a sockeye salmon, and a woodworm, representing the L'eeneidí, L'uknax̱.ádi, and G̲aanax̱teidí clans, respectively, all of whom belong to the Raven side of Tlingit society. Thus, at the very top of the pole is a large black raven, resolute in its gaze, uniting the ancestors who bravely resisted the Russian assault on the Tlingit homeland and serving as an honor guard over the sacred ground of Shís'gi Noow.

"Today is the day that we come together, and it is now time to celebrate," said Al Perkins. Tlingit songs and dances were performed in traditional robes and regalia. Dishes of local native cuisine were served from ornately carved ceremonial plates. Each of the elders told their own clan's account of the Battle of Sitka. Rarely seen clan relics were put on display, including K'alyáan's raven helmet and his blacksmith's cudgel. The guests crowded in to get a closer look at K'alyáan's war crown and favorite weapon. Taking in the day's events, Al Perkins was gratified to see a promise to his people fulfilled. "This is going to be something to remember for a long time to come."

PART ONE

CHAPTER 1

Raven Makes the World

A skein of mist weaves through the columns of spruce and coils around the steep mountain backdrop. The gray vapor settles over Noow Tlein, a cluster of longhouses poised atop a bluff overlooking Sitka Sound. With commanding views of the wooded shoreline and islet-dotted bay, Noow Tlein was the nerve center of a major Tlingit settlement. The Sitka _ḵwáan_, or village, was nestled on the seaside of a rugged island at the western edge of the archipelago that runs along the Alaska panhandle. The Pacific Northwest is a land of snow-capped peaks and ice-chiseled fjords, evergreen forests and cascading streams, orca whales and brown bears, and relentless rain. For thousands of years, it has been the home of Tlingit nation.

The Na-Dene-speaking Tlingit are distantly related to the southern Navajo and Apache people. The Tlingit migration path into the Western Hemisphere started south, turned west toward the Pacific around British Columbia, then back north through the archipelago, eventually reaching the Gulf of Alaska. Bordered in the east by the continent's tallest mountain range and in the west by an infinite sea, Tlingit country is a five-hundred-mile sliver of coastal rainforest. Sitka was one of a dozen major Tlingit settlements within this primeval realm. With access to abundant natural resources and lucrative trade routes, Sitka was a healthy and prosperous community. On the eve of first encounters, in the mid-eighteenth century, the Sitka _ḵwáan_ was home to roughly a thousand people, about one tenth of the total Tlingit population.

Like all Tlingit kwáan, the Sitka community comprised both Raven and Eagle matrilineal clans. To maintain social balance, Raven-descended clans were connected to Eagle-descended clans through networks of marriage and norms of reciprocity. The clans, in turn, were organized into autonomous houses (hít), where extended families lived, sheltering sixty people or more. The Tlingit had a social hierarchy, with the houses of elite families at the top of clan society. The structure was not fixed, however. A house could rise and fall in status, based on family size, accumulated wealth, or strong personalities. There was no all-powerful chief in Sitka. Each clan in the village and each house within the clan had its own elder authority figures—headmen, warriors, and shaman. Village-level decisions, when necessary, were made collectively at a council of elders.

Noow Tlein was the base of the Kiks.ádi clan, one of Sitka's most prominent Tlingit bands. It was the stronghold of Shk'awulyeil, head of the Point House, a long-reigning elite family among the Sitka Kiks.ádi. The Raven-descended Kiks.ádi were aligned with the Eagle-descended Kaagwaantaan. Keeping with Tlingit norms, Shk'awulyeil was the son of a privileged elder of the Kaagwaantaan clan, but raised by his maternal uncle in the Kiks.ádi clan. When he came of age, Shk'awulyeil inherited his uncle's role as clan leader. Now he was ready to stake claim to a higher position for the Sitka Kiks.ádi within Tlingit nation.

As the winter solstice approached, Noow Tlein was in darkness for almost eighteen hours a day. The extended Point House family had vacated their summer camps and were gathered together under one roof. The longhouse was a spacious chamber, with levels leading down to the central fire pit. Smoke billowed out a large hole in the roof above. Along the sides were closeted sections for individual families to sleep and store their belongings. The headman's family lived at the back of the house, behind a form line–painted screen. Here, Shk'awulyeil and his clan relatives were plotting a power grab. But it was neither a military assault nor economic plunder that concerned them. They were planning a party.

Beneath a flickering seal oil lamp, the Kiks.ádi elders were preoccupied with the final details of a potlatch feast. A potlatch was not merely a lavish banquet for friends and relatives, it was a political campaign, meant to reward followers and impress rivals. An uninspiring potlatch would diminish the reputation of the hosting house and its presiding head. A well-orchestrated potlatch would bolster the power ranking of the Sitka Kiks.ádi throughout the northwest archipelago. Shḵ'awulyeil was anxious for the affair to go well.

The elders considered whom to invite. Of course, the village house leaders and families would attend. Invitations would also go out to clan leaders in distant Tlingit settlements, with whom the Sitka Kiks.ádi sought to build security and trade relations. They decided to invite the Eagle-descended Kaagwaantaan from Klukwan on the Chilkat River and the Raven-descended Deisheetaan from Xutsnoowú in Angoon. Shḵ'awulyeil then chose two high-ranking elders to serve as *naa káani*, the official envoys of the clan, who would travel by canoe into the archipelago to entreat the special guests. The Tlingit were a status-conscious people.

Preparations for the potlatch had been ongoing throughout the year. Specialty foods were harvested, cooked, and preserved for the great feast. Fur-bearing animals—such as otter, beaver, and mountain goat—were hunted, skinned, and processed into coverlets and blankets. Rare commodities, such as copper, jade, and caribou antler, were acquired through trade and fashioned into jewelry and tools. The more generous the gifts, the more applauded the potlatch.

All the members of Point House were mobilized for the big event. Other Kiks.ádi house heads came to Shḵ'awulyeil, offering to provide gifts and food as well. Not all families were wealthy enough to host a potlatch, so this was an opportunity to gain recognition for a particular house and to contribute to the clan's overall good fortune. As the solstice drew near, the Kiks.ádi rehearsed songs and dances late into the night in the glow of the large fire pit. Leaving nothing to chance, Shḵ'awulyeil went out in the early mornings for ritual bathing in the cold sea to cleanse the spirit of the Point House.

On the day of the celebration, mad barking on the beachfront roused the occupants of Noow Tlein. All Tlingit villages kept dog packs to guard against wild animals and sneak attacks and to accompany the hunt for deer, goat, and bear. The howling brought a small crowd to the edge of the cliff. The first canoes were arriving from Angoon. The Deisheetaan leader sat prominently in the bow of a large cedar canoe, holding thirty people. His retinue was close to a hundred guests. Soon after, the Kaagwaantaan leader arrived in a wide cottonwood canoe, commanding scores of clan relatives from the large Klukwan village to the north.

The Kiks.ádi ran down to the beach to greet their guests. Still on the water, the visitors stood upright in their canoes, flaunting their finely made robes, headwear, and jewelry. All the guests rose and broke into song. It was the beginning of a familiar Tlingit call-and-response ritual. When the song ended, the Kiks.ádi on land answered with their own salutations. The mutual serenading went on for more than an hour. Finally, Shḵ'awulyeil came forward. He was wearing a lustrous beaver cloak with eagle down sprinkled in his long black hair. The Kiks.ádi summoned their guests to haul their canoes onto the beach and welcomed them to Sitka.

Tell us a story about Raven, grandmother. A clan matriarch, wrapped in a lynx-trimmed robe, gathered the children in a close circle. In the Pacific Northwest, Raven is muse and protagonist of countless stories that entertain and explain. Raven is akin to the coyote in Navajo lore—intelligent, willful, troublemaking, and the central character of origin myths. Raven, or *yéil*, made the tides, the salmon, and the people, although not from any grand plan or benevolent motive. Raven acts from curiosity, self-interest, or comeuppance. The irrepressible raven is a familiar denizen of the coastal rainforest, living on the edge of human settlements and keeping a watchful eye on the happenings therein. For the animistic Tlingit, Raven is the foremost personality among the many spirit companions, who inhabit their world. The grandmother waved her hand and the children hushed. *I will tell you the story of how Raven stole the sun.*

At the beginning of time, there was no world. There was only darkness and Raven. At that time, Raven learned that far away there was a large house, in which a rich man kept the light just for himself. Raven thought over all sorts of plans for getting this light into the world. The rich man living there had a daughter, and Raven said, "I will make myself very small and drop into the water as a speck of dirt, and the girl will swallow the water and become pregnant." When the time came, they made a bed out of soft moss and the baby was born there. Its eyes were very bright and moved around rapidly.

The Tlingit children were rapt, delighted by Raven's shape-shifting transformation.

The old man had hung bundles on the walls of the house. When the child grew larger, he crawled around and cried for many days, pointing at the bundles. Finally, the grandfather said, "Give my grandchild what he is crying for. Give him that bag hanging on the end." The child played with the bundle on the floor. But suddenly he let it go, and it floated up through the smoke hole. It went straight up into the air and the stars scattered across the sky.

Later, the baby cried again and pointed at another bundle. He cried so much that his mother thought he would die. Then his grandfather commanded his daughter to "untie the next one and give it to him." The child played with it for a long while, until he let it also escape through the smoke hole. And there was the big moon in the sky.

Now the only thing remaining was the box that held the daylight. The child cried for it for many days. He turned around and his eyes showed different colors, and his family thought he must be some extraordinary baby. But it always happens that a grandfather loves his grandchild, so he gave in. "Give the last thing to him." The grandfather felt sad when he said this. When the child had his hands on it, he uttered the raven cry—*Ga!* He flew out the smoke hole with the box. Then the old man lamented, "That old raven has stolen all my things!"

This was how Raven stole the sun. Because of Raven, there is light instead of darkness, there is knowledge of the world we live in. The children roared with approval.

———

A Tlingit potlatch exhibited as much pageantry and pomp as a Venetian carnival. The guests from Klukwan and Angoon formed a procession line before Noow Tlein. At the front of the queue stood the guest leaders, donning wide-brimmed spruce woven hats with slender foot-tall conical crowns. The hats were painted with colorful clan crests and embellished with dangling abalone shells, bear claws, and copper trinkets. The headmen were accompanied by their wives, sporting fashionable bone and ivory labrets inside their lower lips to accentuate a protruding countenance.

The Kiks.ádi were arrayed at the entrance in fancy robes, embroidered with animal images and family crests. With enthusiasm, the hosts launched into another welcome song. Then the guests were escorted to assigned places inside the longhouse.

Shk'awulyeil stepped to the front of the crowded room. It was the leader's responsibility to act as tradition bearer for the clan. The potlatch was the main venue to recall departed ancestors and retell the stories of seminal events. For a society sustained by oral tradition, potlatch stories were not simply a form of entertainment—they were hallowed testimonials entrusted from one generation to the next. The stories elaborate a clan's history and sustain a collective memory. Shḵ'awulyeil's face was scarcely visible between his oversized spruce bonnet and the mink-lined collar of his flowing robe. He jingled the puffin beaks tied to a ceremonial rattle and shared the story of the of the Kiks.ádi clan.

"When we were first born, people hated us," he said. "Afterwards some people called the Sky people brought war on us. They destroyed us. One woman saved herself. She dug a hole under a log to conceal herself from the enemy," he said. This lone survivor became the mother of a reborn Kiks.ádi clan. The oral narratives say that the Kiks.ádi originally came from the southern reaches of the archipelago, near Ketchikan. In ancient times, they lived along the shore of a lake near Kiks Bay (now known as Helm Bay). The People of Kiks migrated northward.

They came down the Stikine River, settling for a while near Wrangel, forming the large Stikine ḵwáan. At some point, a faction of Kiks.ádi families split off and moved north again. The phenomenon of hunter-gathering bands splintering and migrating to new territory is the story of the spread of humanity out of Africa and around the world. Sometimes the driver of migration was violent conflict, sometimes it was food shortage, sometimes it was family quarrels. For the Kiks.ádi, the migration was compelled by war.

It was during this migration, Shḵ'awulyeil explained, that the Kiks.ádi adopted the frog as their crest animal. "A man and his wife were crossing the mouth of a big bay, when it became so foggy that they could not even see the water around their canoe. They stopped where they were. Then quite a distance away in the thick fog, they heard singing, and it continued for a long time. The voice was so powerful they could hear it echo off the mountains. When the fog began to rise, they went nearer to the song. They looked about and saw that it came from a little frog. They paddled for some time in the direction that the frog was taking them. Finally, the wife said that she was going to claim this frog. She took it ashore and treated it like a child. She carried it into the woods and put it down by a lake. And that is how the Sitka Kiks.ádi came to claim the frog."

Shk'awulyeil ended the story. For those in attendance, the performance was an affirmation of clan identity. Each Tlingit clan has its own crest, or identity marker—usually an animal. The crest animal is central to a clan's origin myth and its spirit is a source of clan strength. The Kiks.ádi crest embodied a story of survival, as the little frog led the people to safety and prosperity in Sitka. The crest is sacred to a Tlingit clan in the same way that a coat of arms is sacred to a medieval dynastic family or a religious icon is sacred to a community of the faithful.

Archaeologists confirm that humans have inhabited Sitka across the millennia. The defining landmark in the region is Mount Edgecumbe, a snow-capped dormant volcano on an island at the western entrance of the sound. Except for an occasional rumble, geological surveys indicate that the volcano has not been active for more than four thousand years. Yet the Tlingit refer to the cauldron-shaped monument as Lux, which translates as "flashing." The old name likely derives from the time when Mount Edgecumbe was still active, spewing lava and streaking the night sky with bursts of orange. The reference lends credence to the clan's territorial claims. Clan leader Al Perkins asserts that "the Kiks.ádi people were the first people to come to this country. They came up from the south. This is why Sitka is Kiks.ádi country."

—

A team of female servers entered the longhouse, carrying steaming cauldrons and bulging baskets. A Tlingit potlatch is a celebratory feast, with food and drink aplenty, served on the house finery. Special hardwood feasting bowls, decorated with family crests and animal figures, were set down next to large serving spoons, whittled from mountain goat horns. Heaping platters of smoked king salmon, roasted venison, and wild berry sauces were placed before the hungry guests. The Tlingit caviar, herring roe, spilled over the rims of hemlock bowls. Vessels of fish oil accompanied the food. The popular Tlingit drink was made from boiling eulachon, a kind of smelt, in large tubs and ladling out the fatty oil, which was stored in seal bladder sacks until slightly rancid. Throughout the meal, the Point House boomed with caroling, drumming, and laughter. Shḵ'awulyeil intently surveyed his sated guests. It was now time for the main event—the distribution of gifts.

Gift-giving was an institutionalized feature of Tlingit society. In contrast to a market economy, a gift-exchange economy means that valued goods or services are transferred to someone else without immediate or specified compensation in return. It is not an altruistic act, nor is it an economic transaction. Rather, gifts are a social investment. Within the clan, the gifts legitimize internal power relations and the hierarchy of houses. With one's counterpart clan, gifts reinforce norms of mutual support and indebtedness. Beyond that, gifts enhance status and cultivate influence. There is much nuance to the practice. A gift should correspond to social rank, while expectations of reciprocity compel that a gift should not exceed the means of the recipient. Not too extravagant, not too sparing.

The Tlingit did not know the wheel, iron, or gunpowder, yet working with local materials they were highly skilled artisans, engineers, and bladesmiths. Point House members were crafting items all year long in anticipation of the potlatch. The Deisheetaan and Kaagwaantaan headmen were the first to receive their presents. Each was bestowed with a copper shield, a coveted luxury. Made from metals obtained through trade with the northern Tlingit, the copper was heated and molded into a ceremonial breastplate, engraved with form line artwork and crest images.

In descending rank order, the gifts were allocated: stacks of embroidered goat wool blankets, plush otter and beaver fur skins, a metal-bladed dagger with an inlaid abalone pommel, painted bentwood boxes, wooden halibut fishing hooks sculpted in the shape of a sea lion, a taut

deerskin tambourine with seashell jangles. No one at the potlatch was
left empty-handed.

Despite the freezing temperature outside, the Point House was swel-
tering from the roaring fire and presence of several hundred bodies.
Shḵ'awulyeil spoke again about the Kiks.ádi homeland, reminding the
assembled of territorial boundaries. The basic resources for food and shelter,
harvested from the surrounding woods and waters, were held collectively by
the clan. But it was the headman who determined which families worked
which hunting grounds, salmon streams, and berry patches, a prerogative
that reinforced the status of the Point House. Shḵ'awulyeil now conferred
fishing rights on his guests for the spring herring run, when massive schools
of the silver fish arrived in Sitka Sound. The nutrient-rich roe collected from
the spawning herring was a staple in the Tlingit diet. The Deisheetaan and
Kaagwaantaan leaders nodded their approval at the Kiks.ádi concession,
which would be reciprocated in some form on their own territory. While
interclan territorial conflicts were not uncommon, the Tlingit generally
adhered to a well-developed system of property rights.

Shḵ'awulyeil clapped his hands and called for more gifts. Four people with
close-cropped hair came to the side of the host. Shḵ'awulyeil invited his
two guest clan leaders to come forward and make a choice. One pointed to
a tall young man and the other pointed to a strong-looking woman. They
were the gifts.

Even twenty years after the Civil War ended, slavery still existed in
one far corner of the United States. Involuntary servitude was a cus-
tomary practice among the Indigenous peoples of the Pacific Northwest,
including the Tlingit. Slaves were taken as prisoners of war and held for
ransom. If the price was too high, then the captive's freedom was forfeited
and they became property of an assigned owner. As a trade commodity, a

healthy slave was worth as many as twenty furs or a hundred blankets. It was taboo to enslave a fellow clansperson, but all others were fair game. Relegated to the bottom of society, these captives accounted for 10 percent or more of the population in Tlingit villages. The personal treatment of enslaved persons ranged from abusive to affectionate, depending on the owner's disposition. Not until 1886, in a case brought before a US military court in Sitka, was Tlingit slavery outlawed. "The petitioner must be released from the merciless restraint imposed upon him, and go forth a free man," the judge ruled.

Shk'awulyeil had taken possession of these unfortunate souls during a summertime revenge raid on the Tsimshians, an Indigenous people to the south. Interclan and intertribal conflict was a normal state of affairs with the Tlingit and neighboring groups, frequently yielding human prizes. He had been keeping the four captives as servants until now. Slaves were an extravagant gift. By bestowing these people on his peer rivals, Shk'awulyeil was showing off the wealth and power of the Point House.

And what of the other two slaves? Shk'awulyeil raised his hand over the head of a Tsimshian stripling, a lad of noble lineage. He declared that the adolescent was free. The potlatch guests gestured their approval. He then directed attention to the last man, a gaunt Tsimshian warrior, and condemned him to death.

The ceremonial execution of slaves was a climactic moment in a potlatch. The captive was led outside, where a circle of spectators formed around the impassive warrior. A Kiks.ádi shaman entered the circle, wearing a ghoul-faced mask and brandishing a whale-rib baton. He approached the victim from behind and collared him across the neck with the baton. With a ferocious grip, the shaman pulled back and strangled the man to death. The spirit of the deceased was destined to serve the Point House ancestors, while the body was disposed in the bay.

The potlatch festivities reached their finale. The visiting parties assembled to show their appreciation for the gifts and feast. The Deisheetaan and Kaagwaantaan each presented a ritual dance and song of gratitude to the hosts. The guest clans tried to outdo each other with their performances, much to the satisfaction of Shk̲'awulyeil. The potlatch, he believed, was a triumph.

The Klukwan leader announced that his clan had something to present to Shk̲'awulyeil and called on his associate Shuws'aa, a Kaagwaantaan elder. Shuws'aa was married to Shk̲'awulyeil's sister, who resided in the Klukwan village. Her eldest son had reached adolescence, which meant it was time to leave his boyhood home and go to live in the house of his maternal uncle.

Shuws'aa introduced his son. He was K'alyáan, and from this moment, a princeling of the Point House. Shk̲'awulyeil beamed. This was the same path of inheritance that he had followed. Shk̲'awulyeil too was born into the Kaagwaantaan clan, the son of Aankalaseek. The Kiks.ádi leader would groom K'alyáan to become an elite warrior and his heir apparent. Standing together on the cliffside of Noow Tlein, uncle and nephew reviewed the flotilla of canoes, laden with gifts, as they paddled away from Sitka.

At this moment, the Kiks.ádi and their allies were reenacting the familiar rites that had guided Tlingit society for centuries. Unknown to the participants, however, this long-standing order was about to come to an end. At the turn of the nineteenth century, the Sitka *kwáan* would be forcibly drawn into an imperialist plot to seize the Kiks.ádi homeland.

THE LAST POTLATCH

By the end of the nineteenth century, the stated policy of US officials and missionaries was to "civilize" the Alaskan natives, convert them to Christianity, and encourage them to give up their superstitious beliefs and tribal customs. These included their native language, traditional foods, and—chief among these maligned practices—the ku.éex', or ceremonial potlatch.

Governor John Brady, formerly a Presbyterian missionary, supported the goals, but he resisted imposing legal restrictions on these practices. Instead, he implemented subtler coercive measures to encourage the change. In 1904 Brady agreed to allow one last potlatch to settle all debts and imbalances between clans. It was meant to be a sort of farewell to this long-standing tradition.

Brady's allies from the Kaagwaantaan clan hosted this extravagant affair. The governor even secured funding from the US Department of Interior, promising that it would result in lasting good will and good behavior among the Tlingit.

The so-called last potlatch started on December 23, 1904, when Raven clan guests arrived on Japonski Island, south of Sitka, paddling traditional dugout canoes and waving American flags. Then followed four weeks of feasting, dancing, and celebrating, with guests arriving from all over Southeast Alaska. The Kaagwaantaan hosts dedicated five monumental wood carvings that were installed at Eagle and Wolf houses in the area. The local newspaper noted that some elders were "using the opportunity to impress upon the younger members of the tribe . . . the necessity of maintaining their old customs and traditions." Indeed, the Tlingit never did give up this age-old practice, continuing to hold potlatches in secret or in conjunction with more acceptable US holidays.

In recent decades, there has been a resurgence in the practice of potlatch—most notably with the 2004 Centennial Potlatch, somewhat ironically commemorating the "last potlatch" from a century before. Again, the Kaagwaantaan hosted this celebration, which entailed much

feasting and dancing. Several museums allowed use of Tlingit ceremonial hats and other objects from their collections, including some of the
wood carvings that were originally dedicated at the 1904 event.

Tlingit elder Harold Jacobs later recalled the moving event. "It was
a breathtaking sight to see these hats and blankets 'alive' . . . bearing
resonating sounds of 1904 and the ancestors who used them then,
now willed with the words and music and dance of their descendants
100 years later . . . who were told to give up potlatches and their way
of life and their language, who 100 years later were still there to say,
'We never gave up.'"

CHAPTER 2
The Great Northern Expedition

E arly modern Russia missed out on the Age of Science and Discovery. Old Muscovy's boyar elite was a tradition-soaked, self-indulgent cult, shrouded in medieval mysticism. The precocious boy-tsar, Peter Alexievich Romanov, never fit in. Peter's curiosity about the outside world was unquenchable. He spent long hours in the city quarter for foreign merchants, who regaled the young prince with tales of the wonders of the modern age. He became the first Russian ruler to venture beyond the border. Traveling in disguise, Peter and his raucous entourage crisscrossed the continent, meeting with monarchs, dining with dignitaries, and carousing with commoners. His visits to the maritime hubs Amsterdam and London convinced Peter that Russia was still living in a dark age.

In 1689, at the ripe age of seventeen, Peter banished his plotting sister, the regent Sophia, to a convent. The throne was now his alone. Peter vowed to replace superstition with science, backwardness with progress, East with West. He humiliated the old elite, forcing aristocrats to shave their beards and wear Western clothes. He subordinated the church to secular authority. He upended the traditional social order, forbidding arranged marriages and promoting the humble to high rank. He moved the capital from Moscow to St. Petersburg, and moved New Year's Day from September to January. And he made Russia a seafaring power to be reckoned with, earning him the moniker of Peter the Great.

Toward the end of his reign, in 1724, Peter's maritime obsession culminated in a grandiose project of exploration to the still-unknown quarter of the northern hemisphere where Eurasia met America. The Great Northern Expedition was the most ambitious and expensive state-sponsored odyssey the world had ever seen. It revealed the hidden wonders of Siberia, surveyed the continents and mapped the coastlines of the northern Pacific, and took inventory of the plants, animals, and people found therein. He recruited an international team of mariners, engineers, and scientists for the outrageous scheme. It was Peter's signature project to recast Russia as an enlightened Western power and to stake a claim in the New World.

"It is very necessary to have a navigator who has been to North America," the tsar insisted. Peter micromanaged his new navy, from choosing the blue-on-white Saint Andrew's cross for its flag to hammering the iron bolts into its latest warship. And so he dictated a list of instructions to the Russian Admiralty for the Great Northern Expedition. His high commanders scoured the officer roll to find a suitable candidate to lead the expedition. They found their man patrolling the Baltic in the *Lesnoe*, a ninety-gun frigate.

Danish-born Vitus Bering enlisted in the Imperial Russian Navy in 1704, when Denmark and Russia were allied against the reigning bully of the Baltic, King Charles XII of Sweden. The well-traveled Bering had worked on whalers since his teens, taking him to North America, the West Indies, and the Indian Ocean. In the Russo-Swedish War, Bering impressed in logistics and supply, vital skills for transoceanic voyages. His junior officers described him as a dutiful, fair-minded, and sober commander—not the most common combination of traits in the Russian navy. The Admiralty dispatched a messenger to locate the *Lesnoe* and order its master to return to port for reassignment. In December 1724

Peter signed the decree naming Captain Bering to lead his epic journey of discovery, at a salary of 480 rubles per year.

Bering was a reluctant adventurer, a middle-aged officer in the midst of a middling career. He tingled at the prospects of advancement and fame, but was daunted by the scale of the assignment. Upon receiving the commission, Bering hurried home to Vyborg to share the good news with his wife Anna. He explained that his task would keep him away for three years. It was much longer. The Great Northern Expedition was a larger undertaking than anyone imagined, becoming two separate journeys: a six-year trek to find the fabled Northeast Passage between Eurasia and North America, and a ten-year odyssey to scope out and claim a piece of this continent for Russia.

The expedition's mastermind, Peter the Great, did not live to see the final results. In early 1725, just two days after Bering departed the capital, Russia's indefatigable ruler was put to rest by a gangrenous bladder. As obsessed with medical science as he was with naval warfare, Peter was surely disappointed that he could not observe his own autopsy.

In June 1728, after three years of river portages, winter camps, and dogsled treks across Siberia, Bering's company reached the Pacific coast. From here began a voyage into the unknown. Bering consulted his orders: "Sail along the land that lies to the north, search for the place where that land may be joined to America, and then proceed to a settlement belonging to a European power." The problem was that Bering had been given three contradicting maps of the Far East—more speculation than geolocation. The cautious captain ventured into the Pacific and headed north-northeast, always keeping Siberia's coastline in sight. A month later his sixty-foot craft rounded the stark cliffs of Cape Dezhnev and entered the narrow strait that separates America and Asia.

A cacophony of auks and gulls serenaded the crew while the captain pondered. To the west, the top of Siberia and the mouth of the great Kolyma River awaited; to the north, the momentarily ice-free waters of the Arctic deceived; and, to the east, concealed by thick cloud cover, the New World beckoned. Satisfied that no land bridge connected the continents, Bering made his decision: "It is better to return and search for a safe harbor on Kamchatka than to remain in these northern waters, where on some dark night in fog we will become beached and face contrary winds, and not be able to free ourselves." Bering turned around and went home.

Upon his St. Petersburg homecoming, Bering earned the noble rank of captain-commander, a handsome bonus of a thousand rubles, and the sting from a swarm of critics. Having traveled so far, why did the company stop short of North America? Bering, his rivals said, was perhaps a prudent skipper, but certainly a gutless explorer. Bering was shaken by the controversy. He lobbied the Admiralty to support a bigger expedition that would go all the way to America. It was the Age of Empire, Russia was on the rise, and the proposal won over the cabinet. When the scheme was pitched to the new empress, Peter's niece, Anna Ivanovna, she endorsed her uncle's vision of a Russian America. Bering would get another chance.

Bering's first journey was a trial run. The second voyage would make the Great Northern Expedition one of early modern history's most remarkable scientific undertakings. The preparations alone took ten years. The Admiralty, Senate, and College of Arts and Science compiled an ever-expanding list of tasks for Bering, from surveying the vast interior and cataloguing the people, animals, plants, and minerals of Eurasia, to charting the waters of the northern Pacific and exploring the islands and coastline of North America. Bering was even ordered to extend the Russian postal system across Siberia.

"We, your humble servants, will be sailing this spring, if God permits, as soon as the ice melts. We will do our utmost to follow your instructions,"

Bering informed the empress. In early June 1741, two packet-style vessels, the *Saint Peter* and *Saint Paul*, double-masted and medium-sized, weighed anchor from Avacha Bay. The Pacific haven, nestled among Kamchatka's steaming volcanoes, was the starting point for the sea voyage. Aboard the flagship, the *Saint Peter*, the captain-commander stood upon the sun-drenched deck and gazed on the "Three Brothers," the towering rock sea stacks at the entrance to Avacha Bay. Russia's quest for America was underway.

Within a fortnight, the sister ships were separated in a storm and never reunited. Weeks passed without any sign of land. The crew became ornery. Bering fretted about the return voyage, anticipating foul weather and countervailing winds. On July 16, 1741, a cry sounded and the gloom lifted. Three score crewmen scurried across the *Saint Peter*'s deck, gawked, and pointed: through a veil of mist was the unmistakable shadow of land. Next day the clouds parted to reveal the intimidating splendor of Mount Saint Elias (*Yas'éit'aa Shaa* in Tlingit, meaning "the mountain behind the icy bay"). Exultant cheers went up and a merry celebration ensued. The taciturn captain stared at the snow-capped giant for a long while, before returning to his cabin. "They are like pregnant windbags," Bering grumbled," all puffed up with expectations."

Bering duly noted the sighting in his logbook, and was ready to go home. He was a sailor, not a discoverer. His apprehension of being stranded in the North Pacific in winter overrode the crew's eagerness to make landfall and investigate the terrain. He finally dropped anchor on the leeward side of a small island. But it was only to launch a longboat to fetch fresh water. "So, we have come all this way just to bring American water back to Asia," sniped a junior officer. For the next three weeks, the *Saint Peter* plodded westward, following the contours of the coast, taking in the islands, coves, forests, and mountains of southern Alaska, occasionally stopping for water. The scenery was amazing, the pace was slow. In mid-August, Bering ordered a southwest course, away from America and toward Russia.

Back on the open sea, the captain's fears were realized. Strong westerlies stalled the *Saint Peter*'s advance. Water and food ran low. The crew fell to scurvy. Bering too was taken ill, and confined to his cabin. In early October, the ship was battered by a western gale. "In all my fifty years at sea, I have never experienced a storm as this," said the frightened navigator. "The wind charged with such a terrible rage that we were in danger of losing our mast or rudder." The ferocious weather pounded the crew for nearly two weeks. The *Saint Peter* had become a floating deathtrap.

In early November, the teetering vessel approached a stark island. An extraordinary sea council was convened by the officers to debate two high-risk options. Bering made the case to continue to the Kamchatka Peninsula, which must be close, and pray that the ship holds together. The alternative was to beach the ship and make camp on this windswept slab, where at least they would have access to water and food. The captain-commander was outvoted. The *Saint Peter* was run up on the rocks. Unknown to the council, the Kamchatka Peninsula was only a hundred miles west.

The crew was grounded until next spring. Crude shelters and fire pits were dug into the earth on the leeward side. Of the *Saint Peter*'s roll of seventy-seven men, only forty-six survived the winter. The ship's physician took special care of the captain-commander. Bering's scurvy symptoms improved, but he never regained his strength. He was sixty years old and worn down by a decade of battles against Siberian wilderness, Pacific cyclones, and tsarist bureaucracy. He died on December 19, 1741, alone on this remote outcrop, half a world away from home. His passing went unnoticed by contemporaries, but history would eventually include him in the pantheon of great explorers. Yet Bering surely would have traded all his posthumous fame to be with his beloved wife Anna and his sons one more time. Laid to rest in a shallow grave, the ship's doctor, Georg Steller, listed "grief" as the cause of death.

"When Captain-Commander Bering learned of my insatiable desire to visit foreign lands and investigate their conditions and curiosities, he requested that I come meet him," said Georg Steller. "I could see right away that I would be persuaded to join his expedition to America." The boundless opportunity in Europe's newest empire lured the ambitious twenty-five-year-old physician from Wittenberg to St. Petersburg in 1734. Steller befriended another German transplant, naturalist Daniel Gottlieb Messerschmidt, whose Siberian field trips had yielded the first fossil remains of a wooly mammoth. When Messerschmidt died in 1735, Steller inherited his unpublished field notes, rare specimen collection, and grieving young widow. Bering chose well in recruiting Steller as ship doctor and naturalist. The prodigious scientific findings of the Great Northern Expedition were owed primarily to his enthusiasm, stamina, and brilliance, which also explains why his fellow officers could not stand him.

Steller wanted to fit in, expected to fit in, and was dismayed when he didn't fit in. He was clueless about seafaring protocol. Steller was a scientist, not a seaman. In a bookish sense, he was the superior of his colleagues, and could not help to let them know. But in a practical sense, he was their inferior, which they in turn were ever quick to affirm. "They deluded themselves into being highly insulted if anyone should say anything that they did not know." Throughout the voyage, Steller forced his opinion into every critical decision, to the indignation of the other officers. He had earned their scorn early in the voyage by persuading Bering that some floating debris indicated that land was nearby to the south. Bering followed Steller's hunch, but Steller had misread the signs. The *Saint Peter* was nowhere near land and was heading for the Hawaiian Islands, two thousand miles away. After four days, the vexed captain reversed course.

Long before the crew was marooned, Bering had become hostile to advice from his science officer. When the *Saint Peter* at last reached the jagged coast of mainland Alaska, Steller goaded Bering to make anchor in a safe-looking inlet. Mindful of hidden shoals, the captain parried: "Have

you been there already and know for sure?" Bering even refused permission
for Steller to accompany the crew sent to refill the water barrels, saying
that he would be murdered by the natives. The captain offered to make him
a hot chocolate instead. But Steller would not be denied. He threatened
the captain with a negative report to the Admiralty. Bering conceded and
allowed Steller to visit Kayak Island.

Steller took full advantage, gathering rare plants, minerals, and animal
bones and cramming a notebook with illustrations and observations. He
wandered away from his armed companions and into the woods. Steller
discovered that they were not alone when he came across a still warm ash
pit, a cache of dried salmon, and a freshly trodden path. Looking around,
he saw only trees. Bering's warning about hostile denizens flashed through
his mind. Undeterred, Steller continued his investigations, welcoming a
human encounter should it come. When the crewmen had refilled the water
barrels, Steller sent a request back to the captain to allow him an additional
two hours. So came Bering's reply: "Get your butt back to the ship pronto"
or you will be stranded.

It was only at the end of the journey that Steller's expertise was finally
appreciated. Steller was one of the few remaining able-bodied men at the
time the crew ran aground on the island. He salvaged the vessel, built
winter quarters, and hunted for food. But it was in his role as ship's doctor
where Steller excelled, nursing the scurvy-ridden sailors back to health. In
the eighteenth century, little was known about the disease, which was the
main cause of death at sea. Steller scoured the island for herbs and grasses,
from which he concocted an antidote. His improvised remedy marked the
first time that a ship's doctor had managed to reverse the ravages of scurvy
on a long voyage. Steller even won back the confidence and camaraderie
of the captain-commander.

In the annals of natural history, Steller's career was dazzling and brief.
He spent less than ten hours ashore when the *Saint Peter* made stops for
fresh water, yet recorded over a hundred plant species unknown to European

botany. His mineral finds included stellerite, a rare pearly white crystal. But he is best known for a record number of zoological firsts. Birders might be familiar with Steller's jay, Steller's eider, Steller's sea eagle, or Steller's albatross. Among sea mammals, Steller identified Steller's sea lion and Steller's sea cow (the now extinct northern manatee). This ten-ton gentle giant provided the *Saint Peter*'s stranded crewmen an "exceptionally good smelling and nourishing meal, tasting like the meat of young pigs." Steller's most astonishing discovery was Steller's sea ape. "The head was like a dog's head, the ears pointed and erect, the body was longish, round, and fat, with a tail equipped with fins. It was simian-like in habit, movement, and playfulness. It stayed with our ship for more than two hours, looking at us, as if with admiration, raising itself out of the water like a human being." Alas, Steller's "sea ape" was never confirmed, and later dismissed as a young fur seal.

Steller was also a pioneer ethnologist. He befriended Indigenous peoples in the Russian Far East, learning their social habits and survival strategies. His humanistic depictions of native Siberians stood in sharp contrast to the more prevalent subhuman accounts back in the West. The Great Northern Expedition inflicted countless cruelties on the peoples of the Eurasian hinterland, forcibly requisitioning food, livestock, and labor. Steller clashed with Bering about the mistreatment of the Koryak people of Kamchatka before the voyage, and clashed with the government about the mistreatment of the Kamchadal people near Okhotsk after he returned. In fact, Steller's good relations with the Indigenous people so rankled local authorities that an arrest warrant was issued, accusing him of inciting rebellion.

This last vengeful act of provincial officialdom finally broke the spirit of the young doctor. Steller never made it back to St. Petersburg. He died along the way in western Siberia, exhausted and impoverished. But his stacks of notebooks eventually made the trip home, and were published, translated, and disseminated throughout Europe's scientific community. Georg Steller's contributions to natural history place him on par with Alexander von Humboldt and Charles Darwin.

When the storm finally broke and the skies cleared, the captain of the *Saint Paul* scanned the horizon. Alexei Chirikov ordered the ship back to the coordinates where the day before he had been sailing with the *Saint Peter*, before fog, wind, and rain had driven them apart. For the next three days, the *Saint Paul* tacked across the rendezvous spot that the captain-commander had designated. But Bering's flagship was nowhere in sight. Chirikov faced a decision. "In case of separation," Bering had dictated, "each was to look for the other in the places where the boats were last seen." Leaving a crippled companion behind in the uncharted North Pacific was tantamount to a death sentence. The young skipper cast aside his doubt. Eastward ho.

Alexei Chirikov was as closely connected to the Great Northern Expedition as was its more famous captain-commander. Initially, Peter the Great's appointment of the twenty-two-year-old Chirikov to serve as Bering's lieutenant raised eyebrows. Was it based on merit? Chirikov had less than a year's experience at sea, though his expertise in the study of mathematics and navigation was unmatched. Was it nationalism? In a navy top-heavy with foreign commanders, the native son was the pride of Russia's new naval academy. Or was it nepotism? It was rumored that Chirikov was the son of the tsar's favorite carpenter in the royal shipyard. Whatever the reason, the decision proved justified. Chirikov was the unsung hero of the Great Northern Expedition.

Three weeks after giving up the search for Bering, the listless crew was suddenly roused. In the distance, a bird was winging on the horizon and the water surface turned a lighter shade. Signs of land. All eyes strained on the sea ahead. "A number of ducks and gulls, a pod of whales and porpoises, and three pieces of driftwood" were joyously observed. Chirikov ordered repeated soundings and an anchor was readied. The *Saint Paul* drifted forward into the muted glow of the northern white nights.

"At two o'clock," Chirikov recorded in the log, "we saw land ahead of us, upon which was a high mountain and a forest of great growth. We realized without doubt that this was part of America."

Wary of treacherous reefs, Chirikov waited until dawn before daring the shallows for a closer look. "There were great stands of fir, spruce, and pine," he said, "but no human habitations." The crew lined the rail and gazed upon Prince of Wales Island, better known to the local inhabitants as Taan, the island of sea lions. The rocky shoreline intimidated the captain. Chirikov tracked the coast northward in search of safe anchorage. The Russians had arrived in the Tlingit homeland.

The *Saint Paul* came around the mouth of a small bay with a low-lying waterfront and steep snow-peaked backdrop. Chirikov selected his most trusted officer, shipmaster Arvaam Dementiev, to lead an exploratory party, giving him explicit instructions. Sound the depths of the bay and determine if the inlet can accommodate the *Saint Paul*. Go ashore and fill two rain barrels with fresh water. Try to make contact with the local people and learn who lives here. "If you see inhabitants, show them kindness and give them small gifts. But if they are hostile, then defend yourselves and return to the vessel as quickly as possible. Do not vent anger on them." A longboat was lowered into the waves, and the shipmaster with ten armed crewmen ventured forth into the New World.

"Over the next twenty-four hours the wind shifted and it became foggy and rainy," Chirikov noted in the log. The captain lost sight of the landing party. "The wind carried us away from the place where the boat had gone. The boat has not yet returned." For four days, the *Saint Paul* tacked across the mouth of the bay waiting for a sign from the landing party. At last, on the fifth day, smoke was seen coming from the beach. Chirikov ordered a cannon fired to signal Dementiev to return to the ship. Hours passed, but only a walrus swam out of the bay. Aboard the *Saint Paul*, the captain surmised that the longboat was damaged and that it was necessary to send a skiff with the ship's carpenter. Boatswain Sidor Savelev volunteered to lead the five-man rescue party. Five hours later sailors aboard the *Saint Paul* watched the second boat approach the distant beach, then recede from view. Chirikov sounded the cannon to signal Savelev. "We thought we saw someone on shore shooting a gun, but we heard no noise." Two hours later a fire was observed on the beach. Darkness fell. Two lanterns were hung over the rail of the *Saint Paul*.

Early the next morning, two small boats emerged from the bay. As they drew closer, Chirikov realized "they were not our boats. They had a sharp bow and were not rowed but paddled." A man in red clothes stood up in one of the boats, then shouted and waved to the *Saint Paul*. "I commanded the men to wave white handkerchiefs and call them over, but it did no good. They moved away from us and disappeared back into the bay." Shipmaster Dementiev, boatswain Savelev, and fourteen other crew members were never seen again. The *Saint Paul* was without a launch boat and low on water. Chirikov resolved to return directly to Avacha Bay in Russia.

The mystery of the *Saint Paul* sailors remains unsolved. Some speculate that the boats were wrecked in a tidal whirlpool inside the bay, while others suggest that the crew used the opportunity to desert the Russian navy and go native. Most historians, however, agree with Captain Chirikov. "We became convinced that some misfortune befell our men. The weather had been fair. They would have returned," he noted. "The fact that the Americans did not dare approach our ship leads us to believe that our men have either been killed or detained." If indeed this was the fate of the missing men, then the first encounter between the Tlingit and the Russians was a portent of things to come.

The Great Northern Expedition concluded without fanfare. In 1740 the expedition's royal patron, Empress Anna, died and was replaced by Peter the Great's eldest daughter, Elizabeth, via a military coup. Russia then, and now, has never figured out an agreeable system of leadership succession. The new Empress Elizabeth had no interest in empire-building in the Americas. Yet the many discoveries of the Great Northern Expedition would become well-known. The old questions of a Northeast Passage and intercontinental land bridge were finally answered. A wealth of new information would be absorbed by the European Enlightenment.

Bering and Steller, neither of whom survived the quest, would get their due. Chirikov, by contrast, made his way home, only to die in obscurity in 1748, still contesting the Russian government for back wages.

One of the expedition's officers, however, profited from the adventure. Swedish-born Sven Waxell served as lieutenant commander and navigator aboard the *Saint Peter*. He supervised the rebuilding of the broken ship into a seaworthy craft that made it back to the Kamchatka Peninsula in the summer of 1742. Waxell cribbed Bering's diary to compose the final report to the Admiralty. As reward, he was promoted to admiral and put in charge of the Kronstadt naval base. Waxell also ensured that Russian interest in America did not fade, as he had found space in the *Saint Peter*'s hold for a tall stack of sea otter pelts.

BERING'S BONES

In 1991 a team of Danish archeologists made the journey across Siberia to far-flung Bering Island in hopes of finding the gravesite of the island's namesake, Vitus Bering. About twelve years earlier, a Russian team had succeeded in locating and excavating the campsite and dugout dwellings on the Commander Islands, where Bering and the crew of the Great Northern Expedition had spent the winter of 1741, and where Bering had died. The expedition's physician, Georg Steller, had recorded in his journal that "we buried his corpse . . . close to our dwelling with the rites of our church." Armed with these records, the archeologists quickly located a cluster of graves on a sandy ridge overlooking the bay, about sixty-five feet from the dwellings.

Of the six bodies, only one was in a coffin, and this they determined to be the remains of Vitus Bering. They removed the skull for further investigations at the Institute of Forensic Medicine in Moscow. Here, forensic expert Victor Zviagin estimated that the body's age at death was between fifty-seven and sixty-six years, thus confirming that the body belonged to Bering, who was in fact sixty years old when he died (and the only individual in this age range on the ship). Zviagin did extensive studies on the remains, and even used the skull to reconstruct a likeness of the explorer.

The archeological find did not solve all of the mysteries surrounding Bering's death, however, and in fact, sparked some new ones. For starters, the angular face on Zviagin's bust does not resemble an eighteenth-century portrait of Bering. Alas, some historians had already doubted whether the athletic and intrepid explorer could possibly possess the flabby face in the portrait, which has now been attributed to his uncle, the poet Vitus Pedersen Bering.

Another surprise: it was long assumed that Bering died of scurvy, yet the scientists noted the healthy set of teeth in the exhumed skull, which contradicts this conclusion. But Bering's own doctor had actually implied that the commander had recovered from his most recent bout of scurvy, instead recording that he died "more from hunger, cold, thirst, vermin, and grief, than from a disease." Zviagin did determine that the skull was missing six molars, which might well have been extracted as a result of scurvy, even if the disease was not the immediate cause of Bering's death.

Other inconsistencies are not so easily explained. Bering's successor as commander, Lieutenant Sven Waxell, recorded that the corpse was tied to a plank and then buried, yet the archeologists found the body not on a plank, but in a box. Steller recorded that the commander was buried alongside four other crewmen, yet the archeologists found six bodies in total, not five. All of these inconsistencies have led at least one Russian scholar to question the accuracy of the Danish team's findings. "Vitus Bering's burial place is still unknown," Natasha Lind concludes.

Most scholars, however, agree that the forlorn grave on a remote Russian island is indeed that of the celebrated explorer. Bering's bust—as reconstructed by Zviagin—is now on display at the Alaska State Museum. "The amount of his suffering is very visible in the face," the doctor said. "He kept it all inside, internalized it. This is the true face of Vitus Bering."

CHAPTER 3
To the Face of the Clouds

J ust west of Juneau and north of Sitka, Lituya Bay is an inlet that is almost completely closed off from the sea. Its name is Tlingit, meaning the "lake within the point." The glacial fjord is enchanting and devious. Navigators best beware the rip currents at the mouth of the bay, the scene of countless accidents and drownings. Tlingit animists attributed the deadly tides to Kah Lituya, a vengeful water demon. In 1958 the bay made history, when it was deluged by the largest tsunami wave on record, more than 1,700 feet high, taller than the Empire State Building. Lituya Bay is also the setting of a Tlingit legend explaining how the Russians arrived in their homeland.

The account dates back to the time of first encounters in the mid-eighteenth century. The rugged shoreline around Lituya Bay was home to the Coho clan, the L'uknax̱.ádi. Like most Tlingit bands, the L'uknax̱.ádi were adroit traders, working the seasonal markets where coastal and interior peoples mingled. Their baidarka caravans traveled south to Sitka and north to the Copper River, exchanging smoked fish, sea mammals, and woven baskets for metals, minerals, moose, and caribou. According to legend, a convoy of L'uknax̱.ádi traders, paddling across the narrows of Lituya Bay in heavy-laden canoes, was captured by the dreaded riptide.

"The boats had traveled to Yakutat trading for furs," said Charles White, a L'uknax̱.ádi elder. "As they were voyaging back, the tides turned to rapids at Lituya Bay. All ten boats were capsized." Only two men survived, straddling their overturned boat in a back eddy and calling out for help until darkness covered them. When daylight came, they were gone. "They all died." The cargo, however, was not lost. "The furs that they bought were in halibut skin bags. They were like rubber bags, which did not leak. These skin bags were full of sea otter, fox, marten, and mink. The tides swept everything to Russia. When the Russians discovered the bags of fur, they went searching for the mainland from where they had come. So, the Russians came upon this land."

The traditional Tlingit account is consistent with the historic record: it was the prospects of fur trapping that lured the Russians across the Pacific to North America. They came especially for the sea otter, whose pelt is like no other animal. Most marine mammals have a thick lining of fat under the skin to protect their warm-blooded bodies from freezing-cold waters. Sea otters do not have a blubber layer. Instead, this largest member of the weasel family maintains its internal warmth with an ultra-dense fur coat. Sea otter skin has more than a million hairs per square inch. By comparison, a cat has one hundred thousand and a chinchilla has two hundred thousand. The thick hair traps air against the body, creating an insulating buffer between water and skin. Sea otter fur is exceptionally warm and exquisitely plush. "Such is the beauty and softness of the fur that the otter surpasses all other creatures in the vast ocean," wrote Georg Steller.

At a time when the world's rich and powerful conducted their affairs from drafty stone palaces, this incomparably cozy coat was a must-have luxury item. In the second half of the eighteenth century, sea otter pelts became the world's most sought-after commodity, as precious as gold or silver. The demand for the elegant treasure launched a wave of fortune seekers into the North Pacific, beginning with Russia's first commercial ventures into the "Eastern Sea." As Jennie White, of the Thunderbird house in the Shangukeidi clan, recalled in her retelling of the first encounter: "This is why the Russians searched for Alaska. This is how they found the Tlingits. No white man knew of Alaska until the Coho clan boat capsized at Lituya Bay and their bundle of furs floated away to the face of the clouds."

"Siberia is our India, Mexico, or Peru," remarked Catherine the Great, meaning it was rich in resources and ripe for exploitation. Russia's geopolitical rise was sustained by commodity exports from the Eurasian hinterland. In the early modern period, Siberian furs financed the transformation of the minor Muscovy principality into a major European power. Eastward expansion was led by Cossacks, woodsmen, and schemers, all competing for fur-bearing creatures—fox, beaver, marten, and, most of all, sable. In the wake of the trappers came Russia's oligarchs of old, big-time entrepreneurs who founded joint-stock companies, finagled special trading privileges, and coerced the Indigenous peoples. At the apex of this frontier economy was the tsar, who collected taxes and fees and grew rich from the fur trade.

By the mid-eighteenth century, Siberia's bounty was nearing depletion. That's when the stragglers of the Great Northern Expedition returned home, toting a cache of sea otter skins. As it turned out, the Commander Islands, where the crew of the *Saint Peter* was marooned, were home to scores of dense sea otter colonies. "They covered the shore in droves," said Georg Steller. The amateur naturalist was obsessed with sea otters and provided zoology's first comprehensive description of their behavior and habitat. Steller also noted that the boiled meat of the young is "most delicious."

Once the crew recovered from scurvy, they too became obsessed with sea otters, but not for reasons of science or cuisine. Greed was the driver. With nothing much to do, the castaways turned their attention to stalking, killing, and skinning sea otters. "We were living in a state of nature and little work got done," Steller said disapprovingly. "We hunted constantly, making the animals wary of our presence and driving them away from us. Through envy and jealousy, one hunter tried to deceive the other for an advantage, in the hope that he could transport the most pelts back to Kamchatka in spring for the greatest profit." In the evenings, the crew played cards, gambling for pelts. "Anyone who had ruined themselves at cards would try to recover by going after the poor sea otters, which were killed simply for the fur and the meat was thrown away. When this was not enough, some crewmen began to steal pelts from others, causing quarrels and strife in our quarters."

Because the island was uninhabited, the creatures had never known such a predator. "At first, they came right up to our fires, until they learned to run away from us," Steller said. The best hunting time was at twilight or moonlit evenings. The otters came ashore to rest during low tides, when they were more easily ambushed. A small party would steal along the beachfront. When an otter was spotted, one man sprung on the sleeping animal, while the others blocked the escape route to the sea. Armed with clubs, they would chase down their scampering quarry over the rocks. By December, the Russians decimated the colonies near the campsite. By the end of winter, sea otters disappeared from the north side of the island. In spring, the crew trekked thirty miles to the island's south side. In less than eight months, "we killed more than 700 animals and took their pelts back to Kamchatka."

Siberian fur traders were astonished by the sea otter's sublime quality. The color was deep glossy black with silver highlights. The texture was lush and supple. The size reached six feet. The sea otter, they said, was like soft gold. A buying frenzy ensued. The price of sea otter fetched two times, three times, four times the value of the best sable pelt. Rumors circulated of a rocky island chain in the Eastern Sea overladen with the precious pups. The Siberian economy was transformed as the fur trade took to the sea. Coastal settlements sprang up with shipyards, trade houses, onion-domed churches, and vodka-stocked taverns.

In Okhotsk local sergeant Yemelian Basov organized an outing to the Commander Islands, wooing merchant investors to underwrite his costs and recruiting a *Saint Peter* veteran to show him the way. Basov's field trip lasted a year before returning home with more than 1,200 sea otter pelts. The hunters collected unprecedented prices of five to ten rubles per skin, depending on color and size, which Siberian merchants resold on international markets for ten times the wholesale cost.

In the sixteenth century, Siberian fur shipped west to outfit Europe's fashion-conscious dukes and duchesses. A century later, Russian merchants exported pelts south to adorn Ottoman pashas and beys. In the eighteenth century, the epicenter of the global fur market shifted east to Imperial China's aristocrats and mandarins. To protect his heavenly realm from foreign contamination, the Qing emperor channeled all maritime trade through Canton. Russian merchants, however, were banned from the seaport. Instead, they were granted an overland trade post at Kyakhta on the Mongolian border. Russian trade caravans were forced to trek over the Altai Mountains and across the Gobi Desert to exchange Siberian fur for Chinese tea, silk, and porcelain. In the late-1700s, when Russian caravans began carting sea otter skins to Kyakhta, Chinese consumers pushed up the prices to dizzying heights.

Russia's exclusive access to the sea otter was short-lived. Commodity traders from all seafaring nations soon turned their attention to this cold corner of the globe. In the 18th century, a transoceanic voyage was a costly and risky venture, but one consignment of high-quality North Pacific fur sold in Canton could make a merchant captain comfortable for life. The soft gold rush was on.

With the pope's blessing, the Spanish king claimed for his realm the entire western coastline of the New World. Even though Vasco Núñez de Balboa reached the Pacific in 1513, the viceroys of New Spain neglected the Western Seaboard for the next two centuries. But the Great Northern Expedition raised alarm over the Russian tsar's intrusion on the Spanish king's domain. "Is it not natural to think that the Russians in future voyages will come down so low as California?" asked Miguel Venegas, a Jesuit official in New Spain. "How shall we hinder the Russians from making settlements there, unless we do so beforehand." Concern over Russian expansion prompted the positioning of a garrison and monastery in Alta California around San Francisco Bay. In May 1775 Viceroy Antonio Bucareli dispatched an expedition from Mexico to sail up the coast and check for any signs of Russians. Three months later, a Spanish schooner, the *Sonora*, reached the Tlingit at Sitka Sound.

"On 16 August, we saw to the northwest headlands and mountains, one of which of immense height was situated on a cape, the most beautiful I have ever seen." Captain Bodega y Quadra ordered several crewmen to row ashore and mark the territory for Spain. "We prepared ourselves for defense against the Indians. Five of us landed about noon and positioned ourselves at the safest place. We planted the cross with all proper devotion and displayed the Spanish colors. Once we had taken possession of the country, we advanced to our next task to collect water from the river bank, and returned to the ship."

The Tlingit spied on the intruders from afar. They did not intervene, but grasped the meaning of the shoreline ceremony. Bodega y Quadra believed that Spain's ownership claim to the region was duly confirmed and consecrated. The Tlingit were of a different mind. "We soon saw them approach the place where we had fixed the cross, which they took away and placed in front of their own house, while making signs to us with their arms that they had taken our cross." If the Sitka Tlingit were offended by the symbolic land grab, at least they did not attack and kill the trespassers, which the Quinault people to the south had done to a *Sonora* landing party earlier on the voyage. The Spanish, meanwhile, left behind more than just token property markers. Bodega y Quadra's excursion coincided with the first outbreak of smallpox among the Northwest peoples, including the Tlingit.

Satisfied that Russia was not yet a threat to the west coast, Viceroy Bucareli was soon dismayed by new reports of British encroachment into the Pacific Northwest. Two hundred years after the notorious sea dog Francis Drake cruised the California coastline, the British Admiralty sent

Captain James Cook to explore the North Pacific. At Nootka Sound near Vancouver Island, Cook anchored for a month to repair his two ships and resupply his crew. The captain recorded in his journal: "A great many canoes were about the ship all day and a trade commenced betwixt us and them. Their articles were skins of various animals, such as bears, wolfs, foxes, and, in particular, the sea beaver." He was referring to the sea otter. "There is no doubt," Captain Cook said, "there could be a beneficial fur trade here with the inhabitants of this vast coast."

This optimistic assessment encouraged British trader James Hanna, in 1785, to set out in the brig *Sea Otter* for the Nootka Sound, where he collected more than five hundred sea otter skins that earned twenty thousand Spanish dollars in China. More British ventures followed after the London press broke the news of Hanna's big score: "The *Sea Otter* is arrived from the west coast of America after one of the most prosperous voyages ever made in so short a time." In the late 1780s, British traders established a trade post along Nootka Sound on the west side of Vancouver Island. Spain assembled a war fleet to run off the Anglo squatters. Sea skirmishes followed, but a diplomatic solution was eventually reached. Spain conceded that British fur traders could work the Northwest Coast as long as they did not establish any permanent colonies.

The French, meanwhile, had long monopolized the North American fur trade from an interior base in the Great Lakes region. As great power rivalries heated up, King Louis XVI resolved to extend French influence to the western edge of the continent. In 1785 the king dispatched Jean François de Galaup, comte de La Pérouse, to the Pacific Ocean on an expedition of discovery and trade. In the summer of 1786, the French flute *La Boussole* arrived in the Tlingit homeland. "We perceived an inlet which seemed to be a very fine bay, the calmness of the interior of the bay was most seductive," La Pérouse said. The French mission remained a month at Lituya Bay. The local Tlingit welcomed the French frigate, and came out to visit almost every day. "We were continuously surrounded by the canoes of the

Indians, who offered us fish and otter skins in exchange for our iron. Gold is not an object of more eager desire in Europe than iron is here in this part of America." It seemed to La Pérouse that the Tlingit must have had previous contact with European traders. "To our surprise, they appeared well accustomed to the traffic." The Tlingit had entered the global economy.

⚬⚬⚬

In late May 1787, a small Tlingit band prepared for the annual sockeye run at their summer fishing camp on Yakutat Bay. The timeless scene was disrupted by a tall ship appearing in the morning mist on the bay. Captain George Dixon, commanding the *Queen Charlotte*, a three-masted British snow-brig, had journeyed twelve thousand miles to present his credentials as an emissary of the fur trade.

"The people seemed well-pleased with our arrival and a number of them paddled alongside us," said the captain. "They soon understood what we wanted and an old man brought us eight excellent sea otter skins. It seemed no trading party had been here before and we would reap a great harvest." Dixon anchored the *Queen Charlotte* in a sheltered cove, anticipating a rich haul. But the captain's optimism "was built on a sandy foundation." He noted that "the furs that they brought us to sell were few in quantity and inferior in quality. Our trade was inconsiderable." After a week of waiting on promises, Dixon lowered a whaleboat and with a Tlingit guide went exploring upriver. He found more Tlingit houses and people tending fish traps, but "not a single skin of any value amongst them." The disappointed trader returned to the ship and weighed anchor.

The *Queen Charlotte* turned south to Sitka Sound. "The shore here abounds with pines, witch hazel, gooseberries and raspberries," Dixon observed. Once again, the locals paused their summer activities to engage the foreigners. "They came alongside to trade with us at morning daylight, and never failed to spend a half hour singing before the traffic commenced."

The *Queen Charlotte* remained for a fortnight anchored in front of Noow Tlein. The message spread to all the households in Sitka that strangers had appeared seeking to exchange exotic goods for animal skins, especially sea otter. The trading was brisk. "Iron was the staple commodity that we bartered, everything else depended on fancy and caprice." Not all local commodities had a price. In anticipation of a long voyage, Dixon sought to replenish his food stocks. "The inhabitants catch halibut and there was a large quantity of salmon hung to dry, but they were not willing to sell it." When the *Queen Charlotte* finally departed in late June, the captain was pleased: "If our success at this place did not answer our most sanguine expectations, then it was most encouraging. We purchased about two hundred excellent sea otter skins, and more of lesser quality, a hundred good seal skins, and a number of fine beaver tails."

The Sitka Tlingit quickly wised up to the global market and earned a reputation as savvy traders. "Colored glass beads, metal buttons, and all those European toys, for which the islanders of the Great Ocean were so anxious, were hardly accepted here even as a free gift." The Tlingit wanted fashion and firepower. "They are already partly dressed in the European fashion," French captain Étienne Marchand observed. In 1793, when British captain George Vancouver passed through Sitka, his first lieutenant noted that they "prefer coats and trousers more than copper and iron or any other item, except arms and ammunition." But not just any musket would do. New England trader Sullivan Dorr cautioned fellow fortune seekers not to think that they could fool the Tlingit with an inferior product. "These cunning savages are great merchants, and they won't have anything other than good."

The trading itself was a drawn-out affair, which commenced with a chorus of singing from canoes paddling around the anchored vessel. After the Tlingit ascended to the main deck with their wares, the serious haggling got underway. The trade ships employed furriers to vouch for the quality of the pelts. "They examined all the skins, beating them in order to rid them of dust and vermin, and dressing those that were still fresh to assure their preservation until arrival in China." The Tlingit knack for bargaining consistently impressed, and sometimes dismayed. "They are not careless businessmen at all," said one French trader. "They examine everything presented to them with the most scrupulous attention, turning things in every which way; and, they know very well how to spot defects and point them out."

The Tlingit understood that the foreigners were more desperate to make a sale. After all, to reach the North Pacific required a huge investment of time and money. To sail away empty-handed would be ruinous. The locals took advantage. "They remained around the ship for two days with their furs," a vexed French trader complained. "In the end, they carried the furs back to the shore because we refused pay their exorbitant prices, for which they should have been ashamed." The skipper of the *Hope*, out of Boston, observed: "They will not part with a single skin until they have exerted their utmost to receive the best price for it." And British merchant John Meares lamented that "in all our commercial transactions with these people, we were, more or less, the dupes of their cunning."

Aboard the *Queen Charlotte*, Captain Dixon and a Tlingit headman had just struck a deal. "Coo-coo, Coo-coo, Coo-coo," the headman sang out to his entourage in a canoe alongside the ship. "Whoa!" came the immediate reply. The British sailors looked at each other in surprise. "We were strangers to this peculiar custom," said supercargo William Beresford. The call-and-response was a ritual feature of Tlingit trade practice. Generally, clan elders were authorized to negotiate on behalf of their households, but transactions still required collective consent. "The greater or lesser the energy of the response was in proportion to the approval of the bargain," Beresford noted. Trading acumen was a valued leadership trait. One particular Sitka headman earned the nickname "Hard-and-Sharp" from the Americans for his keen eye and tough negotiating style.

Over the next decade, the foreign merchants made Sitka a regular port of call. "If the Europeans set so great a value on furs that they go round the world to obtain them, then these natives show no less eagerness to exchange their superfluous skins for the products of Europe, whose use and convenience they have become acquainted," observed Captain Marchand. The Tlingit had become major players in the global fur trade.

The strategies employed by European traders varied. The British and the New Englanders showed an instinct for commerce, swapping industrial-made goods for locally procured furs. Most prized by the locals were metal tools, household implements, clothing and fabrics, and weapons—especially muskets and powder. By contrast, Spain's New World colonizers brought feudal instincts to the fur trade, preferring to control the labor force. They conscripted California mission Indians to trap sea otters to be sold in Canton. But what might have worked for farming did not work for hunting, and New Spain was an insignificant player in the Pacific fur trade. Like Spain, the Russians exploited the Indigenous peoples as a source of forced labor.

Siberian land-based hunting techniques were not well-suited for pursuing Pacific marine mammals. When the sea otter colonies in the Commander Islands were depleted, Russian hunting parties sailed further east to the Aleutian Islands. Here the Russians met the Unangan people, or Aleuts, as the Russians called them. They were adept boatsmen, maneuvering baidarkas in and around the rocky shoals, and expert marksmen, bringing down quarry with tethered bone-tipped harpoons. The baidarka was a lightweight kayak made from a driftwood frame with a taut sea lion skin cover. Sitting upright in the cockpit, the hunter wore a waterproof bodysuit made of seal intestines. Russian captains at first tried to hire the Unangan to hunt for them. When that failed, they resorted to intimidation. A favorite tactic was to seize hostages from the families of local leaders, who in turn made their people comply with Russian demands. This coercive strategy was so successful that Russia nearly cornered the North Pacific fur market in the late eighteenth century.

One early explorer observed the effective hunting method used by the Aleuts. "A party of anywhere from six to twenty Aleut would take to the sea together for the hunt. Invariably two men went in each little craft, the one in the front hatch using the spear and the one in the back maneuvering the baidarka with a long, double-bladed paddle. Spread out in a line, they would fan out until a sea otter was seen. The hunter who first sighted the animal would raise his paddle into the air as a signal and his canoe would dart forward as quickly as possible to where the animal went down, remaining on the spot while the other baidarkas quickly formed a wide circle around him. Every eye was now alert to catch the otter's reappearance. As soon as this happened, the canoe nearest darted forward in the same manner as the first, while everyone shouted to make the animal dive again, giving it the least possible time to fill its lungs with fresh air. The process was repeated. The sea otter's dives became increasingly shorter as the circle gradually closed in. Finally, a hunter was close enough to throw his spear, and these natives were so expert that a sea otter seldom escaped."

Based in Siberia, Russian merchants had always operated on a one-and-done business model. They raised investment capital, outfitted dodgy sailing crafts, enlisted a nervy captain and crew, and then set them loose into the North Pacific. If the company returned in two years with a cargo hold of fur, the venture was a triumph. But if they wrecked in treacherous waters or were waylaid by resentful islanders, then the venture went broke. One Siberian trader, however, had a different vision of how to do business.

For Grigory Shelikhov, the North Pacific was more than just a surf-splashed hunting ground, it was the future of the empire. There was no good reason why Russia had to stop where Siberia met the sea. Shelikhov imagined the Russian Empire stretching across the Eastern Ocean to the lush shoreline and bountiful woodlands beyond. His obsession was to found Russia's first colony in the New World. "I will succeed to take the American coast all the way south to California," boasted Shelikhov, the self-anointed Russian Columbus.

SAVE THE SEA OTTERS

Before the arrival of the Europeans, hundreds of thousands of sea otters frolicked in North Pacific coastal waters, from the Baja Peninsula all the way up the west coast of North America and over to Russia and Japan. But commercial hunting nearly wiped out the entire lot in less than two centuries. By the time Pacific powers signed an international treaty prohibiting hunting sea otters and other marine mammals in 1911, the population was estimated at only a few thousand. Most of these lived in the Aleutian Islands and a small population remained in central California, but they were essentially extinct in Oregon, Washington, British Columbia, and Southeast Alaska.

Once the hunting stopped, the sea otters made a remarkable recovery. Existing populations grew to about thirty thousand by midcentury. Conservationists then relocated several hundred sea otters from the Aleutian Islands to areas further south, in hopes of filling in the geographic gaps in their historical range. This was also a successful endeavor, and populations exploded in Alaska, with slower growth in California and Washington. Nowadays, more than one hundred thousand sea otters reside along the Alaskan coast.

It's a conservation success story, for sure, but a closer look reveals how vulnerable the sea otter is to changes and disruptions in its ecosystem. The most dramatic example was the 1989 Exxon Valdez oil spill in Prince William Sound, which caused as many as 5,500 sea otter deaths. Further, surviving animals continued to be exposed to lingering oil for decades after the spill. It is estimated that it took twenty-five years for the sea otters' population and habitat to recover after that ecological disaster.

In the twenty-first century, the sea otters are facing a new threat in the Aleutian Islands, where nearly 90 percent of the sea otter population disappeared between 1990 and 2010. The cause is unknown, but some experts think these otters might be getting eaten by orcas, who have lost their traditional prey (great whale calves).

One reason the sea otter is so important is that it is a "keystone species"—that is, a dominant predator that maintains the balance of an ecosystem. In this case, the ecosystem is the kelp forest, an underwater Eden that supports countless species of mammals, birds, fish, and invertebrates, including the notoriously voracious sea urchins. Without predators, sea urchins can decimate a kelp forest—creating so-called urchin barrens, where the sandy sea floor is covered with sea urchins, with no vegetation (and few other animals) in sight. But sea otters are a natural predator for this dangerous echinoderm: where sea otters thrive, sea urchins are kept in check, and kelp forests remain healthy and filled with diverse life. That's why scientists emphasize the importance of continuing to monitor and protect this marine mammal—not because it is so cuddly (although that helps), but because it is critical to the livelihood of an entire ecosystem.

CHAPTER 4
Massacre at Refuge Rock

I was a boy of nine or ten, when the first Russian ship, a two-master, arrived. We had never seen a ship before, we did not know white men," Arsenti Aminak told Henrik Holmberg in 1851. "When we saw the ship far off, we believed it was a giant whale. We went out in baidarkas and saw that it was not a whale, but a strange monster, its stench of tar made us sick. The people on board wore coats with buttons that looked like crabs, they took fire into their mouths and blew out smoke, we could only believe that they were devils."

By occupation, Holmberg was a mining engineer, conducting a geological survey of Kodiak. By passion, he was an amateur ethnographer, studying the island's Indigenous cultures. When Holmberg learned of an Alutiiq elder who knew the old stories, he stopped his surveying and traveled to a remote village to meet him. Aminak was one of "only a few old men from the previous century, who still held childhood images of the hero days of their people." Holmberg was welcomed into Aminak's house, but warned that the things he would hear "may bring danger upon him." For two nights, Holmberg listened intently and scribbled furiously. On the pages of his notebook was preserved the only Alutiiq eyewitness account of the Refuge Rock Massacre.

America was there for the taking. At least that was what Siberian fur trader Grigory Shelikhov believed. It was a big dream for a small merchant.

From an early age, Shelikhov had a knack for making friends and taking risks. He first apprenticed in the vodka business with Ivan Golikov, an on-the-make Kursk kinsman. There was much one could learn from a player like Golikov, a sometimes tax collector, sometimes rogue trader, and frequent courtroom defendant. In 1773, in his mid-twenties, Shelikhov departed the aristocratic order of western Russia for the freebooter tumult of the eastern frontier. He headed to Irkutsk, on the shores of Lake Baikal, capital of the Russian fur trade. Shelikhov soon turned his first profit in a daring expedition to Japan's Kuril Islands. In 1775 Shelikhov made another gainful acquaintance, his future business partner and wife, Natalia Kozhevina, the thirteen-year-old daughter of a well-to-do Siberian shipbuilder. Fortune shone on the young trader, and still he hungered for more. Shelikhov aimed to extend the Russian Empire across the Pacific.

The cheeky merchant crafted a proposal for the empress herself, Catherine the Great. Russia is destined to become a New World great power, Shelikhov enthused. The northwest American coast overflows with riches waiting to be collected and residents waiting to be converted. He vowed to seize this prize for the empire, then asked for an advance. "We will search out unknown islands and lands, inhabited by wild people and valuable animals, and with our labor and patriotic zeal bring them under the Imperial throne." The tsarina was unmoved. It was not that Catherine was averse to expansion. She was, in fact, busy at this time dismembering Poland and conquering Crimea. Rather, she considered America too distant a place and Shelikhov too dubious a man.

Undeterred by Her Majesty's cool response, Shelikhov pressed forward. He formed a joint-stock company with longtime partner Golikov. Together, they smooth-talked investors in St. Petersburg, stockpiled supplies in Siberia, and ordered the construction of three new ships. In 1782 the Northeast American Company came into being. Shelikhov then chose a location for his settlement: Kodiak Island.

The island of the bears, Kodiak (Qikertaq in the native Alutiiq) is the rugged sentinel to the Gulf of Alaska and launch pad into the American mainland. With a moderate subarctic climate, it is abundant in woods and wildlife. For at least 7,500 years, the Alutiiq people were sustained by Kodiak's bounty. In 1741 Vitus Bering sailed past Kodiak Island on the Great Northern Expedition, making note of a "high land" visible through a curtain of fog and mist. It was for the best that Bering's crew did not chance a meeting with the Alutiit. "War is for them a most pleasant exercise," a Russian monk later observed.

In the wake of the explorers came the exploiters. Russian trappers were drawn to Kodiak for fresh provisions and furry creatures. In October 1763 a Russian party led by Stepan Glotov became the first Europeans to make landfall on Kodiak. Glotov sought to persuade Alutiiq chieftains to accommodate a Russian trade post on the island, but was rebuffed. When Glotov settled in anyway, the Alutiit assailed his camp in a line charge behind thick wooden shields and attacked his ship with fire. The Russians hastily evacuated. "These savage-thinking people would not accept anything reasonable that I proposed," bemoaned the foiled Glotov.

One after another, Russian traders seeking to alight on Kodiak were chased off by the Alutiit. In August 1780 Siberian marauder Afanasy Ocheredin anchored on the west side of the island with the intention to deceive. His craft was the "sea monster" that Aminak later described to Holmberg. Under the guise of friendly trade, Ocheredin plotted an ambush. "Upon a signal," Aminak recalled, "they took their weapons out of hiding and killed thirty of our people and stole the sea otter pelts." But Ocheredin's deadly ploy was avenged. His winter camp came under siege, they ran out of food, and his crew perished. "In the spring, they left our island," Aminak said. Once more the Alutiit had successfully defended their homeland.

For centuries, the Alutiit were independent of foreign intervention. Their tenacious reputation spread and European mariners learned to bypass the island. But this situation would not endure. Four years after Ocheredin's retreat, another Russian expedition made landfall on Kodiak, with a leader like none the Alutiit had yet encountered.

<hr />

"In the year 1783, a company of merchants built three galiots in the harbor of Okhotsk. With them, I sailed on the 16th of August, from the mouth of the Okhota River down to the Sea of Okhotsk and then into the Eastern Ocean," Grigory Shelikhov recorded.

Shelikhov's colonization project was underway. For transportation, he built three galiots, smaller-sized sailing vessels that could be rowed galley-style through Alaska's tight fjords. For seamanship, he recruited Gerasim Izmailov, Russia's most experienced captain in the Far East. Izmailov was tutored by Captain James Cook, survived a mutiny and marooning on the Kuril Islands, piloted Russia's most lucrative fur hunt in Pacific waters, and accompanied Stepan Glotov's aborted Kodiak adventure twenty years earlier. When Izmailov cozied up to a bottle of vodka, which was not infrequently, he was soon showing off his numerous scars from arrows and knives. Shelikhov attracted additional talent, including naval navigator Dmitry Bocharov and ship's doctor Sergeant Miron Britiukov. More impressive, he collected two hundred souls, willing to become Russia's first settlers in America. Never mind that his company, according to a Siberian neighbor, "was drawn from the most depraved thieves and bandits in Irkutsk."

In June 1783 the first enrollment of Russian colonists assembled in the Far East town of Okhotsk. The band of rough-cut pilgrims instinctively took refuge in the seaport's accommodating saloons. Among the trunks and barrels stacked dockside was a conspicuous cache of arms—flintlock muskets, gunpowder kegs, and light artillery falconets. Sergeant Britiukov confronted Shelikhov about this arsenal, citing the sovereign's prohibition on the use of force against Indigenous peoples. A defensive precaution, Shelikhov assured.

In mid-August, the convoy departed. "I was aboard the flagship, the *Three Saints*, with my wife, who accompanied me wherever I went, undeterred by the labors and dangers that lay ahead." Standing in the bow of the *Three Saints*, Grigory and Natalia gazed portside at the forested cliffs corralling the sea and starboard at a bowhead whale lounging atop the summer feeding ground. Three weeks later, the flotilla left the safety of the Sea of Okhotsk, passed through the breakwaters of the Kuril Islands, and entered the open sea. "We were met with a violent storm which lasted eight and forty hours," Shelikhov said. "The storm raged so furiously that our ships were separated and we almost lost hope of saving our lives." The *Three Saints* rode out the typhoon and limped northward toward Bering Island, where they spent "a long and severe winter." Where his sister ships were, Shelikhov did not know.

"On 16 June 1784, we left the island and appointed Unalaska in the Fox Islands as our rendezvous point." Nearly a month passed before the ethereal silhouette of the *Saint Simeon* was sighted near Unalaska Island. "We drew our galiots together in the Captain's Haven," Shelikhov said, "refitting our ships and providing ourselves with necessities." It was now late July, and only a month remained to the short sailing season. Before departing, another Russian vessel entered the harbor.

Captain Potap Zaikov was on the return leg of a luckless hunting tour in the Gulf of Alaska. "The local inhabitants did not let us get near to anything to catch, nor could we go anywhere in small groups without our rifles. We lost a number of men to starvation," Zaikov complained. When Shelikhov divulged his destination, Zaikov erupted. "The Kodiak natives are bloodthirsty and unreconcilable." But Shelikhov brushed off Zaikov's reproach. "I have already been warned about the aggressiveness of the Kodiak people," he answered. "I pay no heed to the advice of those who have suffered from their cruelties and I scorn the dangers ahead. My passion for the Higher Throne and our Motherland has encouraged me to overcome my fears." Despite their leader's bravado, the company's mood was somber.

The evening before the *Three Saints* weighed anchor, Shelikhov was visited by an Unangan leader, who tried one last time to dissuade him from landing on Kodiak. But if you must go, he said, there is a man here who may be helpful. He summoned Qaspeq, an enslaved man with Kodiak roots. The meeting of Shelikhov and Qaspeq was a fateful turning point for Russian America.

Qaspeq was a small boy when his village on Kodiak Island was raided by warriors from the Fox Islands. The Aleuts and the Alutiit were longtime neighbors and rivals in the Gulf of Alaska, competing for sea mammals, salmon, and slaves. Indeed, the Aleuts most commonly referred to the Alutiit not by the name of their tribe or the location of their settlements, but as Angadutix, a word that otherwise meant "enemy." After a successful raid, the practice was to torture and kill the opposing warriors and to enslave the women and children. This is how Qaspeq found himself living in an unknown land and serving an ancestral foe. Out of necessity, Qaspeq had learned the local language, Unangan, and—when European fur traders began making appearances in the Aleutians—Russian. He soon gained a reputation among the Russian skippers, who appreciated his linguistic dexterity and his knowledge of the regional seascape.

Qaspeq was a man without a country. He had no allegiance to his Aleut captors. The perceptive servant recognized the military might of the Russians. Several years earlier, when fighting broke out on Unalaska, the Aleuts ambushed a Russian party, then retreated to an offshore site. Qaspeq revealed their location to the Russian captain, who sent a vengeful posse and quashed the resistance. Afterward the Aleuts were forced to do the bidding of the Russian intruders.

Qaspeq was the beneficiary of this regime change. He bragged to his new masters about the riches of his native Kodiak Island, its coves teeming with fur-bearing sea mammals and its forests thick with ancient timber. Now as the *Three Saints* slogged eastward, Qaspeq was honored with a seat next to Shelikhov, who listened thoughtfully to the interpreter's stories.

On August 2, Koniag Peak appeared through the mist. The *Three Saints* and *Saint Simeon* dropped anchor side-by-side in a deep-water fjord, tucked into Kodiak's rocky southwest coast. The shoreline was deserted. The lapping bay was the only sound.

Early the next morning, Shelikhov gathered the company. "I am master of the ship and of all the people thereon," he declared. "I am empowered with the authority to punish and hang not only the islanders, but the loyal subjects of our Most Merciful Empress as well." After the intimidating harangue, the company was compelled to utter their consent. Shelikhov next organized two search parties to explore the southern coastline in either direction. "Try to make contact with the inhabitants," he commanded, "and tell them I want a parley with their chief. Bring your muskets."

But engaging the locals proved a difficult task. Alutiiq scouts easily eluded the Russian hunters, while keeping a close watch. It was not until the third day that three Alutiiq baidarkas paddled into the harbor. Shelikhov rushed to his cabin and emerged with a fistful of glass beads. "We welcomed them aboard with signs of friendship," he said. "I presented them with gifts and we traded some furs for some goods they needed." With Qaspeq translating, Shelikhov began to explain his intention of building a settlement and living in peace to mutual advantage. But this first meeting with the Alutiit was disrupted by a solar eclipse. "Having no idea of the cause, our guests were greatly amazed." The confounded envoys ended the meeting and departed in haste. It was an ill omen.

No Alutiiq representatives returned to the bay. Shelikhov assumed the worst. No one could say he hadn't been warned. The fast-talking merchant had hoped to be able to negotiate his way onto the island, but he was prepared to fight his way, if necessary. "I disregarded all the cautions about the Alutiit," Shelikhov said. "My partners and I were in general agreement that our first obligation was to pacify the savages in the interest of the enterprise." A battle was coming.

News of the Russian landfall shot through the Alutiiq camps along the southwest coast. The elders conferred over the transgression. The late-summer salmon harvest was abruptly postponed. Household members regrouped, gathered a few essentials, and made rendezvous on Sitkalidak Island. There, the Alutiit prepared for combat and summoned reinforcements from neighboring villages. In addition to "swift runners" who traveled by land, they had an elaborate system of signal fires that indicated both the proximity and the strength of approaching enemies. They needed only to hold out for a few days until their allies arrived.

Amid the commotion, an Unangan slave managed to escape his Alutiiq master. The freedom seeker fled toward the Russian camp, hoping to reunite with the company's Aleut hunters. Startling the Russians, the man was seized and taken directly to Shelikhov for questioning. "The Alutiit are expecting warriors in large numbers," the informant said. "They intend to attack the harbor and destroy everything. Already they are discussing the division of slaves and plunder, especially the valuable timber from your ships." A war party was gathering on the far side of Sitkalidak—at Refuge Rock.

Across the southern strait from Kodiak Island, where the Russians were anchored, was the smaller island of Sitkalidak. Nestled along its sheer cliff walls on the south side facing the sea was an inaccessible shelter, known as Refuge Rock. Poised a quarter mile from a sliver of rocky beach in the middle of a frigid cove, this mesa-shaped outcrop rose out of the sea on forty-foot sandstone walls. Its mossy oblong top was the size of two football fields, creased with grooves and pockets. It was a natural fortress—impossible to land a boat on and impossible to scale. This ancient sanctuary had never been breached.

Hoping to avoid a clash, Shelikhov tried to bargain with the Alutiiq leaders. He ordered Qaspeq to act as diplomat: "Attempt to persuade them to agree to friendly relations, assure them that we do not come to quarrel or to hurt them, but on the contrary to gain their good will. Promise them presents."

"Qaspeq had relatives among the inhabitants of the settlement," an Alutiiq compatriot later said. "Qaspeq implored the Alutiit to accept willingly the demands of the Russians, since otherwise they would suffer severe consequences." He had watched Russian brutality transform the once-defiant Aleut tribes of the Fox Islands into a demoralized band of forced laborers. Qaspeq was finally back home, and his loyalties were being tested.

The negotiation failed. The Alutiit rejected the Russian bid. "A multitude had gathered," Shelikhov reported, "and they did not look favorably on my offer. They began to shoot at us with bows and arrows and we were obliged to withdraw." Shelikhov sent Qaspeq back a second time to open communications. But after so long in exile, Qaspeq seemed more a stranger than a brother to the Alutiit. He had no influence, even with kin. His pleas only elicited scorn: "If you return again, you will be treated as an enemy." Qaspeq seethed.

The prodigal Alutiit was rejected by his own people. Qaspeq's allegiance became clear. He returned from this rebuke and went straight to Shelikhov. As it turned out, Qaspeq knew more about Kodiak than he had yet shared. He was aware of the one weakness of Refuge Rock. On Sitkalidak Island, a hidden portage connected a north side inlet with the south side cove. The tight crack through the cliff wall, imperceptible from the water, led out to a narrow pebble-covered beach that faced Refuge Rock. Even from this vantage point, however, the stronghold appeared beyond reach, protected by a quarter mile of punishing surf. Except for one hour at low tide, when a slender rocky spit just below the water surface connected the beach to the fortress. Twice a day it was possible to wade across the cove. Qaspeq betrayed the existence of the secret portage.

"Leave these shores if you want to remain alive," a war chief taunted the Russians. Atop Refuge Rock, the Alutiit readied themselves for battle. The shelter contained several dozen compact houses, dug into the ground and covered with sod. Women were storing food and water in ceramic jars in case of a siege. The men were sharpening slate blades and fixing them to spears and arrows. More kinsmen arrived. The site could hold two thousand people. Only a week after the Russians arrived, the sanctuary was already half filled. The war chief returned to his quarters, a larger structure with a commanding view of the compound and the coast. Inside, he fingered a string of blue beads that Shelikhov had given to his envoy. He summoned a war council.

That night, an Alutiiq scouting party slipped past the sentries of the Russian camp. At midnight, alarm cries sounded and gun shots rang out. We are under attack! The hunters sprang from their bedrolls, clutching their rifles. But the scouts had already vanished into the shadows. The adrenalized company could not sleep. "The likelihood of imminent death gave us vigor," Shelikhov said. Despite the high risk, Shelikhov was unwilling to forfeit his investment. He urged the company to go on the offensive to catch the Alutiit by surprise. "We decided to seize control of the rock before their reinforcements could reach them."

At dawn on August 13, a seventy-man force crept through the secret portage on Sitkalidak and emerged onto the pebble beach facing Refuge Rock. Alutiiq lookouts roused the fortress. The tide was running out, and the Russians were massing for a charge across the spit. With the advantage of higher ground, the defenders assumed positions behind the rock embankments, ready to hurl down a torrent of arrows, spears, and stones. Meanwhile, Shelikhov's artillery team worked on hoisting the falconets onto a ridge above the beach with an unobstructed sightline into the compound. Shelikhov could not wait. If he missed the morning low tide, then the Alutiit would have the chance to outflank him in the north, pin him down on the beach, and obliterate his force. As the tide ran out, the narrow spit was revealed. Russian musketeers advanced.

Though lacking in formal training, Shelikhov's company had had plenty of fighting experience. The veteran trappers in the front ranks had stared down death before and were impervious to the arrows whizzing past them now. Leading the sloshing charge was Yegor Mikhailovich Baranov, one of the rowdiest and roughest members of the company. Baranov reached the base of the fortress: finding a rocky toehold for his thick boot, he began pulling himself upward. Looking up, he saw red-and-black painted faces.

A large rock careened down the cliffside, just missing the head of Baranov, who tightly hugged the wall. A second hunter, Afanasy Liskenkov, scrambled past Baranov, but was struck by a spear and fell backward. A chorus of jeers rang down. Baranov could not use a rifle against his tormentors without losing his precarious grip. A volley of arrows sent the attackers at the base scattering into the chilling surf. The Russians were being routed. Suddenly, a deafening boom cracked over the cove and a sulfurous plume blotted the sky. Stone fragments spilled down the cliff wall and a dust cloud billowed from the fortress entrance. The falconets were in place.

A second falconet launched a two-and-half-pound projectile into the fortress, smashing a house wall and spraying shrapnel with deadly force. A third volley struck where a group of warriors were reassembling, sending bodies crashing to the ground in a senseless blur. The sound of thunder followed by violent destruction. The Alutiit had never faced such a weapon. The organized defense fell into disarray.

Under the cover of five cannons, the Russian assault team scaled the craggy wall. Baranov was the first to reach the top, where he felled an Alutiiq warrior with a musket ball in the entranceway. Shelikhov later wrote that Baranov "was boldly the first to enter the stone fortress with others following behind him. For this he was rewarded with fifty rubles." Many Alutiit fled to the far end of the compound. They tried to claw their way down the steep cliff to the base, where the baidarkas were tethered and an escape route to the sea beckoned. Scores of Alutiit managed to get away from the besieged fortress, but scores more fell to their death on the rocks below or drowned in the sea. Dead bodies floated in the cove.

Inside the compound, malice and mayhem reigned. Russians armed with muskets and bayonets fought off defiant warriors with arrows and clubs. Panic-stricken women and children scrambled into the dugout houses. The invading hunters pursued them as quarry, shooting people in the back or bashing heads with rifle butts. Meanwhile, Russian artillery levelled the compound, its wooden structures set ablaze. In less than an hour, the roughneck army conquered the fortress.

Shelikhov attributed the victory to the falconets. "This experience was new and extraordinary," he said. "It instilled fear and terror in them and gave an awesome impression of us. They abandoned their stronghold."

Roughly five hundred Alutiit surrendered to the Russians. The terrified captives were herded into small groups for evacuation. In stunned silence, they waited for the next low tide. Refuge Rock had fallen.

A battle was won, but the Russians were still a 130-person outfit surrounded by thousands. "The Alutiit felt like they could easily force us off Kodiak Island, down to the last man," Shelikhov said. Yet a united front never formed. "If it had not been for the natives who escaped from the battle, then we would have been totally annihilated by the Alutiit from other villages," Shelikhov observed. "These natives told the reinforcements a story more horrifying than what really happened. They believed we had completely destroyed the stone fortress with our firearms. The reinforcements were so intimidated that they immediately dispersed."

Meanwhile, Shelikhov took advantage of his prisoners. He ordered the survivors to construct a makeshift prison camp near the harbor where the *Three Saints* was anchored. Here they would remain as collateral until the Alutiit agreed to a ceasefire. Shortly after the massacre, a warrior band raided the camp with the aim of freeing the prisoners. "The natives made an attack one night during a wind and rain storm," Shelikhov said. "They assembled in great numbers and made a fierce assault using lances and arrows. We managed to repel them with guns. I do not know how many of them were killed. Six of our men were wounded and they wrecked our baidarkas."

Two Alutiit attackers were captured alive. Shelikhov beat the details of the plot from them, using a whalebone and a rifle butt. According to Sergeant Britiukov, Shelikhov killed them both, one by rifle and one by sword, and put their bodies on display for effect. In retaliation for the assault, Shelikhov then staged public executions of the adult male prisoners. "The men were taken to the tundra and speared to death." Eventually, individual Alutiiq men began coming to the harbor and begging for the release of their family members. Shelikhov consented on the condition that they lay down arms against the colony. A month after the massacre, the prison camp was emptied and the survivors went home.

Shelikhov consolidated his victory. "I took advantage of their amazement of our arms to impress that I wished to live in friendship and that our most gracious monarch only wanted to protect them," Shelikhov explained in colonial doublespeak. He applied the same techniques of imperial conquest that Russians had used for more than a century against Indigenous peoples in Siberia: a complex system of reward and punishment, based on kidnapping.

"After the massacre every chief had to surrender their children as hostages," Aminak later explained. The seizure of family members from the village leaders was an insurance policy, enabling the Russians to settle without fear of attack and to conscript locals into company service.

Hostage-taking as a mechanism of political control had a long history in Eurasia, as the Russians had learned it from the Mongols. If the subjugated community cooperated, then hostages were not harmed and perhaps treated well; otherwise, they were tortured and killed. The taking of hostages was sometimes negotiated with a chieftain and sometimes people were simply snatched. This intimidation tactic was the means by which Shelikhov turned the fiercely independent Alutiit into a compliant labor force.

Russian coercion wore down the Alutiit along the southwest coast. Shelikhov rewarded village heads who conceded with small tokens and favored treatment, and he punished those who resisted with lethal violence. Taking advantage of intra-island rivalries, he co-opted the southwest residents to participate in an assault against the northeast residents, destroying entire villages. Within two years, Shelikhov was ensconced as the boss of an island-spanning protection racket in which the majority of Alutiit were compelled to deliver tribute and labor.

If the Kodiak colony was not thriving, then it was at least surviving. Shelikhov decided it was time to capitalize on his accomplishment. In May 1786 the *Three Saints* was loaded with a cache of furs and a score of Alutiiq chieftains and hostages. Grigory and Natalia headed home in triumph. Russia was now a player in the New World.

Shelikhov was certain that his American colony would be reckoned a success, but for the means by which it was achieved. At least some in the company were aghast at the excessive violence. Notably, Sergeant Miron Britiukov kept a detailed record of abuse, torture, and killing. Wary of antagonizing his cold-blooded commander, Britiukov bided his time.

Shortly before the *Three Saints* left Kodiak, the tension between the two snapped, and the director sacked his surgeon during a red-faced shouting match. Shelikhov was now pressed to return to Russia to preempt a scandal.

Britiukov's damning accusations sent ripples of indignation across Russian officialdom. Catherine the Great was infuriated by reports that Shelikhov's colony engaged in "pillaging, cruelty, and inhumanity against the island inhabitants." The empress vowed that "those found guilty will not escape their lawful punishment." An investigation was ordered. The Admiralty dispatched the report to the Senate for consideration, the Senate immediately passed it on to the State Council for action, and the State Council wasted no time to delegate to the governor-general in Siberia the task of conducting an inquiry. As it turned out, Shelikhov was on good terms with the governor-general, who concluded that the charges were without merit. Thus, after a game of bureaucratic dodge ball, Shelikhov escaped indictment.

Still, the timing could not have been worse. Shelikhov was preparing another pitch to the empress for a royal charter. To bolster his case, he solicited testimonies from regional governors, imperial senators, and court councilors, moved by his embellished tales and generous gifts.

Shelikhov falsely bragged that his colony had added fifty thousand new subjects to the empire, who by "kindly treatment and trust are convinced that the arrival of the Russians has brought numerous advantages." He further claimed to have secured "new locations for Russian settlements along the American coast, south toward California, leaving emblems of our sovereignty to prevent any attempts of other nations to gain this part of the earth." Shelikhov's petition did not skimp. He wanted exclusive rights to the North Pacific fur trade, a long-term loan from the state treasury for two hundred thousand rubles, and on-site protection from the Imperial Russian Navy. Only by such means, he argued, will Russia become a great power in the New World.

Shelikhov was confident that his exploits would be rewarded. But the empress still saw American colonization as an improbable undertaking. She issued an emphatic *nyet*. Catherine likened the scheme to "the proposal of a man who wants to train an elephant to speak in thirty years." She did, however, confer an honorary medal and sword on Shelikhov for "activities very useful to the state." Shelikhov was embittered by this consolation prize.

In July 1795 the raucous frontier town of Irkutsk was subdued by the news that the fearless Shelikhov was "suffering from a long and hard fever." Shelikhov died, at age forty-seven, with his devoted wife and five daughters at his bedside.

Grigory Shelikhov was both the dreamer and driver of Russian America. His death threw into doubt the survival of the colony. His intention was to pass control of the company to Natalia, though he neglected to document this in a legal will. Siberia's conniving merchants seized the opening, especially since it was unheard of that a woman should run a trading firm. Natalia invoked the highest authority. "Most Gracious Sovereign," she wrote the empress, "I remain after my husband's death with only oral instructions not to abandon his activities in America. He was sure that I would be the heiress of his affairs. But if my rights were disputed, he urged me to petition Your Majesty for protection from his jealous detractors. I and my children are wary of becoming victims of their insidiousness. We place hope and trust in Your Imperial Majesty for your motherly support."

In the end, the family's political connections paid off and Natalia was named company head. But even with the capable Natalia in charge, the colony was in jeopardy.

Despite Shelikhov's extravagant claims, Kodiak was hardly more than a lonely frontier outpost. Now, without its zealous defender, the colony seemed destined to wither away. Perhaps Shelikhov's most sagacious hunch was to ask a down-on-his-luck petty trader to look after things on Kodiak until he could find a long-term replacement. If Shelikhov's grand vision of Russian America was ever to be realized, it would fall on the shoulders of the reluctant Alexander Baranov.

For God and Sovereign, Shelikhov set out to conquer the New World. He was consumed by the glory as much as the greed. In 1791 he published a self-promoting memoir of his American adventure with a frontispiece portrait of himself as the "Russian Columbus"—in commanding pose on a Kodiak beach, surrounded by adoring Alutiit and abounding wildlife, and with the god of commerce, Mercury, soaring overhead. In 1800 Shelikhov's family and friends in Irkutsk proposed a towering marble obelisk for his gravesite at the Znamensky Monastery. When the local bishop objected to the monument's sacrilegious scale, Tsar Paul I intervened to assure it was built. The inscription reads: "The Russian Columbus is here buried. He crossed the seas and discovered unknown lands. And seeing that everything on earth is tainted, he set his sail toward the heavenly ocean."

The Russian American colony was founded on bloodshed and exploita-tion. As noted by one Siberian contemporary and avowed critic, Shelikhov was nothing more than a "master robber, sufficiently as cruel as the Span-iards in ancient American history." Columbus, maybe. But perhaps Grigory Shelikhov is more akin to conquistador plunderers Cortés and Pizarro, whose reckless violence gutted long-flourishing Indigenous societies in one decisive battle.

—∞—

Awa'uq—meaning "to become numb"—is the Alutiiq term for Refuge Rock. What was for centuries a vibrant and vigorous island community of more than five thousand people was shattered during one devastating morning. The massacre marked the beginning of "the darkest period of history" for the Alutiit. A free people were defeated, a confident spirit was broken, a new order was imposed.

"When our people revisited the place in the summer the stench of the corpses lying on the shore polluted the air so badly that no one could stay there," Aminak recalled. Still, grief-stricken Alutiiq family members silently crossed over the spit. Atop the cliff, they found the gory ruins of their fortress. The moldering bodies of the slain were scattered among the wild grasses and salmonberries. More corpses were found inside the shelters, where the women and children had been hiding. The houses were burned out. Bereaved Alutiit had come to respect the dead and bury their remains. Before leaving they erected a monument, a cairn of whalebone and small boulders, to sanctify the site as a mass grave. "Since then the island has been uninhabited," Aminak said.

How many were killed at Refuge Rock? On the Russian side, there were no fatalities, and only five men were wounded. On the Alutiiq side, the number is not known with certainty. The main antagonist Shelikhov avoided fixing a number: "I made every effort not to shed blood, but I cannot believe that we did not kill some of them." By contrast, a contemporary Alutiiq source asserts that "between 2,500 and 3,000 Alutiiq people perished" in the attack. More probable estimates come from those who were alive and on Kodiak during the event. The survivor Aminak remembered that "the Russians went to the settlement and carried out a terrible bloodbath. A few men were able to flee in baidarkas, but 300 Alutiit were shot by the Russians." Several years later, Catherine's inquisitors confronted Gerasim Izmailov, who said that about 150–200 persons were killed. Meanwhile, in his exposé, company surgeon Miron Britiukov swore that "armed men murdered about 500 people, and if we count those who ran in fear to escape and were either stampeded or drowned, the number is higher. More recently, Dehrich Schmidt-Chya, a researcher at the Alutiiq Museum in Kodiak, suggested 300-plus deaths, in line with Aminak's estimate. In any case, the number is staggering. Wounded Knee, Sand Creek, Bear River . . . these are among the most violent single-day battles in Native American history since the founding of the United States. Even by the lower estimates, the Refuge Rock Massacre surpassed these infamous events in fatalities.

Until 1784, Kodiak was the bulwark against Russian expansion in North America. "This was the beginning of the end for the Alutiit of Kodiak Island," historian Lydia Black said. "Shelikhov really smashed their military might. It was their first major military defeat." Archeologist Rick Knecht placed the event in historical perspective: "It broke the back of Native resistance; it was the Wounded Knee of Alaska." The Refuge Rock Massacre was the strategic breakthrough that enabled Russian colonization of America.

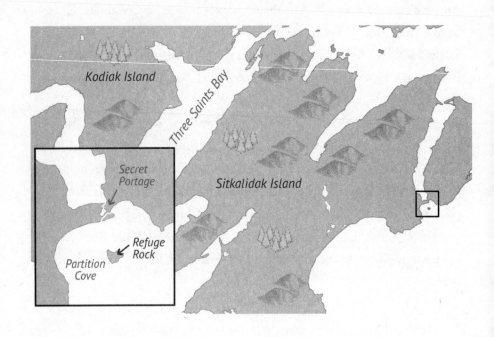

REFUGE ROCK REDISCOVERED

The story of the massacre at Refuge Rock has been an integral part of the Alutiiq lore, recorded by eyewitnesses and passed down through oral histories. Yet the precise location of Awa'uq was forgotten over time. It was only in 1990 that a group of geologists doing a helicopter survey spotted a small refuge island off the southern coast of Sitkalidak Island. From the air, they could see indentations in the earth, remnants of Alutiiq houses on the small island. Most importantly, they noticed the narrow strip of land between Sitkalidak's inland lagoon and its south-facing beach—the "secret portage" that Qaspeq had disclosed to the Russians.

Two years later, a team of archeologists returned to the island to conduct a more thorough excavation. The archeologists uncovered the remains of twenty-eight dwellings, which were similar to but smaller than typical Alutiiq homes from that time. Refuse heaps and hearth rocks were scattered everywhere, implying that there were not nearly enough homes to accommodate the large number of people seeking refuge there. Most of the artifacts found were household items, used for cooking and food storage, as well as weapons. The archeologists also found four glass beads. These types of beads were produced in Russia and Asia during the eighteenth century—confirming that the Alutiit occupied this site after contact with the Russians. One bead was identical to others found during excavations of the Russian settlement site at Three Saints Harbor.

Unfinished blades and lance points indicated that the occupants were in the process of making weapons when they were attacked. Clearly, the Alutiit did not intend to go down without a fight. But, the archeologists concluded, "The terror induced by cannon fire . . . won the day." It was clear how the inhabitants would have retreated to the far side of the island, where there was no escape but into the deadly, icy waters. In the wake of the siege, the Russians probably looted the houses in search of food, as evidenced by the many ceramic fragments and broken pots and storage boxes in disarray. Burned grass and ash and other fire damage suggested that they also burned the homes to the ground before departure.

Most sobering was the discovery of human remains—in particular, the bones of a small child. The scholars wrote that "two hundred years of time and cultural difference did little to erase the sense of grief and outrage that we felt at seeing a child's skeleton on a house floor." Undoubtedly, many more people died as a result of the "needless atrocity" at Awa'uq. The team found possible evidence of a mass grave site as well as several constructions of whalebone and boulders, which may have served as memorial markers. They concluded that the Alutiiq survivors likely later returned to the massacre site to bury their dead.

Two centuries after the Refuge Rock Massacre, the archeological investigations confirmed much of the eyewitness accounts of the siege and clarified some discrepancies. Most importantly, they solved the mystery of Awa'uq, pinpointing a physical location for Alutiiq descendants to honor their ancestors and remember their history.

CHAPTER 5
Into the Land of the Raven

D uring the darkest hours of the night, a mob of armed men surrounded us from all sides and began to stab and slash. Though we had five men standing guard, they crept so close in the darkness that they were just ten steps from our tents when we spotted them. We opened fire but without much effect. They were protected by layers of wooden plaited armor and thick moose hide cloaks, and on their heads were wooden helmets with painted images of animals and monsters. They were more frightful than the most hellish devils." It was June 1792, on Nuchek Island in Prince William Sound, where Alexander Baranov first met the Tlingit.

Seeking to expand operations, Grigory Shelikhov ordered his new company director to explore opportunities for settling the Alaskan mainland. The dutiful Baranov nearly paid with his life. "God shielded me, for though a spear pierced my shirt and arrows fell all around me, I was unhurt." Baranov rallied his men into a defensive circle and withstood the assailants until sunrise when the *Saint Simeon* arrived with reinforcements. The midnight ambush left a dozen men slain and four hostages seized. The beaten crew limped back to Kodiak. It was the deadliest rout Russia had yet experienced in America. Baranov's reputation as a fearless and invincible foe was born. In fact, it was his concealed chain-mail undergarment, which had deflected the Tlingit lances.

Alexander Baranov was born in 1747, in the trading town of Kargopol, along the Onega River in northwest Russia. His merchant father taught him the basics of commerce. A restless soul, young Alexander ran away to Moscow at the age of fifteen, returned home for a spell, then moved to St. Petersburg, before setting out, with a new wife, for Siberia. Baranov readily took to frontier living. His business skills kept him employed in glassmaking, vodka selling, tax collecting, and trading with the Indigenous Chukchi. When Grigory Shelikhov returned to Irkutsk in search of a manager for his American operation, the industrious Baranov stood out. Still, Baranov did not sign up right away. Only after his investments went broke and his wife went home did Baranov consider a move to Kodiak.

In August 1790 Baranov became the Russian-American Company's field manager. The contract stipulated that he would oversee the affairs of the colony and business of the fur trade, defend the company's territorial claims throughout the North Pacific, expand Russian settlements to the American coastline, and foster cooperative relations with the Native peoples and win their allegiance to Empress Catherine. He was even made complicit in a scheme to seize any foreign merchant vessel, whose captain was suspected of privateering on behalf of Russia's rivals. For himself, Baranov negotiated a generous expense fund, a life insurance policy for his wife, and a percentage of the annual fur profits. Most enticing, the benefits included ten shares of company stock, which at the time was worth 2.5 million rubles and included the royal family among the shareholders. It was an eye-watering contract for a mind-boggling assignment. The petty merchant from Kargopol had become the de facto colonial governor of the easternmost edge of the Russian Empire.

Baranov showed his mettle from the start. In October 1790 his transport to Kodiak, the company flagship *Three Saints*, was wrecked in an autumn squall and the crew was marooned on Unalaska Island. Baranov sized up the dire situation and took charge: building winter shelter, finding food, befriending the local Unangan people, and still tending to business by trapping foxes. The biggest threat, he said, was "the great state of boredom, especially when bad weather set in for weeks at a time." The resourceful merchant had learned the basics of boat building in his riverport hometown. By late spring, three makeshift crafts were ready to launch, and despite the crew's desperate pleas to do the safe thing and return to Okhotsk, Baranov pointed the vessels eastward toward America.

—❦—

"My first steps here were met with cruel fate," Baranov said, "but perhaps the end of my efforts will be crowned with good fortune." He conducted an inspection of the colony. The bloom was off Shelikhov's rose. The Russian settlers were aggrieved over failed promises, and threatening mutiny. The Alutiiq villagers were traumatized by their subjugation, and in despair. And British and American merchants were ignoring Russian territorial claims, trading wherever they pleased and reaping big profits. Baranov spent the first year trying to set things right.

For Russian colonists, the main source of discontent was Shelikhov's bookkeeping tricks. Hoping to get rich quickly, company employees signed contracts to receive a salary of a half share of the annual profit, minus personal expenses. The payment was high, the costs were higher. Shelikhov took advantage of his company store monopoly, jacking up prices of food and supplies. Instead of going home at contract's end with a tidy sum, the colonists were obligated to remain in America to work off debt. Baranov was not empowered to dismantle the system, but he earned trust by making the ledger transparent and holding down prices. He imposed on the colonists the same high standards of productivity and dutifulness that he kept for himself. Those who met the mark enjoyed the boss's favor, while those who fell short suffered his scorn.

The chronic shortage of settlers meant that the company was dependent on Indigenous labor. In the quest for sea otters and fur seals, no one could match the prowess of the Aleut and Alutiiq hunters in their lightweight baidarkas. Baranov's predecessors imposed a harsh feudal-style economy on the Natives, demanding tribute in annual quotas of fur pelts and service in hunting parties and work brigades. Shortly after Baranov took charge, the cruel tribute obligation was abolished. Meanwhile, Baranov sought to transform the forced labor regime from a coercion-based to a reward-based system. "It may seem unnecessary to you, but I should like to take the risk on my own account," he appealed to Shelikhov. "I want to gain the goodwill of these wild Americans by making them gifts. We shall not give them the slightest reason for bitterness, and after a while I hope to gain their support."

Much to his relief, Baranov was not compelled to hunt down privateers or confront warships. The tsar's conflicts with rivals back in Europe did not spill over to the Pacific. That was for the best, since Baranov's own flagship was unarmed. But he was confounded to learn that the threat posed by British and US traders was not just economic. "We noticed that the natives had a lot of guns, lead, and powder in their possession. When we asked where it came from, they said that they got the guns from foreign trading vessels." The exchange of firearms for furs was an ongoing source of antagonism between the settled Russian colonists and the visiting merchant captains.

In meeting these challenges, the novice governor benefitted from the counsel and companionship of two allies. At work, Baranov recruited Ivan Kuskov to join him as second-in-command. The pair of voluntary exiles first met in Irkutsk, becoming fast friends. Ivan had arrived in Siberia under dubious circumstances. On the lam from an onerous debt, he found gainful employment on the frontier, with no questions asked. To convince his fellow fortune seeker to accompany him to America, Baranov offered Kuskov an annual salary of one hundred rubles plus one share of the company profit. He also agreed to cover his outstanding debts from his own purse. It was a good investment. Kuskov served as Baranov's loyal sidekick for nearly twenty years, earning praise for his "honesty, zeal, and competence."

Meanwhile, at home, Baranov's wife and children had already departed the frontier and moved back to western Russia. Though he neither divorced his wife nor neglected her financial support, Baranov never saw his family again. Baranov arrived on Kodiak as the island's most eligible bachelor. On a northern tour of the Kenai Peninsula, Baranov met a loquacious Kenaitze chief, whom the Russians dubbed Grigor Razkazchikov, or Grigor the Storyteller. To secure good relations, Grigor presented Baranov with the gift of a new wife, his seventeen-year-old daughter. Baranov was put on the spot by the unexpected offer. Not wanting to spoil the negotiations, he accepted. Besides, marriage was more about status and influence than love and affection. Yet what began as a partnership of convenience blossomed into a lifelong bond. Taking the Russian name Anna Grigorievna, she assimilated quickly to colonial life, while sharpening Baranov's awareness of Native sensibilities. Anna became a trusted confidante, a possessive spouse, and a doting mother. Baranov liked to tout his American Creole family as a model solution for a colony that was always short of new settlers.

Under Baranov, the Kodiak colony acquired a semblance of order. Baranov was now ready to expand operations to the Alaska mainland. The target was a stretch of coastline near Mount Saint Elias, where, he was told, Russian explorers had already converted the local Tlingit into loyal subjects of the Crown. Baranov organized an expedition to Yakutat Bay to call on Yeilxaak.

"In the year 1788, in the month of June, the navigators Gerasim Izmailov and Dmitry Bocharov of the Shelikhov Company arrived on the galiot *Three Saints* to Yakutat Bay, where through the kindness of Yeilxaak and his Tlingit people conducted trade and persuaded them to come under the protection of the Imperial Throne." So read the inscription on the double-headed eagle crest that the Russian mariners presented to the Gaanaxteidí clan head.

Izmailov and Bocharov were the first Russians to venture into Tlingit territory since the Great Northern Expedition. Their mostly friendly encounters with the clans around Yakutat Bay marked an auspicious start for Russian-Tlingit relations. The only negative incident reported in the ship's journal was the theft of a grappling hook. In addition to the imperial crest, the Russians presented a portrait of the heir apparent Tsarevitch Paul to Yeilxaak, "who received it with great joy." Eager to match the gesture, the status-conscience Yeilxaak reciprocated with an ornate metalwork in the shape of a raven's beak, a pair of form line painted wooden panels, and six sea otter cloaks. For the Russians, this exchange of gifts affirmed that the Yakutat Tlingit accepted Empress Catherine as their sovereign. The region "is inhabited by the Tlingit, whom we have brought under our control. We left a sign and emblem there." It was a mistaken conclusion.

Izmailov and Bocharov returned to Kodiak satisfied that Russia had recruited a powerful ally on the mainland. "All without exception obey him." Indeed, Yeilxaak was a vaunted Tlingit chieftain, but the Gaanaxteidí clan were from the Chilkat River, two hundred miles east of Yakutat. Yeilxaak had little influence over the Tlingit living at Yakutat Bay, where the L'uknax.ádi clan was dominant. It was only a coincidence that he was in Yakutat on a trade mission at the time that the *Three Saints* sailed into the bay. Perhaps emboldened by his new Russian partners, Yeilxaak soon after unleashed his ambitions on his clan rivals in Yakutat.

The Gaanaxteidí-L'uknax.ádi war of the early 1790s was driven by two strong-willed clan leaders. Yeilxaak was from an elite Gaanaxteidí household in the village of Klukwan. Their location along the Chilkat River enabled the Gaanaxteidí to control a major trade route between the coast and interior. The prosperous Gaanaxteidí built the elaborately decorated Whale House at Klukwan, later known as the Sistine Chapel of North American Native culture. X̱'unei was a powerful L'uknax̱.ádi leader in the Yakutat region. The Spanish captain Alejandro Malaspina arrived in Yakutat several years after the war and met X̱'unei. "The chief was an old, venerable and ferocious looking man with a long gray pyramid-shaped beard and loose flaccid hair on his shoulders. A large brown bear skin for a cape was gathered in at the waist, leaving entirely bare his breast, arms, thighs, and endowments, very muscular and strong. All gave him a majestic air."

Tensions between the two northern clans reached a breaking point during a potlatch feast in Klukwan, at which the G̱aanax̱teidí hosts offended their L'uknax̱.ádi guests with an arrogant display of wealth. "They spoke so highly that the L'uknax̱.ádi became jealous," one Tlingit elder explained. The proud X̱'unei took offense, and later destroyed the potlatch gifts and mocked the G̱aanax̱teidí. When news of the insult made its way to Klukwan, Yeilxaak demanded retribution. He brought war down on the L'uknax̱.ádi, who suffered a string of defeats. Yeilxaak was triumphant. Hubris led him to send a slave bearing gifts to the L'uknax̱.ádi headmen to gauge their mood. The slave reported that the gifts were accepted with the comment that "the Chilkat are so great that they even give food to the people who are fighting them." Yeilxaak was content that his foes desired peace. "They think that we are even now for all the L'uknax̱.ádi that I have killed," he sneered.

But the L'uknax̱.ádi were not subdued. X̱'unei consulted a shaman, whose vision foretold of "a raven swinging back and forth." The meaning was not clear, but the interpretation was to fight on. A host of warriors was raised from the clans whom Yeilxaak had assaulted. The warriors prepared with ritualistic cleansings and dances. They loaded up canoes with weapons and armor and set out for Chilkat, singing battle songs and beating war drums. When the crafts landed, a column of L'uknax̱.ádi advanced on the G̱aanax̱teidí fortress. They called out their adversaries to fight on the beach. Yeilxaak eagerly accepted the challenge, donning "an extraordinary helmet of wood and copper with the mask of a wolf."

Among the L'uknax̲.ádi was a fierce combatant named Caadisi'kte, who was equipped with a grotesque rat-shaped helmet and an iron-tipped spear. Caadisi'kte stepped forward from the line and invited the swaggering Gaanax̲teidí head to a contest of spears. Yeilxaak drew first blood and wounded Caadisi'kte. But the fight continued until Caadisi'kte pierced Yeilxaak through the heart and he fell dead into the river. His body floated downstream, entangling in thick roots where it bobbed and swayed in place with the current. The L'uknax̲.ádi recognized in this spectacle the shaman's vision: "The raven is moving back and forth, and now we will eat you up." The rout was on, and revenge was theirs. X̲'unei seized Yeilxaak's wolf helmet as a trophy. The Gaanax̲teidí lost their leader and the Russians lost their ally.

In 1794 the Russians returned to Yakutat Bay. Baranov dispatched company officer Yegor Purtov to command a hunting flotilla of several hundred baidarkas. Expecting a show of deference from the locals, Purtov instead encountered defiance. Russia's sovereignty claim over the region was meaningless. He gaped at a British vessel, the *Chatham*, at anchor. Purtov's assertion that the bay belonged to the Russian Empire evoked derision from the British and contempt from the Tlingit. The *Chatham*'s lieutenant commander, Peter Puget, described the Tlingit headman's reaction: "He exerted his utmost eloquence to point out the extent of their territories and the injustice of the Russians in killing and taking away their sea otters, without making them the smallest recompence."

Purtov demanded to know: Where was Chief Yeilxaak? Where was the double-headed eagle crest? The answers dismayed. Yeilxaak was dead. The crest was taken to Chilkat, where the gleaming symbol of Russian power was broken into little pieces and sold. Purtov interrogated the locals about the attack on Baranov's camp on Nuchek Island two summers earlier. The Yakutat Tlingit confessed to the midnight raid, explaining that they initially believed they were attacking their old foe, the Chugach from the north. But when the scouts reported that it was a Russian party, they decided to strike anyway, as Europeans usually had good things to plunder. And what has become of the four hostages? They were sold off as slaves to the southern clans. By now they were probably dead.

Baranov had instructed Purtov to keep on good terms with the Tlingit. He swallowed these setbacks and declared that "Russia wanted friendship." The Tlingit leader responded with an invitation to stay "in Yakutat Sound and the small islands found there." The Russian party lingered in Yakutat for ten days. But the hunting skills of the Alutiit alarmed the hosts. The baidarka teams were harassed by the local Tlingit. A direct confrontation flared up when a daring Tlingit warrior captured four Alutiiq hunters, prompting the Russians to seize several Tlingit hostages in return. The tense standoff was defused through the intervention of a leader from a neutral clan. Purtov reckoned it was time to go home. He headed back to Kodiak with a haul of five hundred sea otter pelts.

Baranov declared the expedition a success. He announced that Yakutat would be the site of New Russia, the empire's first settlement on the American mainland. For the next few years, Baranov sent men and materials to Yakutat to create a palisaded presence on the south side of the bay. But New Russia never prospered. The location was too far north for agriculture. The small band of colonists were unprepared for winter. But what doomed New Russia was Baranov's regrettable choice of supervisor, Ivan Polomoshny, whose arbitrary and abusive manner roused the contempt of Russians and Tlingit alike. One elder complained that "the Tlingit were very angry about the way the Russians were threatening them."

Baranov soon recognized his mistake and sent a scathing reprimand: "I am seriously grieved by the unhappy events that happened at your place and especially by the fate of men who perished ingloriously from laziness and disorder." The disgraced Polomoshny was relieved of duty. On his voyage back to Russia, the vessel wrecked at sea and the bully of Yakutat drowned.

Baranov's first attempt to colonize the American mainland was a flop. In less than five years, Russian relations with the Yakutat Tlingit were damaged beyond repair. By the end of the 1790s, Tanuk was ready to oust the Russians from the bay area. "They are abusing our women. They are taking our children. They are trying to stop the fish from coming up to our smoke houses. We have to do something about these people." Eventually, Tanuk would get his chance.

"The benefits and advantages resulting to Our Empire from the trade carried out by our loyal subjects in the Northeastern Sea and along the coasts of America have attracted our attention and high regard. For this reason, we place the Russian-American Company under Our Highest Protection," proclaimed Tsar Paul I, by imperial decree in 1799.

Four years after Shelikhov's death, his company finally obtained a royal charter. Perhaps the brash new Emperor Paul I was a bigger fan of American colonization than was the more judicious Empress Catherine. Or perhaps the decision was simply another opportunity for the long-suffering son to spite the legacy of his overbearing mother. Regardless, Russia's scrawny American colony was now accorded the perks and privileges of imperial patronage. The tsar granted the company a monopoly on the North Pacific fur trade, authorized an infusion of new capital, and promised the support of the Imperial Russian Navy. While Shelikhov's widow remained in charge of the business in Siberia, corporate headquarters was moved to St. Petersburg, where family confidante Count Nikolai Rezanov oversaw the Crown's interest. The company's faithful field manager was not overlooked. The emperor bestowed on Alexander Baranov the Order of Saint Vladimir and a gold medal.

The tsar's edict claimed all the islands and coastline down to the 55th parallel. It was a bold statement of Russian intentions in North America. Yet Shelikhov's enterprise was already fifteen years old with no mainland settlement to boast of. Baranov knew that the colony must either expand or decline. The future of Russian America, he reckoned, lay in the rainforest archipelago to the south, the heart of Tlingit country. But for good reason, Baranov was wary. Almost every Russian foray into Tlingit territory had provoked hostile reaction. Still, Baranov was inspired by the tsar's blessing. "I was compelled to serve the Fatherland by establishing a settlement at Sitka."

Since 1796, Baranov had been sending scouts to explore the coastal rainforest in hopes of striking up relations with the resident Tlingit. "If you should happen to see the main chief, befriend him and give him gifts of an ermine cloak, a velveteen hat, and ten long strings of blue beads. Ask him if any of his relatives would like to live with us. But be careful, in those parts the people have a passion for deceit." Baranov was encouraged by a report from Ivan Kuskov, upon his return from Sitka. Baranov's trusted lieutenant reported seeing rocky coves stocked with sea otter and meeting a friendly Tlingit nobleman named K'alyáan.

K'alyáan was the oldest nephew of Shk'awulyeil, clan leader of the Sitka Kiks.ádi. His three brothers—K'wáni, Stoonook, and Yeidis'aa—also moved into the Point House in Sitka. From an early age, Shk'awulyeil groomed his eldest nephew for combat. "They did not train him for anything else—not to be the head, but to be a warrior," said Kiks.ádi clan elder Andrew Johnson, a descendent of Shk'awulyeil. K'alyáan embraced the rigorous tests of endurance in freezing cold sea water, tests of pain with thorn branches and wooden clubs, and tests of strength in hand-to-hand fighting. He was especially skilled in knife duels, and always kept a long dagger tethered to his waist. In young adulthood, K'alyáan took a wife and started his own family. According to custom, his Kaagwaantaan clan relatives helped to build K'alyáan a new house along the bayfront, where he and his three younger brothers resided.

The timing of the encounter was propitious. K'alyáan informed Kuskov about a recent confrontation with a British rogue trader. Captain Henry Barber had devised his own triangle trade route between India, Canton, and Australia, peddling whatever he could get his hands on. When Barber got a sniff of the fur trade, he changed course for America's Northwest Coast. He sailed into Sitka Sound on the *Arthur*, announcing that he was willing to pay dearly for sea otter pelts. But Barber brought too few goods to interest the shrewd Tlingit, who withheld their wares. The duplicitous captain lured a local house leader onto his deck with the promise of presents, but the guest was seized and clapped in irons. Barber then demanded a ransom of sea otter pelts for his safe return. The Tlingit complied and their headman was released. Barber then sailed west to Canton with his ill-gotten loot. The incident left the Sitka Tlingit infuriated and frustrated. Ivan Kuskov reported the story to Alexander Baranov, whose eyes widened to the opportunity.

In July 1799 Baranov stood at the rail of the galiot *Olga*, gliding toward the volcano island of Mount Edgecumbe. Tacking eastward, the vessel entered Sitka Sound. Alexander spied Noow Tlein, perched above the waterfront. The sight of the *Olga* navigating through the main channel roused the Tlingit from their summer chores. Two high-prow canoes were launched to investigate. A small crowd gathered on Noow Tlein. From the largest cedar house strode a regal figure to the edge of the cliff. It was Shk̲'awulyeil. A young warrior stood upright in his canoe and called up the hillside. Anóoshi—Russians.

The *Olga* made landfall five miles north of the Tlingit village, on a spruce-clad point, guarding an inland estuary. Here Alexander joined company officer Vasily Medvednikov, who had arrived earlier on the *Orel*. Medvednikov's ship, outfitted with cannons, had been providing cover for a squadron of Alutiiq hunters, working the archipelago in baidarkas. Medvednikov briefed Baranov. Nearly a thousand sea otter furs were collected and the hunters were now paddling back to Kodiak. The Sitka Tlingit so far were tolerating the Russian presence. Two Boston traders had recently departed the sound, after an exchange of nearly two thousand furs for a stash of armaments, including long-barrel muskets, powder kegs, and a set of falconets. This last bit of news alarmed Baranov. He dispatched an emissary to Noow Tlein and requested a meeting with the Sitka elders.

"Despite our weaknesses, I decided to set up an organizational base and make acquaintances with the natives, and then wait for it to bear fruit. It would be a great shame to let the Europeans cut these places off from us and have all our successes wiped out." Baranov convened the heads of the top-ranking households for food, drink, entertainment, and negotiation. While Baranov acted the part of generous host, he was, as everyone knew, the uninvited guest in the room. He plied the Tlingit headmen with clothing and cloth, metal pots and household goods, and baubles and beads. But he also made sure that the Tlingit could see how well armed his company was.

When the songs and speeches were concluded, Baranov made his pitch. He asked for permission to build a small outpost on the site. The benefit to the Tlingit, he said, would come through commerce and defense. An on-site trade post would enable the Tlingit to barter for manufactured goods and supplies on their schedule, rather than the irregular ship traffic. Moreover, the Russians would lend their muscle should Sitka again come under assault from European scoundrels.

The Tlingit were chagrinned by the request. "This place is G̲ájaa Héen, a lot of pink salmon go up stream in this area. It is a dry-fish camp, we smoke salmon there." The late summer salmon run in the estuary was a key source for the community's winter stores. The Kaagwaantaan were especially resistant to a fixed Russian presence on the island. But Baranov was persistent.

"I have been busy all winter with the natives," he wrote. Baranov was astute to the informal power dynamics in the village and recognized that the Kiks.ádi was the dominant clan. He smothered Shḵ'awulyeil with kindness and gifts, including a bronze double-headed eagle imperial crest. He promised that the Russians would always "supply him with necessities and protect him from attack by warlike neighbors." In exchange, Baranov drew up a testimonial for the Kiks.ádi leader to endorse, conceding this little piece of Sitka for the Russian Empire.

Shḵ'awulyeil was flattered. Baranov was satisfied. "It was not without trouble," he said, "but we pacified and subjugated the people at Sitka." A small company remained on site in the fall, clearing the land and making a home base. The first priority was to construct a security perimeter with two guard boxes, a warehouse, and a *banya*. The building frenzy continued through winter with a two-story barracks, a blacksmith house, and a stone-hearth kitchen. The Tlingit came by often to gauge the progress and ask when the Russians were leaving. "They did not expect us to settle permanently," Baranov said.

It was a familiar pattern in the Native American experience. The leaders of a thriving Indigenous people miscalculate the benefits and costs of making accommodation with a scraggy company of European settlers. In October Baranov consecrated the site with a holy procession and naming ritual. He invited the house leaders, who arrived in ceremonial dress through the stockade entrance and were flummoxed by the sight of so many sturdy wooden structures. "This fort created here is under the protection of God's servant the Archangel Michael," Baranov proclaimed. "Glory to our monarch, Paul the Autocrat of All the Russias and Sovereign of America." As the words were translated, K'alyáan grimaced and clenched the dagger hidden under his tunic.

GOODBYE, ALEXANDER BARANOV

In the summer of 2020, waves of angry protests surged across the United States, rallying against the institutions and symbols of persisting racism. Crowds toppled statues of Confederate soldiers and American enslavers. As the movement expanded, it targeted monuments to Christopher Columbus and other European colonizers.

Among these was a statue of Alexander Baranov, honoring his role in promoting the city of Sitka as a center of trade and commerce. Donated by the wealthy local Hames family, the statue was contentious from its erection in 1989, when vandals cut off its nose. In 2020 several groups, including the Sitka Tribe of Alaska and the Alaska Native Brotherhood and Sisterhood, made the case for removal of the statue. "Baranov is a historic figure who is responsible for murder, enslavement, rape and a perpetrator of genocide," claimed one detractor. "This history is still felt by our Indigenous communities today."

Another resident argued, "[The statue] causes me, and many of my people, to feel unwelcome here. And it still causes grief, pain, and it reminds us of our historical trauma." The coalition submitted a petition to the Sitka Assembly with two thousand signatures in support of moving the statue.

Proponents of keeping the statue in place remained relatively quiet, although there was a counterpetition. This effort was started by the Russian Community Council, which promotes the interests of Russian-speaking peoples in the United States. It garnered some six thousand signatures, but the city assembly did not give much consideration to this point of view. "Frankly I really don't care a bit what the Russians think," said one assembly member.

As it turns out, the statue was moved only a few feet—from a central public place in front of Harrigan Centennial Hall, to the Sitka History Museum, which happens to be inside the hall. The museum director said this solution represents "a respectful compromise in a difficult, somewhat divisive discussion." He emphasized that the museum exhibit will provide important context about Baranov and his place in Sitka history.

For members of the Tlingit community and other local Native Americans, the decision was a win. "It is more than a statue," explained Alaska Native Sisterhood president Paulette Moreno. "It is the doorway to us exerting our sovereignty as a Native nation."

PART TWO

CHAPTER 6

Fortress of the Bears

C ircumstances do not permit me to remain here and share in local efforts that require much care. I need to leave for Kodiak, and I appoint you as superior and entrust all the settlers and hunters to your command," Alexander Baranov explained in a letter to Vasily Medvednikov. Thanks to Baranov's perseverance, by the spring of 1800, a viable Russian colony was established at Sitka. Now he committed to ink and paper a list of instructions to the acting head of Fort Saint Michael. He devised a dual-track scheme to indulge the local leaders with acts of friendship and to intimidate them with displays of force. Of utmost concern was that the Sitka Tlingit should not be provoked.

The key to the colony's survival, the departing governor believed, was to appease the headmen at Noow Tlein. "Pay special attention to the newly unanimously elected head of the Kiks.ádi clan 'Mikhailo' (Shḵ'awulyeil)," Baranov said, "as well as Skhates, his brother, the shaman, and other honorable men; and, from the nearest bay, the rich and hospitable nephew of Mikhailo (K'alyáan) and his brothers." The Russians liked to assign a Slavic Christian name to local leaders with whom they had close relations. The Tlingit were not offended, as they commonly accumulated multiple names as they grew to maturity.

Baranov urged Medvednikov to be as generous as possible with the Tlingit leaders. "When occasion arises offer them food, and when provisions are plentiful treat them together with their crews. When the chiefs visit and meat is plentiful, they should be given a portion to take home." Also, the colony must share "in small quantities" the manufactured goods acquired from trading ships. Baranov made clear that this was not a matter of choice, but a necessary condition for the safety of the colony. "Small gifts should be given to show kindness at all times, taking into account that our occupation of their land demands gratitude from our side."

Baranov also addressed security measures at the fort, specifying who should be allowed inside the compound. It was one thing to entertain friendly leaders, but quite another to give access to their unruly crews or to their relatives from distant villages. "If they come in large numbers exercise extreme vigilance, especially if the Kaagwaantaan are among them." In Sitka, the Kaagwaantaan were considered "the most war-like of all." Baranov's effort to woo the Kaagwaantaan clan was scorned by their leader, "the malicious and arrogant Chief Scar."

Baranov reminded Medvednikov of the fort's no weapons policy for Tlingit visitors. The policy did not apply to the temperamental leaders, and Baranov was repeatedly unnerved at the sight of K'alyáan's dagger swaying at the hip. Most of all, Baranov implored Medvednikov to keep the colony on high alert. Settlers should not go into the woods alone or without firearms. Men should always be stationed at the front sentry post and the raised lookouts. Mounted cannons facing the beach and the back-woods should be primed and loaded. Gunpowder and cartridges should be well stocked and easily accessible. And, an alarm signal calling the men to arms should be practiced.

Baranov made it clear that coercion should only be used in defense. But any act of Tlingit aggression should be swiftly met with Russian aggres-sion. Otherwise, the Tlingit would be emboldened to strike against the colony. One episode, in particular, seemed to justify this assumption. At Eastertime, in the spring of 1800, Baranov sent an interpreter to the Tlingit village to invite the headmen to a celebration. "The woman interpreter was beaten and robbed by some natives who were visitors to Sitka. We had to show them that we were not afraid." Baranov led twenty-two men with guns and two falconets into the center of the village, where three hundred Tlingit men were gathered. The Russian posse went straight to the house where the offenders were staying and demanded satisfaction. Bloodshed was imminent. "They had boasted that they wanted to fight us, but after only two volleys they took fright and instead tried to get rid of us by offering food." Baranov's brazen display of force defused the conflict. But he cautioned that "our strength is inadequate and so we must use diplomacy and leniency."

Baranov not only had firsthand experience with the Tlingit penchant for fighting, he had an understanding of the Tlingit sense of dignity. "These people have enjoyed natural freedom since the beginning of the world," he wrote. "They have never thought about and do not know how to placate foreign will. They cannot bear the least offense without retaliation." Indeed, Baranov was aware that the tenuous peace in Sitka was more likely to be shattered by his own Russian settlers than by the Tlingit inhabitants.

"Punish anyone who jokes with the community's peace, even the sharp shooters," Baranov implored Medvednikov. The sharpshooters were a select group of company hunters. Their skill with a musket for both profit and provision accorded them special status. The sharpshooters were a privileged fraternity within the Russian colony, a raggedy warrior elite. Imperial Spain had its conquistadors, Imperial Russia had its *promyshlenniki*.

Tsarist Russia featured a strict social hierarchy, with the high aristocracy at the top and the peasant serfs at the bottom. The *promyshlenniki* were a breed apart. They were frontier folk, free men, living outside the formalities and constraints of the Russian caste system. Cossacks, fur trappers, and runaway serfs, whose self-driven exploits pushed the empire ever eastward across Siberia. They were an exclusively male society, not unlike the cowboys, mountain men, and rustler gangs of the American West. Men of dubious means and on the make. The *promyshlenniki* were the shock troops of Russian imperialism. They fought with the Indigenous people, trampling over their homelands, and comingled with them, begetting a Siberian Creole population. In the late eighteenth century, when the Russian fur trade went maritime, the *promyshlenniki* adapted. They learned how to navigate sailing ships, shoot atop teetering waves, and survive in the North Pacific.

The Russian American colony was composed of two distinct groups: higher-status *promyshlenniki*, Russians and Creoles, who served as fur hunters and skilled workers, and lower-status Indigenous conscripts, predominantly Alutiit and Aleuts, who served as forced laborers, fur hunters, and domestic servants. The Indigenes outnumbered the *promyshlenniki* by more than two to one. On Kodiak, the *promyshlenniki* employed the conscripts in various personal service roles. The men were hunting guides and baidarka drivers, while the women were food preparers and sex partners. The relationship between the two groups was fundamentally unequal, based on coercion, and reinforced by a colonial mentality of ethno-superiority.

Now, as Baranov departed, his biggest fear was the culture clash of "rudeness and ignorance" between colonists and Tlingit. "The Russians must keep their coarse superstitions in check as much as possible," he said. Moreover, he knew that the mere presence of so many Alutiiq hunters, traditional Tlingit antagonists, was an offense to his Sitka hosts. "Our side, Russians and native hunters, must not give any reason for dissatisfaction. Contact should be minimized, especially in view of our present situation of little power." Baranov's forebodings were justified. The company sharpshooters would become the main culprits in the breakdown of Russian-Tlingit relations at Sitka.

⎯⎯⎯

On a jagged outcrop at the edge of Sitka Sound, a harem of sea lions basked in the December sun. A hundred yards away, a two-man baidarka drifted silently. Aleksey Eglevsky readied a long-barreled musket: pouring sixty grains of black powder from a sheep horn into the barrel, pressing a steel ball into a cloth patch, and shoving the ball and patch down the barrel with a ramrod, sprinkling fine powder grains into the flash pan, and cocking the flintlock hammer. Eglevsky's deformity, a permanently crooked forefinger, was perfectly suited for priming a musket. He handed the weapon to his partner, Vasily Kochesov, who casually took aim at a four-hundred-pound golden brown female, basking upright. A loud crack, and the sea lion toppled over. Frightened barks and frantic dives, the harem dispersed. The baidarka skimmed over the waves to claim its prize.

As winter fell upon Fort Saint Michael in late 1799, the new Russian colony faced an existential threat from sickness and hunger. "Two died, but we were only short of food for two months," Baranov said. "The rest of the time we had abundance. We killed forty-five sea lions and 250 seals. Almost all were shot by the two Kochesovs."

Vasily and Afanasy Kochesov were Russian-Aleut Creole brothers from the Fox Islands. They were sharpshooters, *promyshlenniki*, who had worked for the Russian-American Company in Kodiak since Grigory Shelikhov's time. Sitka's acting director Vasily Medvednikov had known the brothers for nearly ten years. No one in the company was more skilled with a long carbine than Vasily Kochesov. He was an unrivaled fur hunter, food provider, and all-round tough guy. He was also the bane of the Sitka Tlingit. Tall, haughty, and sneering, Kochesov never missed a chance to provoke his hosts. The Tlingit referred to him as Gidák, and both feared and despised him.

"The behavior of the Russians in Sitka did not make a very good impression on the Tlingit," noted visiting naval cadet Gavril Davydov. "The hunters committed many unjust acts. They embittered the savages, and no one was powerful enough to prevent them from doing so." Generations later, Kiks.ádi elder Andrew Johnson said, "The Russians were very cruel to the Tlingit. They treated us like dogs and laughed about it."

Medvednikov did not enforce Baranov's warning to avoid contact between colonists and Tlingit. After Baranov departed, there were recurring clashes and several killings. Vasily Kochesov, in particular, was accused of murder. But Medvednikov ignored the appeals of the Tlingit headmen to mete out justice. In principle, the acting governor had the authority to rein in the sharpshooters; in practice, he dared not antagonize the colony's main protectors. "The Russian officials made promises to the Tlingit," Andrew Johnson said, "but they could not keep them."

As was their wont, the sharpshooters solicited local women into service at Fort Saint Michael. In some cases, house leaders allowed enslaved women to go to work for the Russians as servants, concubines, and interpreters. But in other cases, young Tlingit females were either enticed or forced to serve at the fort. "The hunters started taking away their young girls," Gavril Davydov observed, "and offending them in other ways." It was one thing to take a Tlingit wife, but quite another to do so in disregard of clan protocol and gift-exchange expectations. "When the Tlingit walked in the woods, the Russians hid in the thick vegetation," Andrew Johnson explained. "They attacked the Tlingit men and knocked them unconscious, and violated the Tlingit women." The widespread practice of Russian-Tlingit cohabitation at Fort Saint Michael rankled local sensibilities.

Meanwhile, from their base at Sitka, Russians colonists roused Tlingit indignation all over the archipelago. Each summer, Fort Saint Michael served as the rendezvous point for a baidarka fleet of a thousand Alutiiq and Aleut hunters, who systematically ravaged the sea otter colonies and robbed the Tlingit of their most valuable trade commodity. The plundering was not confined to sea mammals. Russian hunting parties raided the dried fish stores that the Tlingit stocked for winter survival. And one Alutiiq baidarka squadron out of Sitka committed the ultimate sacrilege of ransacking ceremonial furs, weapons, and relics from a Kuiu Tlingit graveyard in Chatham Strait.

But what most incited the elders was Russian insolence toward the elite clan families. The company sharpshooters were not discriminating about whom they insulted. In the summer of 1801, an altercation between the fur hunters and the Angoon Tlingit led to the headman's nephew being roughed up and locked in iron cuffs. Further south, a confrontation with the Kuiu Tlingit led to the killing of a clan leader, his wife, and his children. Meanwhile, back in Sitka, a high-status Kaagwaantaan shaman Héendei was falsely accused, incarcerated, and humiliated for the sadistic pleasure of the sharpshooters. Two years after the founding of the Russian colony at Sitka, Tlingit elders had had enough.

Red-and-black painted canoes rolled lazily upon Sitka Sound beneath a silver-and-gray sky. It was early autumn and the last days of halibut season. On the pebble beach at the foot of Noow Tlein, an older man was loading a canoe with bulging spruce-woven baskets. Shuws'aa was a Kaagwaantaan elder of the Chilkat Tlingit, and the father of K'alyáan. He was on a business trip, trading goods between Klukwan and Sitka. K'alyáan's younger brother Stoonook ran down to the beach. "Father, I would like to go to Chilkat too," he asked. The noble Shuws'aa was pleased to have his son as a travel companion and as a surprise treat for the boy's mother.

"When they came to the place, his father's people were overjoyed to see the son." His cousins prepared a special dinner for Stoonook, with a place at the head table, "elevated next to his older clan brothers." Shuws'aa, meanwhile, went off to his own house. He offered Stoonook advice as they parted. "Be brave, my son, this is the time when things can fail." Stoonook washed his face and hands in a basin at the entrance to the longhouse. His hosts served dried fish and bowls of cranberries. "He was eating very well," when another cousin arrived. Kak̲áayi was also of aristocratic

Kaagwaantaan lineage. "He did not know diplomacy, he had a very loose mouth." Kak̲áayi positioned himself next to Stoonook.

"Let me ask you, Stoonook, is it true what people are saying about what happened with that man down there, that some fine Russians had him sitting in a jail?" Kak̲áayi said, referring to the incident with the shaman Héendei. "What kind of sons of Kaagwaantaan do you have in Sitka?" Kak̲áayi jeered. "They just keep sucking up to the Russians."

Stoonook went quiet. He pushed the bowl away and stood up. He stormed out of the longhouse, insulted and humiliated. He found his father and fumed. "You go around like a noble man. But I want to leave this evening or float out on tomorrow's tide." Shuws'aa tried to calm the boy down. "My poor son! What happened to you?" In the morning, the pair headed back to Sitka. All the way, Stoonook brooded in silence over Kak̲áayi's affront. The canoe appeared on Sitka Sound as a storm was breaking. A young villager saw it and ran to find K'alyáan.

"Your older brother wants you," Stoonook was told. He went directly to K'alyáan's house, where other family members were already gathered. Stoonook informed K'alyáan about his mistreatment from their Kaagwaantaan relatives. "The insults are not meant for you, younger brother," K'alyáan said. "But what do you want to do about it?" Stoonook railed that he did not want to hear such slurs. "That's right," K'alyáan agreed. He picked up his musket and shot it into the flames, the burning embers sprayed over the room. K'alyáan picked up the hot ash and rubbed it on his chest. Stoonook did the same, and so did the others. Outside, the wind howled.

East of Sitka, deep within the archipelago lies the Tlingit village at Angoon, Xutsnoowú, the Fortress of the Bears. In winter, the darkness lingers and the days are still. But in December 1801, Xutsnoowú was alive with activity. A conspiracy was unfolding. For several days, pairs of cedar canoes arrived to the protected deepwater inlet, where a Yankee trading ship, the *Globe*, was at anchor. Esteemed guests wrapped in thick fur cloaks were ushered into a Deisheetaan longhouse. Inside Tlingit leaders from a half dozen villages in the central and southern archipelago assembled around a blazing fire. There were even representatives of the Kaigani Haida and Tsimshian peoples, whose communities were adjacent to the southern Tlingit. They were summoned to the Fortress of the Bears for an extraordinary event, a council of war.

"No one comes into your land until they have an agreement or until they have been invited. If you go into anybody else's land, it's a battle. That's one of the strongest laws of the Tlingit," explained George Ramos, a Tlingit culture-bearer from the L'uknax̱.ádi clan. By summer's end in 1801, Russian fur trappers had managed to antagonize nearly every Tlingit village in the archipelago. Whatever vague agreements the Russians thought they had with the Sitka and Yakutat Tlingit, they certainly did not extend to the hunting grounds of the Hoonah, Angoon, Chilkat, or Kuiu communities. One by one the headmen stood before the fire and related their experiences with Russian broken promises, misdeeds, and high crimes. They have plundered our sea otter colonies. They have raided our dried fish stores. They have assaulted our women. They have insulted our honor. When the speeches were finished, a grizzled man obscured in shadow cleared his throat with a cough and then stepped into the light to speak. The captain of the *Globe*, Irish-born and Boston-based William Conyngham, told the Tlingit that the Russians were robbing them poor. Once the sea otter were gone, the traders would move on, he asserted. Defend what is yours.

The council agreed with the *Globe* captain and now considered its options. It was a daunting challenge. No North American Indians had yet succeeded to uproot and drive out a European colony once it became established. While particular clans could boast of daring raids or one-off skirmishes, the Tlingit as a whole had never waged war against a European power. At least some of the elders urged caution, pointing to Russia's firepower and large force. "What will happen afterwards?" they demanded. "There are more of them than blades of grass." Besides, it was argued, the Yakutat and Sitka villages have co-existed with the Russians and have yet to be attacked.

But this view was countered by an ominous prediction. "The Russians act kindly at first, but then they will prevent us from taking sea otters and later they will enslave us. They will take us to Kodiak and other distant places for use in heavy labor." The pro-war argument was led by Kanyagit of the Dall Island Tlingit in the southern archipelago. Kanyagit divulged that he could supply the northern clans with guns, powder, and small cannons, which he had acquired from British traders. As the speeches became more animated, one course of action gained favor: the Russians must be removed from the archipelago. Thus, in late December 1801, at the Fortress of the Bears, the extraordinary council of Tlingit elders voted to go to war.

The conspirators next devised a tactical plan. Rather than challenge the Russians in a full-scale battle, they would divide and conquer their foe. The Tlingit knew that each summer two large hunting parties made up of hundreds of baidarkas, one from Kodiak and one from Sitka, combed through the archipelago looking for sea otter. During these weeks, the Russian forts would be undermanned and vulnerable. The plan was to coordinate a set of simultaneous attacks. In the north, the Angoon, Hoonah, and Chilkat Tlingit would ambush the Kodiak hunting party in Icy Strait, while the Yakutat Tlingit would lead a land assault against the New Russia compound. In the south, the Kuiu, Kake, and Stikine Tlingit would ambush the Sitka hunting party in Chatham Strait, while the Sitka Tlingit would lead a land assault against Fort Saint Michael. The Tlingit would confront the Russians in four theaters of war, in which they would possess a force advantage and the element of surprise.

The war plan required a strategy that had never been tested before: nationwide mobilization and multiclan coordination. The Angoon war council dispatched envoys to Yakutat and Chilkat in the north and to Sitka

in the west. The declaration of war against the Russians was not unexpected, and for many was welcomed. With Fort Saint Michael serving as
command central of Russian America, the plotters all knew that the key
to the plan's success rested on the Sitka Tlingit.

A Russian sentry hollered up to the second-story window of the commandant's office. "Vasily Grigorievich, a party from the Tlingit village is
approaching the stockade. It is Shk'awulyeil." Fort Saint Michael's acting
boss, Vasily Medvednikov, closed his accounting ledger and clambered
down a ladder to greet his guest, mindful of Baranov's order to indulge the
Kiks.ádi leader whenever possible.

The unexpected visit was prompted by grim news from Angoon. A canoe
messenger had informed the Sitka elders of the meeting at the Fortress of
the Bears "It was agreed that they will all assemble on a certain date in the
spring at Xutsnoowú," the messenger said. "Then they will proceed
toward the Russian fort and join with the Sitkans to attack it. And, if the
Sitka Tlingit refused to participate, then they too will be annihilated."
Shk'awulyeil immediately summoned all the house heads to discuss the war
council's ultimatum. The Sitka elders were sensitive to the reproach "for
letting a small number of Russians get control over them and turn them
into slaves." By this time as well, the accumulation of Russian-perpetrated
indignities had reached a tipping point among the Sitka Tlingit. The mood
was overwhelmingly belligerent. Shk'awulyeil consulted the Kiks.ádi
shaman, who saw that war was coming.

Still, it was not a light decision for Shk'awulyeil to join the conspiracy.
The Point House had benefitted from friendly relations with the Russians. He went to talk to the fort commander. Medvednikov welcomed
Shk'awulyeil into the Russian compound and ordered a meal prepared. The
headman then surprised his host with a passionate plea for the Russians to

vacate Sitka and return to Kodiak. Without giving away the details of the Tlingit war plan, Shḵ'awulyeil said that the colony may be targeted for a raid and that it was in everyone's interest for the Russians to abandon the fort. Medvednikov dismissed the suggestion without a second thought. After the required hour of socializing, he sent Shḵ'awulyeil away and returned to his chores.

In the weeks that followed, there were more Tlingit attempts to warn the colony. "Throughout the winter rumors spread," Kuskov later reported to Baranov. "The women interpreters Daria and Aniushka heard that the distant Stikine and others were planning an attack on the fort." Even the Alutiiq and Creoles living in the compound were contacted by the locals and informed of the plot. But Medvednikov insisted it was "all much ado about nothing." The acting commander had long since forgotten Baranov's instructions to stay vigilant. As spring arrived, Gavril Davydov observed that Fort Saint Michael remained "badly equipped and constantly careless."

Shḵ'awulyeil was not eager to take up arms against the Russians, but neither could he hold back the fury that was coming. Andrew Johnson explained the decision of the Kiks.ádi clan to go to war. "When a Tlingit is abused, he has enough patience to endure for a while. He might even plead to be left alone. But if they continue doing this, he never forgets it as along as he lives. There will be a time when he will avenge. This is what happened." The expulsion of foreign invaders was a goal that Native peoples across the New World had had for three centuries, without success. But the Tlingit were ready to take their chance. And the main strike would come at Sitka, led by Shḵ'awulyeil and K'alyáan.

THE BOMBARDMENT OF ANGOON

In October 1882 a harpoon gun exploded on board a whaling ship that belonged to the North West Trading Company. The accident injured several crew members and killed one—a Tlingit shaman named Tilxtein from the village of Angoon.

The other Tlingit workers mourned their brethren and—according to Tlingit tribal law—demanded two hundred blankets from the Oregon-based company as compensation for his death. They seized the whaling boat and some other equipment to hold until they received payment. By some accounts, they also took two hostages, although this claim is disputed by the Tlingit. The captain of the whaling fleet feared the worst and fled to Sitka to request assistance from the US Navy.

Just three days later, two well-armed naval ships sailed into the shallow waters around Angoon. The villagers promptly turned over the company's property and the hostages. But this did not bring resolution. Instead, the ship's commander demanded a payment of four hundred blankets "as punishment and guarantee of future good behavior." The Tlingit were not able to comply: they could only supply eighty-two blankets.

Retaliation was swift and harsh. The navy shelled the Tlingit village, smashed the canoes, set fire to the houses, and destroyed the food supplies. Most residents managed to flee, but six children died of smoke inhalation and Angoon was obliterated. The Tlingit villagers were left without food and shelter, with the onset of winter close at hand. Resident Billy Jones later recalled "the people of Angoon nearly starved to death, all of them . . . How much we suffered."

In 1973—nearly a century after the incident—the Indian Claims Commission awarded the Angoon clans compensation for the property destroyed by the bombardment. The amount was miniscule, as it was based on the 1882 value of the property, but it was accepted as a tacit admission of wrongdoing. Since then, the state of Alaska has acknowledged the atrocity by proclaiming a Tlingit commemoration day on the anniversary of the bombardment and requesting an official apology from the US government.

But the federal government is noticeably quiet on the subject, save for a weak statement from the US Navy. "The destruction of Angoon should never have happened," wrote Assistant Secretary Herrington, "and it was an unfortunate event in our history." The Tlingit may never receive an official apology for this "unfortunate event," but they did regain a piece of their heritage—and a powerful symbol of their resilience.

In the winter of 1882, after the bombardment, Angoon village had only one remaining functional canoe, which allowed them to hunt and survive the winter. The prow of the canoe bore a carved beaver, representing the crest of the Deisheetaan clan of Angoon. As the years passed, the canoe was considered sacred because it had been so critical to the community's survival. When the vessel was no longer seaworthy, the beaver carving was removed and the canoe was cremated with the same honor afforded a human being.

More than a century later, a group of Tlingit repatriation specialists discovered the so-called Beaver Prow in the collection of the American Museum of Natural History in New York City. It's not clear how it arrived there, but it was immediately recognized and welcomed back to the tribe. The piece was returned to the Angoon village in 1999.

"The impact was so powerful," said Leonard John of Angoon. "The realization that had it not been for this war canoe, I probably would not be here . . . Just this one war canoe is what kept our village alive." Some Tlingit were hopeful that the return of the Beaver Prow might "bring healing to our people." Others were skeptical: "We won't breathe good until there's an apology," one clan leader stated definitively. "We will always remember."

CHAPTER 7
Retaliation

D uring the night a fleet of canoes went out to the far side of the islands in the sound," Andrew Johnson said. "The men hid there and kept watch on the fort. From Indian River, another company of men went overland. They followed the trail to Gájaa Héen, which the Russians called Saint Michael. For the way that the Russians had treated the Kiks.ádi, this was retaliation."

The 1802 Tlingit uprising was an unprecedented collective action campaign with multiple objectives. It was a territorial conflict—to drive out the Russian settlements in Sitka and Yakutat from Tlingit property. It was a sea battle—to end Russia's large-scale predation in Tlingit waters. And it was a revenge war—to redress the accumulated abuses that Russian colonizers had piled on the proud Tlingit elite families.

The Tlingit way of war was unlike the Russian way. In early modern Europe, war was bureaucratized and command was centralized. Human and material resources were mobilized on a mass scale in order to fight for extended periods—the Seven Years' War, the Thirty Years' War, the Hundred Years' War. War was impersonal. A soldier did not know his opponent, nor have a personal grievance. War was not a private matter, but a public affair, concerning the entire realm. The nature of fighting was large-scale pitched battles. Artillery and infantry replaced archers and knights; the weapons of the gunpowder revolution reigned supreme.

By contrast, in Native North America, political power was decentralized and personalistic. Leaders could not compel others to fight: they needed to persuade combatants to take up arms. Clan alliances were the exception, not the norm. Such alliances—when they did come together—lasted for one or two battles, then dissolved. The authority to command was temporary. The scale was more limited and more local. The reasons to fight were personal, family driven, or clan specific. Family feuds might endure, but ongoing warfare was not sustainable because of seasonal cycles. The war makers were also the economic producers, and the outcome of a battle was irrelevant if winter food stores were not collected. Pitched battles with big armies were rare. Instead, brief skirmishes and surprise ambushes were the most common modes of combat.

In North America, once a European power became settled in the homeland of an Indigenous nation, the disparity of resources and capabilities tipped the coercive balance in its favor. When the Tlingit went to war in the early 1800s, their hope was that the Russians were not yet sufficiently entrenched to be able to mobilize their full arsenal. The Tlingit had two additional advantages. First, the war would be fought in the familiar terrain of the rainforest, where Russian settlers feared to tread, and on the narrow straits of the archipelago, where Russian ships could not easily maneuver. Second, the Tlingit had assembled a coalition of clans, united by the desire to expel the Russians. More often, Indigenous communities in North America did not team up against a common foe until it was too late. But in the Tlingit-Russian war, more than a half dozen autonomous and sometimes adversarial Raven- and Eagle-descended clans joined together before their would-be oppressor became an unmovable force.

The Sitka Tlingit prepared for war. Each house organized its own fighting team with captains. K'alyáan and Stoonook were assigned leadership roles in accordance with their status as the favored nephews of the Point House. Their uncle Shḵ'awulyeil had trained the boys since childhood, mastering particular weapons and fighting skills. Now they were expected to assume command, organize troops, and devise tactics. They led by example, poised at the front of their respective crews. The Tlingit warrior elite was fearless to the point of reckless. "It was an honor and duty to defend their land," said Tlingit culture-bearer Ellen Hope Hayes. The individual was transitional; the clan was eternal.

Stoonook paddled his canoe downriver to the silverberry bushes. "Bind up twenty bundles of silverberry branches," he directed, "and place them in the bow of the boat." The psychological preparation for war began with physical and spiritual rituals. Warriors tested their stamina by crouching in icy cold water for long periods, and upon emerging were beaten by their elders with the silverberry's whip-like branches and razor-sharp leaves. They went alone into the forest to fast and purify their bodies, and to summon ancestral spirits for added strength. Each warrior brought out their personal weapons, stored in bentwood boxes adorned with clan crests. The artfully crafted objects were the warrior's most treasured possessions: a sharp handpick carved from jade stone, a heavy club made from caribou antler, a wooden truncheon with a row of embedded bear teeth, a double-bladed steel dagger, a long copper knife with animal-carving pommel. These traditional weapons were supplemented by muskets and gunpowder, courtesy of their New England trading partners.

On the eve of war, K'alyáan came to Shḵ'awulyeil seeking permission to wear the raven-head helmet, *sheey-kaa-shkut-yeil.* The war helmet was a sacred clan object of the Kiks.ádi. "Hand it over. Let me wear it so I may go out and do battle with them." For the Tlingit, the inspiring image of K'alyáan leading the charge in the raven-head war helmet would become an enduring icon of the Tlingit-Russian war.

The prelude to war occurred in May 1802, fifty miles from Yakutat at Dry Bay. Ivan Kuskov was leading the first summer hunting party of two hundred baidarkas into the northern archipelago. At the mouth of the Alsek River, several baidarkas overturned, sending their fur cargos into the sea. "The ermine pelts got wet, and since ermine rots quickly, it needed to dry out. Taking precautions, we made camp intending to leave the next day." But before moving on, the camp was surrounded by Tlingit from nearby Aakwei village, whose leaders confronted Kuskov in his tent. "They complained about our native hunters in rude terms, saying that they caused offenses and plundered graves. Moreover, they said we hunt in their waters and take too much. We don't leave enough for them to barter with the Europeans. They threatened to break friendly relations with us."

Kuskov was a diplomat, not a fighter. He talked his way out of scrapes with the Tlingit and Europeans alike up and down the Northwest Coast. But this time his conciliations were no use. "I strove to justify myself with kindness, and offered gifts of tobacco. But there was little hope in calming them." Trying to provoke a fight, Tlingit men harassed the hunters and grabbed their equipment and furs. Ivan reorganized the camp into a protective ring and made preparations to leave early the next morning.

At midnight, the forest came alive with a Tlingit raid. The frightened men bolted for the baidarkas on the beach. Kuskov stood his ground and mustered the sharpshooters, who repelled the assault. A Tlingit ruse tempted the Russians to chase them into the woods, where a deadly ambush awaited. But Kuskov was wise to the stunt. Instead, he seized the moment to beat a hasty retreat through a hail of gunfire and spears. Kuskov regrouped across a small channel in a wooded grove on higher ground. He positioned the falconets toward the shoreline and dared the Tlingit to charge him. After an edgy standoff, Kuskov secured a cease fire and his hunting party retreated back to Yakutat. The Russian company lost three men, including an Alutiiq chieftan, and hundreds of fur pelts. The Aakwei Tlingit lost ten warriors. They were the first deaths of the Tlingit-Russian war.

At Yakutat, Kuskov placed the fort on high alert, mobilizing cannon crews to the stockade mounts and forbidding individuals from straying outside the fence. At the Tlingit village, Ivan observed an unusually large number of visitors from Angoon, Kuiu, and other communities. "I learned from an old man that in the Icy Straits a big party of Tlingit from various settlements had gathered and were waiting to barter with us," Kuskov said. "This seemed doubtful as these people seldom leave their settlements. The old man then casually mentioned that some clans from the south were planning a raid on Sitka." Kuskov dispatched his fastest six baidarkas to give warning to Vasily Medvednikov at Fort Saint Michael. War had begun.

Abrosim Plotnikov grumbled. It was a lazy Sunday afternoon at Fort Saint Michael. Most of the men had gone off in baidarkas with Ivan Urbanov to Chatham Strait to hunt sea otter. Vasily Kochesov and Baturin were hunting sea lions on the sound. The remaining settlers were enjoying a day of rest. So why was it, Plotnikov wondered, that commandant Medvednikov had chosen him to traipse down to the creek to tend to the newborn calves. Making himself comfortable on a sun-soaked patch of moss, Plotnikov was suddenly roused by shouting at the fort. He scrambled back up the path. The colony was under attack.

Atop the ridge overlooking the settlement, Shk̲'awulyeil was standing in full battle dress, directing a company of Tlingit warriors in a two-pronged attack on the fort. From the back forest trail, favorite nephew K'alyáan was leading a force of several hundred Tlingit, rushing the unguarded stockade gate and pouring into the compound. From the waterfront, younger brother Stoonook was leading a squadron of sixty war canoes, converging on the beach and cutting off a sea escape. Scores of colonists, more women than men, were trapped inside Fort Saint Michael. A shaman's drum thumped ominously, as Tlingit insurgents closed around the perimeter.

The first structure adjacent to the main gate was the blacksmith's forge. Following K'alyáan's prominent raven helmet, a Tlingit troop pounced on the Russian smithy, Klokhtin, who was hammering hot metal into knife blades in the open doorway. "They killed this man while he was pounding away," Andrew Johnson said, "and they carried off his blacksmith hammer." K'alyáan seized the smithy's cudgel to use against his foes. By this time, Stoonook's team had already breached the stockade walls. The cook Tumakaev darted from the kitchen across the compound, yelling to all: "Trouble. Get to the barracks. The Tlingit are coming with guns." The two-story barracks was a fortified garrison, containing the main sleeping quarters, a small armory, and the chief manager's office. Medvednikov rang the alarm bell for all to retreat to the garrison at once. With the Tlingit bearing down, he shuttered the heavy door, ordered the women into the cellar, and positioned the men in the upper casements with firearms.

Not everyone made it to the garrison. From a window, Ekaterina Pinnuin observed the mayhem outside. "The Tlingit were stabbing everybody on the street." Abrosim Plotnikov rushed back to his comrades. "I ran to the barracks but the door was already locked. I could not get in, so I went to the barn for a gun. Four Tlingit broke in and I shot at them and missed. I jumped through a back window and ran into the woods. Two Tlingit pursued me. But I hid myself inside a hollow tree trunk."

The Tlingit laid siege to the two-story stronghold. The colonists inside shuddered with each splintering thud, as the invaders brought their axes down on the door. The cornered settlers loaded a cannon and pointed it at the entrance. Impatient warriors hacked slits into the side walls, pushed through rifle barrels, and fired blindly inside. With a terrifying crack, the door broke open. Tlingit elder Alex Andrews shared the story he learned from his father: "When K'alyáan charged in a cannon was fired in his face and he fell. When he came to, he jumped up and sounded like the brown

bear. He growled and charged inside the big house and the Russians began
screaming. His men charged in behind him."

There was a flash and a deafening cannon shot. Bodies were scattered,
the room was thick with smoke. For a moment, it was quiet. Then the
warriors leapt over the threshold into the sulfurous haze. Close-range rifle
shots dropped the first attackers dead on the floor. K'alyáan took a musket
ball in the thigh. Stoonook staggered and fell. Medvednikov led the sharpshooters from their second-floor perches down the ladder into the melee
below. Ekaterina Pinnuin caught a final glimpse of her husband, Zakhar
Lebedev, as he disappeared in the fray. She later recalled that "the Russians defended themselves by shooting, but were hopelessly outnumbered."

K'alyáan, Stoonook, and other commanders wore red sashes, signifying
leadership on the battlefield. "Before the battle started, they passed out
red sashes for the aristocrats to wear," Andrew Johnson said. "A son of
the Chookaneidí clan named Duk'aan asked for a red sash, saying that
he too was a brave warrior. So they threw him one to put on." In the perilous charge on the garrison, Duk'aan moved to the front ranks. "As they
rushed in, two sons of the Kaagwaantaan were the first through," Johnson
explained. "Those two fell from gunshots, and then Duk'aan jumped in. He
was the third man through, and he also was shot. But he fell ahead of the
other two, so that Stoonook would see that he was at the head of the line."
An individual who fought bravely inspired collective pride with the clan.

K'alyáan's army included a squad of older veterans. "The young warriors tried to discourage them, telling them to go back because they were
too old to fight," Andrew Johnson said. "We will fight in our own way,"
the old-timers answered. The veterans collected and carted large bundles
of dried sticks coated with flammable resin. As the attack on the garrison
unfolded, the senior squad's moment arrived. "When the battle began the

old people broke all the windows in that large building, then they lit the pitch and threw it through the openings. The large building was enflamed."

The blaze forced the Russian defenders out of the garrison into the open yard, where they were attacked with spears and daggers. "From my hiding place, I saw Nakvasin jump from the second-floor balcony and start to run for the woods," Plotnikov recalled. "But he was not fast enough and he fell. Four Tlingit lifted him on their spears and brought him back to the barracks and cut off his head." The conflagration spread. "There was still more pitch wood, so the old fighters started a fire at the foot of the stockade. It also began to burn. Every bit of it was burning." Fort Saint Michael was turned to blackened ash. Not one single structure was left standing.

The Tlingit plundered the compound. The entire inventory of four thousand furs wrapped in large bales were rolled out of the warehouse onto the street. The armory was raided for cannons, guns, and powder kegs. Another coveted prize was people: roughly thirty hostages, mostly women, were rounded up. "As the women were forced out of the cellar hole in the ground, the young men grabbed them in front of their husbands and violated them," Andrew Johnson said. "An eye for an eye and tooth for a tooth. That is the Tlingit way." Ekaterina Pinnuin was among those taken prisoner: "When it was over, the Tlingit divided among themselves the company's supplies, furs, and us girls. They dragged us to their baidarkas. They took me first to their winter village and after that I was made a slave in another village."

The plunder-laden war canoes pushed off from G̲ájaa Héen. Later, when the canoes approached their home villages, they showed off their triumph by propping up spears in the bow with the skewered heads of their victims. They paid tribute to their fallen brothers by fixing upright paddles next to vacant seats in the canoe.

ABOVE: Sitka sound from the seat of a kayak. *Cedit: ID 99540710 © Edmund Lowe | Dreamstime.com.*
BELOW: *View of an Indian Village in Norfolk Sound,* by Sigismund Bacstrom, depicts Noow Tlein
in Sitka Sound in 1793, one of the earliest recorded views of the Tlingit village. *Image courtesy of
Beinecke Rare Book and Manuscript Library.*

ABOVE: This Russian possession plaque reads "Land owned by Russia." Early Russian traders left such plaques in Alaska in the eighteenth century to stake the empire's claim on the territory. *Image courtesy of Sitka National Historical Park, SITK 1650.* LEFT: Illustration of an eighteenth-century Russian hunter, or *promyshlennik*, by David W. Rickman. *Image courtesy of Sitka National Historical Park, SITK 9691.*

ABOVE: *Aleut at Sea Hunt*, by Mikhail Tikhanov, 1818. *Copyright © Scientific Research Museum of the Academy of Arts of Russia.* BELOW: Illustration of sea otters on land and in the water, by Georg Steller, 1751.

Колумбы Росскіе презрѣвъ угрюмый рокъ,
Межѕ лъдами новый путь отворятъ на Востокъ,
И наша досягнетъ въ Америку, Держава,
И во всѣ концы досягнетъ Россово слава.

Shelikhov considered himself the "Russian Columbus," as depicted in this illustration which was the frontispiece of his memoir. *Image from the Alaska State Library P20-177, Alaska Purchase Centennial Commission Photo Collection.*

ABOVE: Aerial view of Awa'uq, the Refuge Rock near Sitkalidak Island, and the site of the 1784 massacre of Alutiiq people. *Image courtesy the Alutiiq Museum & Archaeological Repository, Kulluk Survey Archive, AM714.* BELOW: View of Grigory Shelikhov's settlement at Three Saints Harbor on Kodiak Island. Lithograph from *The journey of Captain Sarychev's fleet through the northeastern part of Siberia, the Arctic Sea and the Eastern Ocean*, by Gavriil Sarychev, 1802. *Courtesy of Alaska and Polar Regions Archives, Rasmuson Library, University of Alaska, Fairbanks, C0015 pg 057.*

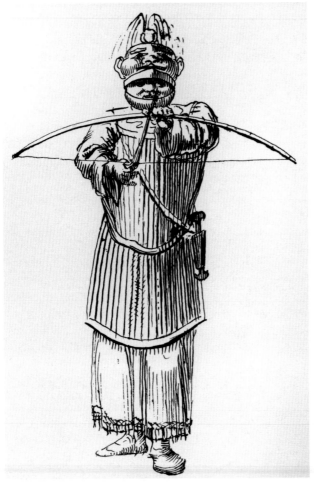

ABOVE: *Potlatch guests arriving at Sitka, Winter 1803*, by Bill Holm, exhibiting three different types of canoe used by the Tlingit. *Image from the Alaska State Museum, ASM-92-22-01.* LEFT: A Tlingit warrior at Port Mulgrave (Yakutat Bay), 1791. Illustration from the journal of Tomás de Suría, a member of Alessandro Malaspina's scientific expedition. *Copyright © Granger 0175296*

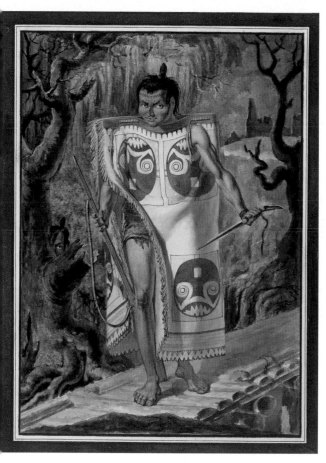

LEFT: *Kolosh Chief from Baranov Island in War Outfit*, by Mikhail Tikhanov, depicts a Tlingit warrior in 1818. *Copyright © Scientific Research Museum of the Academy of Arts of Russia.*
BOTTOM: *Kolosh family from Sitka Island*, by Mikhail Tikhanov, depicts a Tlingit family in 1818. *Copyright © Scientific Research Museum of the Academy of Arts of Russia.*

ABOVE: Tsar Paul I (pictured) bestowed this medal on Alexander Baranov in 1799 for "expanding Russian trade in America." *Image from the Alaska State Museum, ASM-III-R-348-P02.*
RIGHT: *Portrait of Alexander Baranov, Chief of the Russian-America Company,* by Mikhail Tikhanov, depicts Baranov in 1818. *Image from the Russian State History Museum, Moscow.*

Sitka Island Chief Katlian with his Wife, by Mikhail Tikhanov, depicts K'alyáan in 1818. *Copyright © Scientific Research Museum of the Academy of Arts of Russia.*

Battle of Old Sitka, 1802, by Ray Troll, depicts Tlingit warriors in masks and armor, launching their attack on the Russian fort St. Michael. *Copyright © Ray Troll.*

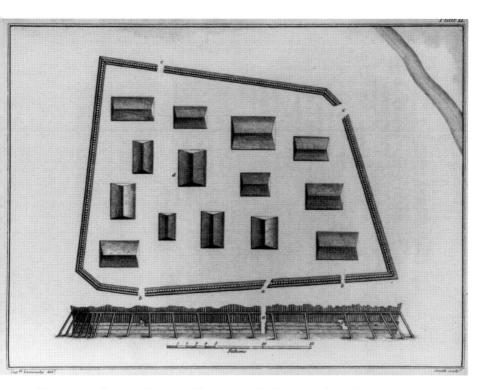

ABOVE: Illustration of Shís'g'i Noow, the Tlingit fort at Indian River from the Battle of 1804, drawn by Yury Lisyansky, from his book *A Voyage Around the World*, published in 1814. *Image from the US Library of Congress.* BELOW: Raven helmet worn by K'alyáan during the Battles of 1802 and 1804. *Image from the Sheldon Jackson Museum, #SJ-I-A-131.*

ABOVE: Russian sailors rowing from the battleship *Neva* to the Tlingit fort during the Battle of 1804. Aleuts in their baidarkas in the background. *Image courtesy of NPS Harpers Ferry Center.* BELOW: "For the journey around the world." Tsar Alexander I rewarded Yury Lisyansky and the crew of the *Neva* with this medal, in honor of the first Russian voyage around the world in 1803–1806. *Image from the Alaska State Museum, ASM-III-R-349.*

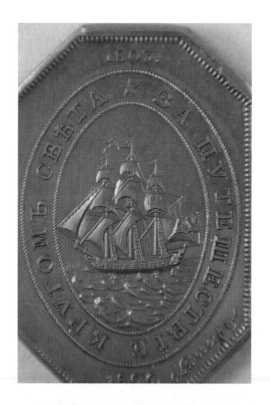

ABOVE: Wearing the raven helmet, K'alyáan leads Tlingit warriors against Russians and Aleuts during the 1804 Battle of Sitka. *Image courtesy of NPS Harpers Ferry Center.* BELOW: Bronze plaque of the double-headed eagle crest, symbol of the Russian Empire. According to oral tradition, this particular crest was presented to a Kiks.ádi clan leader in Sitka as part of the peace negotiations that followed the Battle of Sitka in 1804. *Image from the Alaska State Museum, ASM-III-R-150.*

ABOVE: A contemporary view of Sitka, with St. Michael Cathedral at the far right and Mount Edgecumbe in the background. *ID 251883215 © Steveheap | Dreamstime.com.* BELOW: *Novo Arkhangelsk*, by Alexander Olgin, depicts New Archangel (Sitka) in July 1837, with St. Michael Cathedral at the center right and the Tlingit village in the lower left. *Image courtesy of the State Archive of the Russian Navy, St. Petersburg.*

ABOVE: Mark Jacobs and other Tlingit elders greet Irina Afrosina, a descendant of Alexander Baranov, at the 2004 Reconciliation Ceremony in Sitka. Kiks.ádi clan at.óow and historic artifacts are on display in the foreground. *Copyright © Daily Sitka Sentinel.* BELOW: The raising of the K'alyáan pole, carved by Tommy Joseph and erected in 1999 on the site of the Battle of 1804, now part of Sitka National Historical Park. *Copyright © Daily Sitka Sentinel.*

Close-up of the K'alyáan pole, with the Kiks.ádi clan crest (the frog) at the base of the pole, holding K'alyáan's raven helmet. *Copyright © Mara Vorhees.*

Throughout the carnage, Plotnikov remained hidden in the hollow of a large cedar tree. Late in the evening, when all was quiet, he crawled out. "I went to look on the pitiful heap of ashes and ruin, even the poor dumb animals had spears stuck in their flanks. Two Tlingit saw me and I was forced into the woods again." Plotnikov wandered alone in the forest for two days before encountering an elderly Alutiiq man and a mother and child. Hunger drove the pitiful survivors under darkness to scrounge through the burned-out compound for morsels of food. "Every night I would go back to the place of the massacre and weep over the fate of my comrades who perished there." In the daytime, Plotnikov crept through the shoreline foliage in hopes of spotting a rescue ship. The Tlingit also kept their eyes on the water. The campaign was not over.

Curls of smoke rose from the charred ruins of Fort Saint Michael. Razing the fortress was a big victory, but only one battle in the Tlingit-Russian war. At this moment, two large hunting parties—led by Kuskov out of Kodiak and Urbanov out of Sitka—were somewhere on the water.

Canoe teams were dispatched into the archipelago to locate the whereabouts of the Russian fleets and to spread the news of the demolition of the Russian colony. In Sitka, Kiks.ádi patrols remained on alert to intercept any stray colonists.

The next day, the Tlingit got their revenge on Vasily Kochesov, better known as Gidák. The despised Russian-Aleut Creole and his sidekick Baturin returned in baidarkas from hunting sea lions. "What has happened to the large building?" they wondered. "It could not have been pulled up to heaven?" The startled pair was spotted by a canoe patrol. Baturin frantically paddled to a wooded stretch of shore and escaped into the forest. The Tlingit instead went after their main nemesis. Kochesov was no longer the hunter, but the hunted. Oral histories recall how "the canoes came after him, and he fled to the sea. He paddled, but the Tlingit were right behind. The Tlingit did not paddle fast, so he could feel the sting of being chased." Kochesov beached the canoe at the foot of a protected cliff. "Gidák was known as a marksman and he shoots rapidly. The Kiks.ádi tried to get close, but they had no chance." Concealed in the rocks, Kochesov killed five warriors before finally running out of powder. "Then they came with full force and caught Gidák and took him prisoner to an island with a Kiks.ádi village. They stripped him of his clothes and hung him upside down. They had the little children line up with small bows and arrows to see who could break the eyes." Kochesov's legacy of cruelty was avenged.

Meanwhile, a hundred miles southeast of Sitka, Ivan Urbanov had led a fleet of ninety baidarkas with nearly two hundred men. They combed the spruce-topped islets and rocky outcrops of the inner archipelago looking for sea otters. Urbanov was pleased with their haul of 1,300 skins, taken without any protest from the local Tlingit. These waters belonged to the Angoon, Kuiu, and Kake communities, who, in fact, were closely monitoring Urbanov's hunters. When news of the events in Sitka reached the eastern villages, they launched the next phase of the Tlingit offensive. A multiclan force stalked the hunting party as it reassembled near Kake for the journey home. The weather turned stormy and Urbanov's men made camp on a desolate beach. In the blackness of night, the Tlingit surrounded the exhausted party and attacked with daggers, spears, and muskets. The baidarkas on the beach were destroyed and the bundles of fur were seized. Only two dozen hunters escaped the death trap.

Further north, Ivan Kuskov was still waiting for his messengers to return from Sitka. In the meantime, he fortified the baidarka fleet with more guns and falconets and headed back into the archipelago. The weather was frightful and the harvest was meager. The nervous hunters were reluctant to paddle too far away from one another. Near Yakobi Island, less than eighty miles from Sitka, the fleet encountered two Tlingit canoes, whom Kuskov hailed for information.

They were the heralds of the news of Fort Saint Michael's destruction and were not anxious to hang around. "They promised to come ashore and talk with us, but then they left in a hurry." On the next day, five of the baidarkas dispatched to Sitka caught up with Kuskov. "We were stunned by the unhappy news that our fort at Sitka was reduced to ashes and all the people there exterminated." The five baidarkas had been chased by Tlingit patrols in Sitka Sound. A sixth baidarka was overtaken and never heard from again.

Kuskov now grasped the full extent of the campaign as well as his own exposed position. "In order to avoid being caught in the pincers and subject our party to an unfortunate fate, there was no course but to return to Yakutat," Kuskov determined. "Besides the Alutiit were greatly disturbed by the news from Sitka, lamenting and sobbing over the attack on their kin." The company traveled at night to avoid detection on the open water. Kuskov arrived at Yakutat just in time to foil a Tlingit mob that was moving against the small Russian fort.

Through a combination of wits and luck, Kuskov managed to thwart Tlingit plans to rid Yakutat of the Russians. Medvednikov in Sitka was not so fortunate. The Tlingit multifront war delivered a crippling blow to Russia's imperial ambitions. Before they could celebrate the victory, however, events at Sitka took an unexpected turn.

"On the last day of our pitiful wandering in the mountains, I heard two cannon shots and was cheered," Abrosim Plotnikov recalled. "I told the old man and the girl to take cover and wait for me, and then I went down to the banks of the creek. As I approached the shore, a ship sailed around the island. When it came closer, I saw that it was English."

On the bridge of the *Unicorn* stood the notorious captain-swindler Henry Barber, returning to Noow Tlein to trade weapons for furs. "I arrived on the sound and was a good deal surprised at seeing nothing of the Russians or their Kodiak hunters." The Kiks.ádi had good reason to distrust Barber. Still, an opportunity to replenish firearms and gunpowder could not be passed up. Besides, Shk'awulyeil believed that Barber would be pleased to see that the Russians had been run out of Sitka. The rogue captain openly disdained Russia's presence in America. Baranov and Kuskov considered Barber as nothing more than a pirate. Shk'awulyeil approached the brig with caution. He brought along as translator a runaway sailor from the *Jenny*, an American merchant vessel. The captain and the headman exchanged greetings. Believing that it was safe to trade, Shk'awulyeil returned to Noow Tlein, leaving his translator behind.

The *Jenny* deserter was inspired to shift loyalties once more. He delivered "a melancholy account of the destruction of the Russian compound and massacre of the Russian commandant." Barber had to see for himself. "I went in the yawl with the American, well-manned and well-armed, to the cove where the Russian compound had stood. I found the place entirely destroyed by fire, and mangled bodies of about twenty men scattered among the ruins, prey to the ravens and the beasts of the forest, as shocking and horrid a sight as a human could witness." Startled by a distress call from the woods, the crewmen aimed their weapons as a wretched figure stumbled into the clearing. Plotnikov was rescued. Soon Barber gathered a half dozen Fort Saint Michael refugees from their hiding places in the woods. "We were very glad to see one another and told our adventures," Plotnikov said. Back aboard the *Unicorn*, Barber fed the survivors and listened to their stories. Stroking his chin, the captain hatched a plan.

Three days later, Shk'awulyeil returned to the *Unicorn* with a canoe escort for trade talks. He was accompanied by his wife and K'alyáan, still limping from the musket shot that had pierced his thigh. Barber amiably welcomed the esteemed guests onto the main deck, then sprung his trap. On a signal, gun-wielding sailors leapt from the hold, disarmed K'alyáan, and clapped the two men in iron shackles. The captain issued an ultimatum to the alarmed Tlingit in canoes: return to me all the hostages and furs taken from the Russian fort or your chief and his nephew will hang from the yardarm. Thus began five days of threats, appeals, and feints. The Tlingit dragged out the negotiations, delivering only one hostage a day and spoiling for a chance to rush the crew.

Barber's position was bolstered when two Boston merchantmen, the *Alert* and the *Globe*, sailed into Sitka Sound and joined forces with the *Unicorn*. Incensed by the Tlingit revolt, the captain of the *Alert* loaded grapeshot into the cannons and began blasting the canoes. Several Tlingit warriors were killed in the skirmish that followed. Tired of the delay, Barber announced that the long guns would next take aim on Noow Tlein and obliterate the Kiks.ádi compound. The Tlingit capitulated. "In the morning, we were visited by several canoes," Barber reported. "They brought one Russian man, ten Kodiak women and two children, whom we accepted in exchange for the Chief and his wife." Plotnikov was outraged. "The commander released the chief and the nephew, despite our pleas to bring them to Kodiak," he fumed. The liberation of the two principal leaders of the uprising stoked Russian suspicion that the devious trader was in some way to blame for the catastrophe. Without spending as much as a shilling, Captain Barber's well-timed visit to Sitka yielded a large bundle of furs as well as twenty-two new passengers.

Barber then implemented the second part of his plan. The *Unicorn* proceeded straight to Kodiak Island to pay call on the director of the Russian-American Company. Baranov was devastated by the news about Sitka. He had told Medvednikov repeatedly to stay vigilant and maintain good relations with their hosts. Barber moved quickly from condolences to compensation. "From humane motives, I rescued the prisoners from the hands of savages, fed and clothed them, and neglected my own business." He submitted to Baranov a bill for fifty thousand rubles to cover the costs of his compassion.

Baranov was flabbergasted. It was less a reward than a shakedown. Barber stubbornly refused to release the Fort Saint Michael survivors until Baranov paid up. Baranov seethed with hatred for the conniving captain, whose demands would bankrupt the colony. At last, they came to agreement on a rescue fee of ten thousand rubles, payable in fox and beaver skins.

Baranov also splurged for an additional twenty thousand rubles worth of desperately needed supplies, including the cache of rifles, falconets, and gunpowder that Barber was intending to sell to the Sitka Tlingit. Baranov was already plotting his revenge.

The *Unicorn* sped to Canton, where Captain Barber reaped a windfall profit, a sizable portion of which went directly into his private account. There was no need for his investors to know about the side deals involving hostages and stolen goods. Barber then sailed back to New South Wales, where he posted a fancifully embellished account of the events in Sitka. Along the way, he stopped in the South Sandwich Islands and learned that back in Europe, Great Britain and Russia were on the verge of hostilities. What rotten luck, if he had only known earlier, Barber would have blasted the Kodiak settlement into oblivion and rid the North Pacific of the Russians once and for all.

For more than two decades, the Russian Empire had steadily advanced from its Eurasian base across the Pacific to North America. The sacking of Fort Saint Michael brought Russian expansion to an abrupt halt. The Tlingit multifront offensive against the Russian Empire was an extraordinary event in Native American history. It marked the worst defeat that Russia would ever sustain in its bid to become a New World player. The cumulative death toll, including settlers and hunters, was roughly 250 victims, comparable to the number of dead cavalrymen at the iconic Battle of the Little Big Horn. While Shk̲'awulyeil and K'alyáan are mostly unknown in American popular culture, their role as Native resistance fighters, who pushed back a foreign invasion of their homeland, is on par with the accomplishments of Sitting Bull, Crazy Horse, and Red Cloud three quarters of a century later.

RAINFOREST WARRIORS

Among the North American Native cultures, there was no defensive weapon comparable to the Tlingit suit of armor. It deflected arrows, knives, and even musket balls. The fantastically carved helmet was as dramatic a display as the most resplendent Plains Indian eagle-feather war bonnet.

In the early twenty-first century, Tlingit artist and master carver Tommy Joseph set out to learn what made his forebears' defensive costume so formidable and so frightening. He traveled throughout the United States and around the world to examine Tlingit weapons and armor held in various museum collections, from Philadelphia to St. Petersburg. He studied the materials and methods that were used hundreds of years ago, and eventually he was inspired to try his own hand at this traditional craft. His pieces make up *Rainforest Warriors*, an exhibit that appeared at the Alaska State History Museum. Joseph outfitted six mannequins in full, fearsome battle gear and regalia, complete with copper daggers and jade war clubs.

The fully uniformed Tlingit warrior was a sight to behold, a rainforest variation of a herald-emblazoned medieval knight. Toughened moose hide undergarments covered the torso and legs. A spruce-wood armor tunic was layered over the moose hide, reaching from the shoulders down to mid-thigh. The tunic's pleated wooden slats were overlaid in multiple rows and stitched tightly with deer sinew to provide upper-body protection and flexibility. Wooden armor sleeves guarded the forearms, while also allowing free movement of the elbows and shoulders.

"It was the Kevlar vest of the day," Joseph explained. "One layer isn't going to stop a bullet but multiple layers woven together, and the slat armor over that . . . they were pretty well protected."

Joseph discovered (and re-created) a version of the Tlingit armor that used coins for an extra layer of protection. "The Tlingits got Chinese coins through trade . . . The money didn't mean anything to the Tlingit, but having that handy hole in the middle, they were able to sew it to the hide, kind of like chainmail."

This walking shield was topped by a high wooden cowl and low-resting helmet, with a narrow opening for the eyes. The hardwood helmet featured a full-scale head carving of a fierce animal or semi-human fiend, making the attacker seem a frightening foot taller. According to Joseph, "These helmets were like your spirit helpers. You brought your ancestors with you into battle and they helped to protect you." The overall effect was relatively impenetrable and thoroughly intimidating.

Tommy Joseph is one of many contemporary Tlingit artists who have taken inspiration from the elaborate arms and armor used by their forebears—from Preston Singletary's glass shark helmet to Tanis Seiltin's woodcut prints. "This art is not a dead art form," Joseph observed. "It continues to evolve the way it always has."

CHAPTER 8
Voyage of the *Neva*

I am sorry, my brother, when you go. I will see you again, for I may die soon." In low voices, tributes were sung to the fallen warriors outside the longhouses during the week of mourning following the battle at Gájaa Héen.

The Russian colony was destroyed. The foreign menace was driven out of the homeland. No longer would the Tlingit live in fear of an encounter with armed Russians in the woods or on the water. No longer would the Russians trespass and poach on Tlingit hunting grounds. No longer would Tlingit women and children be forced to serve inside the Russian compound. It was a time to exalt, and a time to grieve.

The Tlingit frontal assault inevitably resulted in many casualties. K'alyáan was wounded in the battle, but he survived. Brother Stoonook, however, was fatally struck. So too was the young warrior Duk'aan, who wanted to wear the red sash. Both were killed leading the rush on the garrison. The widows of the dead painted their faces black and fasted, while their clan relatives managed the death rituals. The bodies were cleansed, dressed in fine clothes, and covered in blankets and furs. The faces of the dead warriors were painted with red ochre. Their family crests, personal possessions, and water vessels were arranged around the body, while a dagger was placed in clenched fingers.

In Tlingit culture, death was a transition. The animating soul departed the physical body and returned to the spirit world, until a later time when it was called again to live in the earthly realm. The corpse was placed on a cedarwood pyre and burned to ashes, which were stored in the pillars of the house. For a leader or warrior, the head was lopped off the body first, wrapped in a fur blanket, and placed in a splendidly painted bentwood box. The box was later fixed to a totem pole or clan crest, infusing the sacred marker with an ancestral spirit. Fallen warriors traveled a special path to Keewakowanne, a heavenly paradise somewhere above the homeland, which occasionally could be glimpsed from earth in the form of a rainbow or the northern lights. To die in battle was the highest honor.

In the Point House, the Kiks.ádi leader Shk̲'awulyeil and eldest nephew K'alyáan sat on mats next to the fire, smoking a tobacco pipe and reciting the names of departed clan members. It was an invitation to the ancestral spirits to come and guide the fallen Stoonook on his afterlife journey. "A funeral pyre was built above the tideline," Alex Andrews said. "The Tlingit dead were brought there to be cremated. The prisoners who were going to be killed were all brought there too."

When the mourning period ended, the victory celebration began. The pounding of drums resonated down from Noow Tlein, calling the Sitka Tlingit to gather at the Kiks.ádi longhouse. It was now time for feasting, singing and dancing, and speeches. The assembled sat around the fire by order of rank. Shk̲'awulyeil and K'alyáan were at the front. The feast would mark the first occasion, when the story of the 1802 war against Russia was told by the principal participants. These narratives would be retold year after year and passed on to successive generations in each clan house, preserving the Tlingit version of the events and personalities. The speeches delivered on Noow Tlein would endure as a spoken history for more than 150 years before it was finally recorded in writing.

After the recitations, Shk̲'awulyeil distributed gifts to the attending families and clans. There was much to share from the huge pile of plunder salvaged from the ruins: firearms, knives, tools, iron, clothes, blankets, furs, and slaves. (Not all the hostages were returned to Captain Henry Barber.)

The Kiks.ádi leader was the recipient of a most welcome prize—the long-barreled musket belonging to the Russian Creole Gidák. "They killed him and broke off his head, and then they brought it to the funeral pyre and shot his eyes out with his own rifle," Alex Andrews said. "The rifle was a muzzle loader, the kind that when the bullet fits in snug, it hits the target well. They took Gidák's musket as booty for the noble man Shk'awulyeil." Andrew Johnson adds that Gidák's body was not cremated but thrown into the sea, so to bring further indignity on their foe.

Toward the end of the feast, Shk'awulyeil asked the Kiks.ádi shaman if the Russians were truly defeated. An anxious silence fell over the longhouse as the seer fell into a trance. He clutched a raven-carved talisman, a soft rattling was heard. At last, the shaman opened his eyes and uttered a prophecy: "The Russians will return in a huge schooner to seek revenge for the loss of Fort Saint Michael."

Far from Sitka, the royal patron of the Russian American colony met with his own misfortune in St. Petersburg. In March 1801 the reign of Tsar Paul I was cut short by drunken palace guards, who strangled the emperor to death with his bedroom curtains. Paul I was succeeded by Catherine the Great's favorite grandson. Tall, blue-eyed, and curly blond, Alexander I was eager to signal Russia's ascent to the rest of Europe. In summer 1802, as Fort Saint Michael was burning, the new tsar received a proposal for a grand imperial project—Russia's first transoceanic circumnavigation.

The idea was to send two ships around Cape Horn into the Pacific on a mission of scientific discovery, commercial enterprise, and great power display. Along the way, the expedition would visit and resupply the Russian American colony in Alaska. The scheme was dreamed up by naval captain Ivan Krusenstern, nudged forward by the lord admiral, mulled over by the minister of trade, and seized upon by the chief executive of the

Russian-American Company, Count Nikolai Rezanov. The count pitched the tsar, who loved the idea. A high-profile circumnavigation fit perfectly with Alexander's global ambitions. The emperor authorized a 250,000-ruble loan for the venture. The well-travelled Krusenstern was enlisted as mission commander, who, in turn, recruited Yury Lisyansky to be his sailing sidekick.

Representing the finest of Russia's cadet corps, Lisyansky had graduated at the top of his class at the Imperial Naval Academy. The fifteen-year-old midshipman was immediately sent into action in the Baltic, after the king of Sweden, Gustavus III, declared war on his second cousin, Catherine the Great. Having distinguished himself in the Battle of Reval, Lisyansky was selected for a prestigious six-year apprenticeship with the British navy. He served in the Atlantic, chasing French pirates, escorting British traders, and press-ganging American sailors. After a bout with yellow fever sidelined Lisyansky in the Caribbean, he went on a sightseeing tour up the coast of the newly independent United States, stopping for tea with George Washington. In 1802, back in St. Petersburg, Lisyansky lobbied his friend Krusenstern for a role in the emperor's circumnavigation project.

For his first assignment, Krusenstern handed Lisyansky a packet of promissory notes signed by the tsar and sent him off to find two stout vessels for a grueling three-year ocean voyage. The quest took Lisyansky back to London, to the Royal Navy's used shipyard in Gravesend. He purchased the *Leander*, a three-masted sloop and ex-slaver, and the *Thames*, a three-masted two-hundred-foot frigate. The whopping cost of 22,000 pounds sterling for two ships in need of major repair raised eyebrows at company headquarters. It was hoped that Lisyansky was better at seamanship than he was at haggling. The ships required Russian names, so the *Leander* was rechristened the *Nadezhda* (*Hope*), while the *Thames* became the *Neva*.

By July 1803 the refurbished ships bobbed in place next to Kronstadt naval base, where the Neva River empties into the Gulf of Finland. The expedition was ready to launch. Under the eternal glow of the midsummer Baltic sky, a lavish send-off party tippled over the decks of the *Nadezhda*. Krusenstern's wife Julianne was an attentive hostess. The guest of honor, Tsar Alexander, conferred God's blessing on the enterprise. The next day the history-making convoy was underway.

At the behest of the emperor, company chief executive, Nikolai Rezanov, was a reluctant passenger on the *Nadezhda*. The count was conscripted by the tsar to lead an embassy to the shogun of Japan, in hopes of establishing diplomatic relations with the reclusive East Asian empire. Krusenstern's flagship was crammed with scientific instruments, goods for trading, supplies for the colony, and a cache of luxurious and kitschy gifts for the Japanese emperor, including a huge woven portrait of Tsar Alexander made by the master craftsmen at the royal tapestry shop. Newly promoted Lieutenant-Commander Lisyansky stood tall on the quarterdeck of the *Neva*, the smaller of the two ships, armed with fourteen cannons and a hundred barrels of vodka. The *Neva* may have begun the odyssey as an escort vessel, but it was destined to become the most renowned Russian ship of the age of sail.

Alexander Baranov was, if anything, stubborn. The Tlingit offensive in the summer of 1802 wiped out three years of hard work at Sitka. He was confounded that Medvednikov had not followed his explicit instructions. He was devastated that his comrades had met a gruesome fate. He was worried that the company had incurred staggering losses. But mostly, he seethed that the Sitka Tlingit had betrayed and attacked him. Baranov vowed to avenge this bitter defeat.

In early September, Baranov was heartened to see the *Ekaterina* cruise into Saint Paul Harbor in Kodiak, delivering Ivan Kuskov and Ivan Urbanov. Thankfully, the New Russia fort at Yakutat was still standing.

The pair briefed Baranov on their summer in the archipelago battling the Tlingit. Kuskov relayed the key details of the uprising, gleaned from Native informants at Yakutat, including which clan leaders instigated the rebellion. Baranov was dismayed to learn that almost all the Tlingit villages in the archipelago were involved in the offensive. His campaign to exact punishment would have to be deferred. The colony at this time was not strong enough to challenge the Tlingit alliance.

By year's end, Baranov's situation began to improve. In late fall, the *Zachary and Elizaveta* arrived from Okhotsk, bringing much-needed supplies and 120 new settlers. Even though it meant more mouths to feed, the colony was reinvigorated by this infusion of humanity. On the ship's return to Okhotsk in early 1803, Baranov delivered a shipment of furs worth more than a million rubles. He dispatched two additional fur cargos to Okhotsk before the year was over, including 15,000 sea otter pelts and 250,000 fur seal skins, worth a million and a half rubles. At least Baranov's reputation remained in good order among Siberian merchants and St. Petersburg shareholders.

During this time, Baranov made a new friend, Boston-based Irishman Joseph O'Cain, who arrived in Saint Paul Harbor aboard his ninety-three-foot eponymously named schooner. O'Cain bartered supplies for furs, which he sold in Canton for a rich profit. The inspired trader journeyed back to Kodiak with a proposition. O'Cain offered to transport a party of Alutiiq hunters with baidarkas southward, beyond Tlingit country, in search of sea otters along the California coast. The captain and the governor would split the take. With the archipelago now off limits to his fur trappers, Baranov readily agreed. Six months later, the *O'Cain* returned from California with six hundred sea otter pelts for company coffers.

Finally, Baranov began investing in warfare. He amassed a stockpile of rifles, artillery, lead balls, and gunpowder from every Yankee trader who stopped in Kodiak, without quibbling over the price. He ordered trusted assistant Ivan Kuskov back to Yakutat to construct two small sailing ships with cannon mounts, using iron and rigging scavenged from an old wreck. Kuskov brought several dozen workers with him, bolstering the Russian presence along Yakutat Bay.

Baranov was biding his time before the next round of battle.

"From Noow Tlein, they kept watch for when the Russians would retaliate," Alex Andrews said. For weeks following the destruction of Fort Saint Michael, the Kiks.ádi remained on alert for a Russian counterattack. Shk'awulyeil continued to send out canoe patrols and stayed in close communication with the other Tlingit villages in the northern archipelago. But there were no signs of the Russians. All indications suggested that the enemy had been routed. Life returned to normal in Sitka.

The Tlingit New Year begins with the July moon and the return of the salmon. By late summer, the Sitkans had all but forgotten about the Russians. The community prepared for the winter. Now was the time that the men caught salmon with bone-point spears and weir traps and the women gathered berries in spruce baskets. In autumn, the men pursued new quarry, as deer and halibut were at their fattest and mountain goats moved down below the timberline. The women processed the harvest. The fish were gutted and smoked, the berries were preserved and stored, the venison and goat were cut into strips and dried in the sun, the hides were cut and dressed for leather.

By the end of November, the extended clan families gathered in the largest wooden longhouse for the winter roost. At last, the time had come for feasting and storytelling. The old stories were shared and new stories took shape. Each house celebrated its role in the war against Russia with its own version of the main events and personalities. Winter was also the time that the Tlingit tended to handicrafts. Around the warm fire pit, the women wove mountain goat wool into blankets and thin spruce strips into baskets and the men carved mountain goat horns into spoons and deer antlers into clubs.

As the nights grew longer, so did the gambling games. The most popular game, and most obsessive, was the devilfish stick game. Played with a set of several dozen pencil-thin sticks, uniform in size but painted differently. Two men kneeled on opposite sides of a mat and built piles of sticks before them, hiding the devilfish stick in one of their piles. (Devilfish was a squid used as bait to catch halibut, so the object of the game was to catch the bait.) In turn, a player guessed where the devilfish was hiding and then drew sticks blindly from a leather pouch, throwing them down one at a time onto the mat. Depending on which particular painted sticks came out of the pouch, the player either won the devilfish pile, rolled again, or passed their turn.

The goal was to collect all the sticks. Gaming sticks were treated with as much care as weapons. They were carved from hard maple or alder wood, finely polished, ornately decorated, and stored in soft leather bags. The stakes were usually blankets and furs. Gambling games kept the men occupied throughout the long winter nights.

In early spring 1803, a high-prow canoe appeared in front of Noow Tlein. The occupants raised their paddles and chanted in unison, asking to be invited to land. Shk'awulyeil recognized the crest images painted on the bow and welcomed the visitors ashore. It was the L'uknax̱.ádi clan with news from the north. New life was stirring in the Russian compound at Yakutat. The previous summer, a Tlingit war party had come close to overrunning the fort and driving the Russians out. Now the savior of New Russia, Ivan Kuskov had returned with reinforcements. The compound now sported a pair of big cannons, aimed at the approach to the fort and at the Tlingit village across the bay. Inside, the settlers were hard at work, building two new warships. "The Russians are coming to kill you." Shk'awulyeil grimaced at the news. He summoned the Kiks.ádi shaman and his nephew K'alyáan.

"The wind was now favorable and I waited, with some considerable impatience, for Mr. Rezanov," Captain Krusenstern said. In September 1803 the *Neva* and the *Nadezhda* were anchored off the coast of Falmouth, at the southwest tip of England. Count Rezanov was in London, on an errand to procure navigation instruments for the expedition. Taking advantage of his liberty, he decided to do some extra shopping and drop in on some old friends. Krusenstern, meanwhile, fretted. Fair weather was wasting. The captain's appointment with history was delayed.

From the beginning, the military man and the businessman clashed. The disciplined Krusenstern envisioned a voyage of discovery of new lands and peoples. He modeled himself after Captain Cook, and even kept a copy of Cook's published diaries in his cabin, which he consulted routinely. Krusenstern was inspired by scientific glory. By contrast, the impetuous Rezanov envisioned a commercial empire in the North Pacific. He had married his way into the Russian-American Company, as son-in-law to company founder Grigory Shelikhov, and then artfully won the confidence of a bevy of wealthy patrons. Rezanov was on a quest for riches. The conflicting motives were a source of tension throughout the journey. It did not help matters that Tsar Alexander had told each separately that they were in charge of the expedition.

Aboard the *Neva*, Yury Lisyansky was thankful to be away from the drama. He used the layover to recaulk the seams of the thick oaken hull and to stock up on Irish corned beef. In the age of sail, the key to circumnavigation was to minimize the number of lengthy voyages. Ships skittered from one landing spot to another, pausing to repair leaky frames and tattered sails, and to replenish empty water barrels and food stores. From Falmouth, the team would head south to the Canary Islands off the coast of Africa, and then westward across the Atlantic to Santa Catarina Island off the coast of Brazil, before making the dangerous passage around Cape Horn.

On the morning of October 5, Count Rezanov finally returned from London with a cartload of gadgets, a sextant, porcelain snuffboxes for the officers, and assorted personal items that one simply could not find in Russia. "The same day we sailed at high tide from Carreck Road with a fresh northerly breeze," Krusenstern said. "All officers remained on deck until past twelve. Upon entering the ocean, the night was as fine as could possibly be, clear and not a cloud to be seen. It appeared to everyone a good omen for our long voyage."

The trip through the South Atlantic was without incident, excepting the *Nadezhda* getting bruised by a gigantic finback whale and a mischievous Brazilian monkey getting loose in the captain's quarters. Even the stormy cape passage was unusually calm. In March 1804 the *Neva* and *Nadezhda* entered the enchanting South Pacific, where they were greeted by a cyclone. The furious storm hurled the ships onto separate paths. A month later, Lisyansky's crew became the first Russians to gaze on the giant stone idols of Easter Island. The *Neva* caught up with the *Nadezhda* in the Marquesas Islands. Captain Krusenstern was flaunting a new tattoo. The reunited explorers sailed on to Hawaii.

By now, the bickering of the *Nadezhda*'s twin commanders was a full-blown battle. Krusenstern intended to conduct a scientific survey of Hawaii's exotic flora and fauna. But Rezanov insisted that they quickly load up on provisions and sail on to Japan for his diplomatic mission. The company boss prevailed over the ship captain. Krusenstern was forced to abandon his "hopes of making a new discovery." The Hawaiians were eager traders. The captain acquired fresh potatoes, coconuts, and suckling pigs, but declined an offer of "an old man's young daughter, whom I incorrectly perceived was still innocent." In early June 1804 the *Nadezhda* weighed anchor, hoping to stay ahead of the monsoon season. Krusenstern should have stayed in Hawaii. The Japanese emperor declined to give an audience to Rezanov, and refused to accept the bundle of gifts or the tsar's personal letter.

Lisyansky, meanwhile, lingered in Polynesian paradise. The *Neva* toured the Kona coast on the Big Island. He bartered iron for hogs, axes for fruit, and clothing for yams. He traced the footsteps of his hero Captain Cook on the beach where the legendary explorer was killed.

Unfortunately, Lisyansky missed the chance to introduce himself to Hawaiian strongman King Kamehameha, due to an outbreak of sickness on Oahu. Instead, he directed the *Neva* to Kauai to meet local big-shot King Kaumuali'i. The island chieftains were fierce rivals. Kaumuali'i tempted Lisyansky with a political proposition: Kauai's pledge of allegiance to the Russian emperor in exchange for Russian military support against King Kamehameha. Lisyansky politely declined, saying that "he was not in a position to agree to the king's plan." The Kauai chief's attempts to draw Russia into his feud with Kamehameha would be revived at a later date with a more open-minded emissary.

Lisyansky rowed back to the *Neva* in Waimea Bay and received startling news. "On our return to ship, we found some sailors belonging to the United States, one of whom had been on the Northwest Coast of America. He informed us that the Russian settlement in Sitka had been destroyed by the natives." Lisyansky cut short his tropical rambles and ordered the crew to make sail. The *Neva* headed north into the land of the Raven.

Atop Noow Tlein, a war council convened. The Sitka house leaders and representatives from other villages discussed the foreboding news out of Yakutat. Shk̲'awulyeil warned that the Russians were plotting a new advance into the archipelago. The Kiks.ádi shaman retold the prophecy that the Russians would return in a huge schooner seeking revenge. It was necessary to prepare, the shaman said, by constructing a new fortress at Sitka and reviving the wartime alliance. But not everyone agreed. Now was not the time to organize for another battle, some said. It was the season to prepare for winter. The Russians had abandoned the archipelago, others insisted. Then K'alyáan spoke. He was convinced of the shaman's words, and he argued for a mobilization of resources and strengthening of defenses. Shḵ'awulyeil deferred to his nephew, and K'alyáan was appointed as Kiks.ádi war commander.

"K'alyáan was an extraordinary person," said Tlingit culture-bearer Herb Hope, "because he was the one who could see the danger of the change that was coming." K'alyáan's first task was to construct a defensive stronghold. Noow Tlein was on a hilltop, protruding into the bay. It may have given the Tlingit a tactical advantage against canoes and foot soldiers wielding spears and arrows, but it was vulnerable to the long-range cannons of the European ships. Even the Russians had pointed out to Shḵ'awulyeil the defensive shortcomings of Noow Tlein: "You built this fort wrong. Your guns are in the wrong place. There is no water up here." K'alyáan now considered the alternatives, and chose a site one mile south of the main village.

"That is why the Kiks.ádi built their fort at Indian River, in a level place where there is water," Alex Andrews said. "On the beach side, logs were piled high. Ten houses were built inside and a huge pit was dug." The compound was built out of Sitka spruce. "The Tlingit people had names for the different size spruce trees. Those that are two feet in diameter are called *shisg*. The fort was made of *shisg*, the young trees," Andrew Johnson explained. Hence, the Indian River stronghold became known as Shís'gi Noow, the Fortress of the Saplings. Its ingenious design would stymie the Russian Empire's firepower and prove a marvel of Native North American engineering.

In April 1804 Alexander Baranov climbed aboard the *Ekaterina* and gazed with approval upon the armada assembled at Saint Paul Harbor. Three hundred baidarkas, carrying eight hundred Alutiiq and Aleut hunters, were poised behind Baranov's flagship and the accompanying *Alexander Nevsky*. From Kodiak, they would sail to Yakutat to strengthen their force with two additional armed vessels. Against the backdrop of Snowy Mountain, Baranov gave the signal and his crusade was underway.

In late May Baranov's flotilla arrived at Yakutat. His cannon-toting ships were battle ready as the Alutiiq fur trappers set up a mile-long campsite around the bayfront. The Yakutat Tlingit were dismayed by the confrontational display, and too intimidated to interfere. Baranov greeted Kuskov and inspected the two newly built ships—small sailing crafts that could be rowed galley-style, well suited for the tight passages of the inner archipelago. Baranov commandeered the vessels and christened them the *Yermak* and the *Rostislav*. He then instructed the *Alexander Nevsky* and *Ekaterina* to continue on to Sitka without him. Baranov would catch up after leading a hunting party into the archipelago, where the governor had unfinished business.

The *Yermak* and *Rostislav* headed into Icy Strait, acting as armed chaperones to the baidarka teams. In their swift and steerable crafts, the Alutiiq systematically ransacked every colony of lounging sea otters they came upon, accumulating more than 1,500 skins. A thick fog arose and the two ships became separated. The *Yermak* was trapped in a drifting field of glacial ice. "Death appeared to encircle us," Baranov reported, "but after a torturing twelve hours in mortal danger, we finally escaped." On the other side of the frozen gauntlet, the two ice-damaged ships were reunited. Baranov was defiant. He ordered the flotilla deeper into the archipelago, southward into the hazards of Peril Strait. Baranov was on a mission to punish the Kake and Kuiu clans for the 1802 attacks. But the Tlingit avoided direct contact with the Russian force.

Instead, Baranov had to slake his vengeance by setting fire to a handful of abandoned villages. The message was clear, however. Retribution awaited any clan that dared to oppose the Russian Empire.

By late June, the signs were unmistakable: the *Neva* was getting close to Kodiak. "We met with an amphibious animal about three-feet in length with a bushy tail and sharp muzzle. It played around us for an hour. We supposed it was a sea otter." Glacier-capped mountains were visible to the east. The air was chilled. In early July the *Neva* arrived at Three Saints Harbor, the site of Grigory Shelikhov's original colony. A squadron of baidarkas surrounded the ship and addressed them in Russian. "These were welcome visitors," Lisyansky said, "especially because they brought us a quantity of very excellent fish." The next day several Alutiiq pilots led the *Neva* through impenetrable fog and treacherous shoals to the main settlement. The *Neva*'s entrance into Saint Paul Harbor was announced with an eleven-gun salute from the Russian fort.

A boatload of happy colonists rowed out to congratulate the captain and crew of the *Neva*. "It is not easy to express what I felt on this occasion," Lisyansky said. "To be the first Russian to perform so long and tedious a voyage gave me a degree of religious fervor mixed with satisfaction and delight." Kodiak's acting head, Ivan Banner, briefed the captain on the Tlingit aggressions against the colony. Governor Baranov, he said, had already set out on a mission to take back Sitka. "I had supposed my voyage was at an end for the present year, but it turned out otherwise," Lisyansky said. "Mr. Banner begged my assistance in opposing the savages." Although Lisyansky's orders did not require him to participate in hostilities, he could not leave Baranov on his own. Lisyansky was a patriot and a romantic. "I complied with the request, and resolved to prepare to sea immediately."

In late August Lisyansky set eyes on the snow-rimmed cauldron of Mount Edgecumbe. "From our entrance into Sitka Sound, nothing pre-sented itself except impenetrable woods, reaching from the waterside to the very tops of the highest mountains," Lisyansky observed. "I never saw a country so wild and gloomy."

The captain of the *Neva* observed another sailing ship across the sound. It was the *Alexander Nevsky*, followed by the *Ekaterina*, which had already arrived from Yakutat. The nervous Russian crewmen were thrilled that a naval frigate was joining their armada. "I learned that they were waiting for Mr. Baranov, and that the inhabitants of Sitka had fortified themselves and were resolved not to suffer the Russians making a second settlement without a trial of strength."

In mid-September the *Yermak* sailed into Sitka Sound. Lisyansky was relieved: "We had begun to doubt that Mr. Baranov was still alive." Baranov was overjoyed to see the *Neva*, converted into a sloop of war and at his service. Behind Baranov came the Alutiiq hunters. "At eight o'clock in the evening, sixty baidarkas arrived under the command of Mr. Kuskov, who fired a salute of muskets on passing us, in answer to which I ordered two rockets to be sent up," Lisyansky said. The *Rostislav*, however, had fallen behind and its party did not go unscathed. "The Sitka natives caught a baidarka in the hunting party, shot the two Alaskans in it, and cut off their heads in full view, frightening the others."

From the vantage point of Shís'gi Noow, the Sitka Tlingit closely monitored these first arriving Russian vessels. They harassed their crews and prepared to defend their homeland. And then, through the early autumn mist, the *Neva* appeared on the sound. The two-hundred-foot, three-masted, cannon-toting frigate sent an air of dread through the community. The shaman's prophecy was confirmed. The Russians had returned in a huge schooner to seek their revenge.

WRECK OF THE *NEVA*

Some say that the 1812 voyage of the *Neva*, from Okhotsk, Russia, back to Sitka, Alaska, was doomed from the outset. According to one version of the story, a Kiks.ádi shaman foresaw the destruction of the ship some eight years before it occurred. Others say the shaman actually cursed the ship in retribution for its role in the conflict between the Russians and the Tlingit.

In any case, the return voyage certainly didn't start out well. The newly appointed captain drowned before the ship even left port, when his skiff capsized during an inspection. Throughout the journey, fierce storms damaged the ship, and the next-in-command lieutenant became too ill to do his job. Some fifteen crewmen died before the ship reached the safety of Prince William Sound. Desperate to reach Sitka before experiencing more death and destruction, Navigator Daniil Kalinin—who was now in charge—made the fateful decision to continue to Sitka in the depths of winter. During the final leg of the journey, Kalinin went below deck to get some rest, and that's when fog engulfed the *Neva* and the ship veered off course. She foundered on the rocks, which tore apart the keel, and everyone aboard tumbled into the surf, causing thirty-two people to drown. The remaining twenty-eight passengers and crew barely made it to shore at Kruzof Island.

Just ten miles west of Sitka, this island is a sacred place for the Tlingit. Its main feature is the extinct volcano Mount Edgecumbe, and according to Tlingit lore, their ancestors were drawn to Sitka by the mountain's smoke. The fact that the *Neva* wrecked at a location so meaningful to the Tlingit is sometimes offered as evidence that the disaster was the work of a shaman.

The *Neva* survivors endured three weeks of winter weather in this remote outpost before they were finally rescued. But not before two more men died, including the high-ranking Tertii Bornovolokov, who was coming to Sitka to replace Baranov as manager of the Russian-American Company. The exact site of this tragic interlude—isolated and unsettled—was forgotten.

Nearly two centuries later, an international team of archeologists found traces of the survivors' camp on Kruzof Island, including the remains of cooking fires and a stash of axes. Later searches turned up additional cooking fires, food bones, and gunflints used as fire starters. Researchers found one lone coffin, crudely crafted with salvaged lumber, interred in the traditional Russian Orthodox manner.

The artifacts gave some clues as to how the castaways survived. It appeared that they utilized any materials they could find, fashioning makeshift tools from scrap metal and boat parts. They managed to find ways to hunt, fish, and cook, as well as send out search parties (which eventually led to their rescue). Underwater searches revealed no evidence of the ship itself, which had been a mystery. But large nautical pieces were found washed up on the shore and even in the forest, indicating that the ship had been broken apart and dispersed around the island. It was a tragic end for the once-triumphant vessel.

Upon completion of the excavation, Tlingit elders and Russian Orthodox clergy together blessed the survivors' campsite. It was "a poignant gesture of forgiveness and healing," bringing closure to a small but significant piece of history.

CHAPTER 9

Battle at Indian River

T he appearance of the *Neva* triggered a state of emergency in Sitka. The alarm was sounded up and down the rivers and streams, where the salmon harvest was underway. Families stopped their winter preparations, quickly found one another, collected a few essentials, and headed for Indian River. The community gathered inside Shís'g̲i Noow. K'alyáan assumed the role of war commander. "He was a real strong leader, one of those individuals who takes over in crisis situations," said Tlingit culture-keeper Bill Brady. He rallied the Kiks.ádi warriors. He ordered swift couriers into canoes to alert clan relatives in Angoon, Klukwan, and elsewhere. Tell them that the Russians have returned. Sitka needs reinforcements, weapons, and gunpowder. Tell them that the clan alliance must be reformed. The reckoning has come.

─────

With his armada reassembled in Sitka Sound, Governor Alexander Baranov went to confer with Commander Yury Lisyansky. Baranov divulged his plan of conquest. He would first give the Sitka headmen the opportunity to reach a peaceful resolution. It was, in fact, an ultimatum. Allow the founding of a new settlement or endure the wrath of the Russian Empire. This time Baranov desired a better location for the colony. Long covetous of Shk̲'awulyeil's home base on the hilltop overlooking the sound, Baranov insisted on taking possession of Noow Tlein. "And if they refuse, I will compel them by force," Baranov told Lisyansky.

From the direction of the Tlingit camp at Indian River, a lone canoe paddled across the bay toward the Russian fleet. A Kiks.ádi envoy requested to know Baranov's intentions.

Baranov scoffed. He would not bandy words with a lowly messenger. He sent him away, stating that the Sitka house leaders must come in person to sign a peace treaty, agree to cede territory, and give up their sons as insurance hostages. "And if your chiefs reject this offer, then their former treachery will be punished with the utmost rigor."

While Baranov waited, a reconnaissance party returned to the *Neva* with surprising news. The Noow Tlein compound appeared to be abandoned. A launch approached the beach. Wary of an ambush, Lisyansky buzzed the hilltop and surrounding woods with cannonballs, but no fire was returned, no one stirred, no dogs barked. A boatload of sailors landed and ascended the cliff. The Tlingit were gone. A naval squad swooped down on the space. "By noontime, we had several field pieces and two long six pounders on the hill," Lisyansky said. "Baranov went ashore with a number of armed men to raise his flag on the high hill of the abandoned village." From their viewpoint at Indian River, the Sitka Tlingit seethed at the sight of the Russian flag planted atop Noow Tlein.

The next morning the same envoy delivered an Alutiiq hostage, captured in the raid on Fort Saint Michael. Unmoved, Baranov and Lisyansky considered the gesture a stalling tactic. Later that day, K'alyáan led a contingent of Sitka headmen and three dozen armor-clad warriors on a march along the shore toward Noow Tlein. Russian cadets on the hilltop braced. But the Tlingit company stopped just out of range of their muskets. K'alyáan with several clan leaders came forward, requesting a parley. Baranov was reacquainted with his former-ally-turned-enemy. He told them that he was willing to forget the past as long as the Tlingit agreed to his demands, including the takeover of Noow Tlein. K'alyáan responded that he too was willing to forget the past, as long as the Russians promised to never again settle in Sitka.

"They were feeling very brave and did not think of making peace with us," Baranov said.

The negotiation lasted several hours. Neither side budged. "Arrogant villains," Baranov chafed, in response to the Tlingit speeches and demands. Finally, K'alyáan got up to leave. Baranov railed that his armada would rain hellfire down on his fortress. K'alyáan remained impassive. He called down to his company of warriors outside, who sprung to attention and "retired in military order" back to Shís'gi Noow.

Behind a band of spruce trees along the Indian River, a war canoe was hidden from the Russian ships on the sound. A team of young warriors was assembled on the embankment, planning a covert operation. "When it begins to get dark, come by boat to the beach at the fort," K'alyáan said. There was no doubt now that a full-scale Russian assault was coming. It was imperative for the Tlingit defenders to retrieve the reserve stores of gunpowder, flint, and firearms concealed in their underground armory on a nearby islet in the bay. The dangerous mission would expose the big war canoe to the Russian ships in front of Noow Tlein. A cohort of young fighters volunteered for the assignment, including K'alyáan's nephew. K'alyáan and squad leader Kaagwáask', a Kaagwaantaan veteran, knew that it was best to wait until nightfall to launch the canoe. But scouts reported that a Russian yawl, armed with a mounted swivel gun and crewed by uniformed men, was making a reconnaissance of the shoreline. A sense of urgency gripped the camp. The Russian attack might come before they could retrieve the munitions. The young warriors strained with impatience. "Let's go now. We are wasting time." Reluctantly, the senior commanders agreed.

The war canoe pushed off into the cold current and silently entered the bay. Kaagwáask' charted a wide path using outcrops and islets to cover their passage. The team safely reached the hidden armory and loaded the powder kegs and weapons into the canoe. "Shall we start back now?" a young warrior asked. "No, not now. We can be seen clearly. They might fire on us with cannons on the open water," Kaagwáask' answered. The young ones were eager to mix it up, and argued back, "We have enough ammunition in the canoe." As dusk fell, Kaagwáask' relented. "We shall start back now. But don't do anything until I give you a command. You're just to paddle as fast as you know how, and we'll try to zig zag." The young team scrambled into the canoe, and in unison chanted, "Huh, Huh, Huh," the familiar Tlingit callout before a fight.

On the return run, they were spotted from across the bay. "A large canoe was observed at a distance, lurking among the islands," Lisyansky said. "Our launch attacked it." In the Russian yawl, Lieutenant Arbuzov pursued the war canoe. He ordered the gunners into position. The warriors paddled mightily to reach the far beachfront as cannonballs splashed around them. The roar of the Russian falconets sent K'alyáan running to the forest side of the Indian River to observe the skirmish. "My nephews are being chased and bombarded over there!" he called out, pointing toward the back channel. If the canoe could get close enough, then the Tlingit on shore could send a volley of musket balls to cover its landing.

The Russian yawl bore down on the canoe. Gunshots splintered the wooden hull. Several warriors were hit, but continued to paddle the heavy vessel toward the beach. Kaagwáask' was the team's best shooter. He loaded his rifle and took aim at the Russian yawl. But the Russians still advanced. One of the young warriors stopped paddling and picked up a musket. He pried open a powder keg to load the flintlock and shoot back. From the stern seat, Kaagwáask' fired again. "When the hammer hit the flint, a spark landed right in the powder keg and blew up the whole canoe," Andrew Johnson said. Loud booms, fire flashes, and smoke clouds exploded over the surface as each powder keg ignited. The war canoe was smashed to small pieces and the occupants were hurled into the black waves. Arbuzov's yawl arrived on the scene, finding three men already dead. "With great difficulty six of its crew were saved, of whom four were very badly wounded," Lisyansky reported. "It was amazing that they had defended themselves as long as they did and still paddled: some of them had as many as five bullet wounds in the thighs."

Inside Shís'gi Noow, the Tlingit were gutted. On the eve of battle, their army was robbed of its most capable young warriors, who had been groomed to lead the fight. Moreover, they would now have to muster a resistance without a stockpile of weapons and powder. The close-knit community was torn with grief, having witnessed the horrific debacle on the bay. K'alyáan bemoaned the death of his young nephew, yet another close family member killed by the Russians.

Kaagwáask' was pulled from the water half-drowned and unconscious. He was made a prisoner aboard the *Neva*, and slowly recovered from his wounds. "Later he was taken to Kodiak Island," Andrew Johnson said. "He finally returned to Sitka many years after the war was over, and became one of the leaders." The martyr death of the young warriors in the canoe would be preserved in Tlingit memory through a patriotic song, told from the perspective of a soldier's mother: "All the spirits of the dead have come down. It has even touched me. And I could not weep and cry anymore. I now give up all hope of ever finding you again."

———

Early the next morning, Baranov fitted his chain mail tunic under his shirt and coat and went out to meet Lisyansky for final preparations. "Gathering together we decided to take decisive action against our enemies, the barbarians, who were in a fine fort built in an inaccessible place," Baranov said. Baranov deferred to Lisyansky to organize the armada. Lisyansky maneuvered the vessels into classic naval warfare formation. "We carried our threats into execution by forming a line of four ships before their settlement."

The *Neva* summoned the Tlingit to battle with a thunderous volley from the six-pounders. Believing this display of firepower might cause the house leaders to reconsider, Lisyansky then raised a white flag on the *Neva*'s mast, indicating that there was still time to surrender. "Presently we saw a similar white flag on the fort of the enemy. I was not without hope that something would yet occur that might prevent bloodshed." But the Tlingit made no signs of capitulation. Unfamiliar with the symbolism of the white flag, the Tlingit were simply mimicking the Russians.

Lisyansky grew tired of waiting. "I ordered several ships to fire into the fort," the *Neva* commander said. More than a dozen long-range guns were primed, loaded, and fired at Shís'gi Noow. But the cannons appeared to have little effect on the fortress. Because of the extensive mudflats off Indian River point, the fleet remained more than a mile away. "The water was so shallow that our ships could not approach closely," Baranov complained. "Our bombs and grapeshot were almost harmless."

Lisyansky dispatched Lieutenant Arbuzov to take the yawl and sail in closer to the stronghold. A heavy four-pound cannon in a carriage was lowered into the yawl. Arbuzov used the big gun to rake the shoreline, obliterating the canoes overturned on the beach and blasting a food storage shed into flames. Still there was no response. Arbuzov's crew was emboldened. They rowed the yawl onto the rocky beach and lifted the cannon out of the boat and lugged it closer to the fort. The sailors were dumbstruck by the scene before them. Black ravens and crows were perched all around and actively feeding at the compound. No sound other than caws and squawks came from within. Perhaps the mighty Russian armada had caused the Tlingit to flee.

But inside the sanctuary, a war battalion lay in wait. They were outfitted in full armor, war paint, and weapons, hidden from sight. All morning they kept a close watch on the Russian movements, ready for the moment to put their plan into action. The day before, K'alyáan had instructed the men to catch a large quantity of salmon, plentiful in the river in September, and told the women to cook the fish and cut it into large chunks. In the dead of night, they placed huge trays of freshly cooked salmon on the rooftops of the dwellings, attracting the ravens and crows at daylight and giving the appearance of an abandoned compound.

When the Russians were ferrying toward the beach, K'alyáan rose to speak. "This is going to destroy me," he said, but he would rather die on the battlefield than surrender to his enemy. "Who is with me?" he asked. Still consumed with anguish over the loss of the young warriors in the canoe, there was at first a cold silence. "I am with you, my good man, I am with you," said a brother-in-law of the Kadakw.ádi clan. The other warriors rose one by one and gave their assent. K'alyáan tied the raven helmet under his chin, strapped the blacksmith's hammer to his wrist, motioned to his crew, and quietly slipped out of the back of the compound.

The Kiks.ádi commander led a platoon to the edge of Indian River, where they stripped off their body armor and waded into the chilling waters. For the past few days, the Tlingit had been throwing logs into the river, which the current carried out to the bay. The Russian patrols were now used to seeing debris in the river. K'alyáan's crew lay flat amid the logs and floated in the current, undetected by Arbuzov's men. They climbed out downstream in a thick undergrowth of devil's club, outflanking the unsuspecting Russian sailors.

K'alyáan shouted the Tlingit war cry, "Huh, Huh, Huh," and they charged the sailors, who were too surprised to form a line and ready their guns. With his left hand, K'alyáan pressed his dagger into the chest of one opponent, and with his right hand began swinging his hammer with lethal force. One Russian fighter with a hand axe came at K'alyáan and took a ferocious swipe. He dodged the blow, which deflected off the black raven's beak of his war helmet, just above his eyes.

More warriors rushed out of the fort. Several sailors made it back to the boat and retreated into the surf. The rest were encircled, repeatedly struck and stabbed, and fell dead on the beach. The warriors hoisted up the dead on the tips of their spears and yelled triumphantly at Baranov's armada in the distance. Then the women came out and ripped the clothes off the fallen to cause further humiliation to the enemy. "The dead bodies looked like a lot of halibut on the beach," Andrew Johnson said. Scanning the battlefield, K'alyáan ordered his warriors to confiscate the cannon. "Afterwards, they ran back inside the fort and barred the door behind them. They were not even scratched."

Aboard the *Neva*, Baranov was aghast watching the Tlingit ambush unfold. "We made a mistake in sending the landing party," he admitted. "Too late we went to join the attack." Baranov hastily mustered reinforcements to rescue Arbuzov's party. All available boats were lowered and crammed with musketeers and artillery. The Alutiiq hunters followed in their baidarkas. A fighting force two hundred-strong went swiftly over the waves toward Shís'gi Noow. When the Russian company made landfall, the Tlingit were barricaded inside the fortress.

From the *Neva*'s quarterdeck, Lisyansky nervously followed Baranov's reckless charge. "The Tlingit kept perfectly quiet except an occasional musket shot," Lisyansky observed. "This stillness was mistaken by Mr. Baranov; and, encouraged by it, he ordered the fort to be taken." Baranov was in a fury. He barked orders to the company to ready their flintlocks and form fighting ranks. He commenced a march over the mudflats toward Shís'gi Noow. He was fixed on storming the compound and inflicting defeat on his foe. "But this maneuver nearly proved fatal to the expedition," Lisyansky said. "For as soon as the enemy perceived our people close to their walls, they collected in a body and fired upon them with an order and execution that surprised us."

The sharp crack of the Tlingit musket volley was followed by the ear-splitting discharge of a falconet from inside Shís'gi Noow. The men in the Russian front line stumbled and fell.

Panic shot through the company. The Alutiiq chieftain Nakok turned on his heels, almost knocking down Baranov, and sprinted to the baidarkas with his kinsmen right behind. Baranov's disciplined march became a dis-ordered scramble. The fortress gate was unbolted. Through the doorway K'alyáan—wearing the raven helmet and gripping the blacksmith cudgel overhead—pounced into the smoking chaos. Right behind the Kiks.ádi commander poured hundreds of Tlingit warriors, costumed in ghoulish war helmets and body armor. They descended on the fleeing remnants of the Russian assault force. The beachfront was engulfed in thick black smoke and sulfur fumes. Bodies collapsed in the surf.

Governor Baranov and the naval officers stood their ground against the Tlingit onslaught. But as their troop fell into disarray, they withdrew to a position nearer the waterfront to cover the retreat and save the cannon. But even this line of defense was broken when Baranov was struck in the arm by a musket ball. Baranov staggered and dropped his weapon. Two cadets rushed to the governor's aid, shielding him from further harm. They helped him reach the safety of a boat. The Tlingit seized the moment and charged across the flats to finish the job.

Suddenly, a booming cannonade from the *Neva* pounded the shoreline and halted the rout. Having let Baranov take the lead, Lisyansky was flabbergasted by the disastrous counterattack on the beach. "If I had not covered this unfortunate retreat with my cannons, probably not one man would have been saved." The bloodied Russian force escaped the death trap. The Kiks.ádi had won the day.

Darkness fell over Sitka Sound. The combatants returned to their bases to take account of the dead and wounded and to regroup for the next round. Shivering and weak, Baranov was rowed back to his squatters' camp on Noow Tlein. Nakok came to check on the governor and apologized for abandoning the frontline. "I know that you won't advance," Baranov said, "but at least do not flee to the rear as an example to your followers." By candlelight, a naval surgeon carefully peeled off Baranov's bloodstained jacket and chain mail to tend to his broken arm. The injury was not fatal, but Baranov was unfit for battle. He dictated a message to Lisyansky.

Aboard the *Neva*, the crew was subdued. They had walked blindly into a snare. There were numerous casualties and two officers were dead. Lisyansky lamented his decision to allow a civilian to assume command. "Mr. Baranov was anxious to terminate the affair quickly, and that anxiety led him into the error of placing too much reliance in the bravery of his people, who had never engaged in a warfare of this kind before." The Russians lost their swagger. "The events disquieted us considerably," Lisyansky said. "But from the stillness of our enemies during the night, we inferred that they had suffered perhaps more than ourselves. Though this was of little comfort."

Inside Shís'gi Noow, the warriors gathered around the fire pit. They had repelled the offensive and inflicted lethal damage on the enemy. But there was no celebration. It was one battle in a long war. The Russian force was a thousand strong. And the *Neva*'s cannons were still trained on their fort. The women made up a ground paste of the cure-all devil's club plant, which the warriors applied to their injuries. K'alyáan dictated a message. His couriers sneaked along the shoreline to hidden canoes and under the cover of darkness paddled off to the inner archipelago, begging the other clans for help.

The next morning Lisyansky was distressed to learn that one of his wounded sailors had died overnight. He felt responsible for allowing the battle to get out of hand. Meanwhile, a Russian launch arrived alongside the *Neva*, delivering Baranov's message. "He informed me that he was unable to come on account of his arm; and, he begged me to take upon myself the future management of the contest, acting as my judgement dictated." Lisyansky was relieved—this was the mandate he had hoped for. "I resorted to the plan that I wished to adopt from the first." Lisyansky had no intention of staging another frontal attack on the stronghold. Instead, he put his trust in the firepower of the Imperial Russian Navy. "I would annoy the enemy from the ships, and I instantly ordered a brisk discharge of guns on the fort." Lisyansky's plan was simple: to pound the Tlingit relentlessly with the *Neva*'s cannons. Shís'gi Noow was under siege.

But the strategic location of the Tlingit fortress across the tidal flats kept them beyond the range of the Russian ships. After watching several wasted rounds, the frustrated commander ordered the cannons to cease fire. The officers huddled in the captain's quarters. The solution, it was agreed, was to get the artillery closer to the fort. It was suggested that they could construct wooden rafts and ferry the cannons pontoon-style across the shallows. But that would give the enemy time to resupply. Lisyansky had a different idea.

Lisyansky consulted with the Alutiiq chieftains. Soon scores of baidarkas were paddling around the sides of the *Neva*. Thick nautical ropes were thrown down to the hunters. The kayaks were tied to the ship, like reins to a horse-drawn stagecoach. With a tremendous heave, the baidarka team began to tow the war machine. "The *Neva* could not have reached its station without the united assistance of upwards of a hundred baidarkas, though small in size pulled with uncommon strength." From inside Shís'gi Noow, the Tlingit watched with apprehension as the *Neva* slowly entered the shoals in front of Indian River point.

Lisyansky strode confidently behind the gunners as they primed the *Neva*'s fourteen long-barrel guns. The conflict would soon be over. For the next few hours, more than a hundred cannon shots pounded the ramparts and rooftops of the Tlingit hideout. But even at this close range, Shís'gi Noow did not yield. The cannonballs did not even dent the spruce wood façade. Instead, the shots ricocheted harmlessly over the compound. "The Russian fleet came, anchored in the front, and opened fire," Andrew Johnson said. "As they hit the slanting outside logs, the cannon balls would glance off and land in the Indian River."

Lisyansky studied the oddly designed structure, looking for a weakness. "It was constructed of wood so thick and strong that the shot from my guns could not penetrate it at the short distance of a cable's length." Moreover, the Russian frigate was now within reach of the falconets inside the fort. Shís'gi Noow roared to life and falconets found their mark. "Our rigging was much damaged by them," Lisyansky grumbled. The captain of the *Neva* was utterly confounded.

Frustration ran high inside Shís'gi Noow as well. When the tide receded and the Russian cannons were out of reach, the clan leaders gathered. K'alyáan preferred hand-to-hand combat, but his warriors were now hunkered down in an artillery duel. No one dared to venture into the open with the *Neva*'s bombardiers and snipers at the ready. Whenever a boom thundered over the sound, the families scrambled into their dugout shelters as twelve-pound grapeshot rained down on the compound. The Tlingit were not prepared for a long standoff. They had plenty of food, except much of it was hidden in storage boxes outside the compound. More concerning, they were low on gunpowder. But most of all, siege warfare was alien to Tlingit experience and sensibility. Just one day of waiting was making the warriors restless.

The headmen summoned the shaman to a council and pressed him on their fate. Had their plea reached the other clans in the archipelago? Which clans were sending warriors and gunpowder to fight the Russians? But the shaman could see no one. "There is only darkness," he said. The mood was bleak. The Tlingit alliance had unraveled. Sitka was on its own. K'alyáan must devise an alternative course.

The next morning an emissary from Shís'gi Noow paddled out to the *Neva* to discuss terms of a truce. The negotiations faltered from the start. The Tlingit ambassador claimed victory and demanded the Russians leave the sound. Lisyansky was bemused and encouraged. He issued a counterproposal. Hostilities would cease when the Tlingit agreed to allow the Russians to resettle in Sitka, surrender their fortress on the Indian River, liberate the remaining Alutiiq slaves, and deliver hostages from the families of the clan leaders. The envoy departed. The *Neva* fired a salvo over Indian River point for emphasis. "This had the desired effect." Late in the afternoon, the peace negotiator returned to the *Neva*, consenting to the demands. "I received this overture amicably," Lisyansky said. His optimism was misplaced.

The process dragged out for five days. An elderly Tlingit brought one boy to the *Neva* as an insurance hostage, and said they needed time to round up more. Over the following days, the same Tlingit boatman brought out several more hostages and three Alutiiq slaves. The *Neva* crew mocked the ferryman as Charon, the Greek psychopomp who transports the souls of the dead to the underworld. Meanwhile, Lisyansky insisted that no one was allowed to use the canoes. "We kept a good look-out on the fort, aware of the treacherous character of the enemy, but nothing much materialized. I was occasionally obliged to shoot on the fort." By now, Governor Baranov, impatient as ever, rejoined the officers on the *Neva*. On the fifth day, two Alutiiq women captives were delivered. "One of whom informed us that the enemy had sent a messenger to Angoon soliciting assistance." K'alyáan was playing the Russians for time while waiting on reinforcements.

At least some of the headmen were still urging a fight to the death. Baranov too was spoiling for a rematch. But Lisyansky was now in charge of the battle. He would not allow his crew to attempt another beach landing. Instead, the *Neva* discharged booming cannonades at the fortress. Baranov tried a different tack, issuing a personal plea to K'alyáan. He promised to quit the war and forget the sacking of Fort Saint Michael if the Kiks.ádi commander promised to cede the hilltop location and evacuate the riverside stronghold. With this initiative, the negotiations gained momentum. "Finally, the chief asked us for permission to spend the night in the fortress, giving his word that all its inhabitants would vacate it by dawn." That evening the sailors were drawn to the rail of the *Neva*, haunted by the hypnotic drumbeat and mournful chorus wafting above Shís'gi Noow.

The Battle at Indian River lasted a week. The Russians amassed a force of about a thousand settlers, hunters, and navy crewmen. Roughly eight hundred Tlingit were huddled inside Shís'gi Noow, including three dozen house heads and three hundred warriors. There were many wounded on both sides. Among the Russian dead were a dozen *Neva* officers and crewmen, while the Tlingit death toll was believed to be thirty or more warriors. Intimidated by Baranov's threats, the clan relatives throughout the archipelago and in the north withheld their support. The Sitka Tlingit faced the Russians alone.

On the seventh day of the conflict, Lieutenant Commander Lisyansky alighted the *Neva*'s deck in dress uniform and greeted the sun, climbing over the mountain peaks and casting a copper sheen on Sitka Sound. "Early in the morning, seeing no movement at all, I assumed the Sitkans were busy moving out of their fortress," Lisyansky said. "When I noticed many ravens congregating there, I sent the interpreter ashore to investigate."

FINDING THE SAPLING FORT

The territory around the mouth of the Indian River was declared a national monument—and later the Sitka National Historical Park—due to its significance as the site of the consequential Battle of Sitka of 1804. But the precise location of the so-called sapling fort, Shís'gi Noow, was forgotten after it was destroyed by Russian attackers. "The fort's definitive physical location had eluded investigators for a century," said Thomas Urban, an archeologist who finally solved the mystery in 2021. "Previous archaeological digs had found some suggestive clues, but they never really found conclusive evidence that tied these clues together."

The Russians left behind the first important clue: a sketch of the fort, which depicted an unusual trapezoidal shape, measuring approximately 240 x 165 feet, and fourteen houses contained within.

Archeologist Frederick Hadleigh West conducted a rudimentary survey of the area in 1958, claiming to find some remains of two walls of the fort. Based on this information, the National Park Service designated a probable location in a cleared area of the park (aptly known as the "fort clearing"). However, West did not find artifacts to support his claim. Nor did he find any hearths or other features of the homes that should have been contained within the fort. The inconsistencies led some historians to question the conclusions.

Continued research over the next fifty years located musket balls, grapeshot, and even cannonballs, which helped to pinpoint the location of the 1804 battlefield. But none of the studies was successful in confirming the location of the fort. The question became more complex when alternative sites were proposed.

Finally, in 2020 Urban and his team addressed the puzzle with new technology: ground-penetrating radar and electromagnetic induction. The latter is a technique that measures variations in the soil's conduction of electric current in order to identify materials and shapes under the surface. These methods are useful for conducting surveys in densely forested areas.

The geophysical surveys revealed the buried foundations of the fort walls in the shape of a trapezoid, with similar dimensions that the Russians had recorded. The findings were consistent with Tlingit oral histories and West's earlier conclusions. The team was also able use remote sensing to cover a larger area and rule out other potential locations. The study concluded that "the geophysical survey has yielded the only convincing, multi-method evidence to date for the location of the sapling fort."

For the Tlingit—and especially the Kiks.ádi clan—Shís'gi Noow is an indicator of their resistance to colonial incursions. As one Tlingit historian explained, "At that time, the Battle of Sitka of 1804 clearly showed the rest of the world that the Russian forces in Alaska were too weak to conquer the Tlingit people." And now the fort's location is revealed, solving a long-standing mystery about this history that is integral to the Tlingit identity.

CHAPTER 10
Survival March

The siege of Shís'gi Noow was unrelenting. The Tlingit resort to delay tactics was at an end. The options were stark: a suicidal last stand or submission to foreign overlords. The house leaders agreed, "We cannot surrender and become slaves of the Russians. We will fight alone if we have to."

As the headmen debated, a new proposal was put forth: "Abandon Shís'gi Noow. Live to fight another day! We cannot be defeated on the battlefield, if we are not on the battlefield." The suggestion of giving up the fortress would have been unthinkable at the beginning of the contest. But since the loss of the young warriors and reserve munitions, the mood inside the compound had turned fatalistic. K'alyáan and the war council considered the ploy. It was agreed that withdrawal was preferable to the alternatives. The move did not mean that they were conceding the territory to the Russians. The war was not over. But the tactics must change. They would opt for a strategic retreat. Later, when the time was right, the Tlingit would return to Sitka and reclaim their homeland.

The maneuver presented an awesome challenge to the house heads. At least eight hundred people were huddled inside the fort. They ranged from the elderly to the newborn, and from the healthy to the frail or wounded. Meanwhile, the Russian armada had the Tlingit pinned down. The community's large canoes were already destroyed, and the shorefront was covered by the *Neva*'s long guns. If the Kiks.ádi chose to escape, they would have to go overland.

The Sitka Tlingit lived at the far west of the archipelago, along the Pacific coast. Their lifestyle revolved around the sea, the tidal flats, and the wooded shoreline. Their large island home was covered in dense forest. Few inhabitants had ever ventured far into this inner sanctum of beasts and spirits. In between their settlement on the west side of the island and the inner archipelago coastline on the east side was a steep wall of ice-capped mountains. The Tlingit did not use pack animals. When the Sitkans visited relatives or conducted trade, they did so in canoes, paddling around Sitka's interior barriers. To move an entire village across the island by foot was a logistical nightmare.

Once the decision was made, the headmen worked out an evacuation plan. Each house leader was responsible for organizing the retreat of their families. They would move under the cover of darkness, over several nights, in small groups with warrior escorts. The older people and mothers and children would be the first to flee, heading inland along the right bank of the Indian River to the backwoods trail, then turning north. The main body of warriors would hold down Shís'gi Noow until the end. The first rendezvous point was set at Gájaa Héen, on the ruins of Fort Saint Michael. The instructions were emphatic: take only what you need and what you can carry on your back, bring blankets and warm clothes. We are going over the mountain.

To gain precious time, K'alyáan gave promises to Yury Lisyansky that the Tlingit would give up Shís'gi Noow the next day, but then offered new excuses as to why they could not yet leave. "We sent an inquiry to the inhabitants if they were ready to quit the place and received the answer that they were waiting for high tide," Lisyansky said. "But when the flood was at its height, the natives made no preparations to leave and gave no reply." An envoy paddled out to Lisyansky to say that the Tlingit needed access to their canoes in order to move out of the fort. The impatient commander denied the request. Finally, a message came that the Tlingit would leave the fort early the next morning and would signal their readiness by singing out in the night.

During the last evening in Shís'gi Noow, the headmen prepared the remaining family members and warriors for evacuation. This would be the main exodus. Before setting out, the community assembled one last time as undisputed sovereigns of Sitka. The clan elders praised the warriors for their heroic defense and mourned their slain brothers. When the emotional tributes ended, the drumming began: steady, solemn, echoing. Soft voices gradually became louder—a weeping refrain, drifting across the tranquil bay. "It was an extremely sad song from the heart of everyone in the fort," Herb Hope said. "It expressed pain and anguish at the outcome of the great battle and at the loss of their tribal houses, their many canoes, their ceremonial regalia. And it gave vent to all the grief they still felt for the loss of so many friends and relatives." After midnight, K'alyáan secured his dagger to his belt and silently ushered the last team of warriors out of Shís'gi Noow, into the black woods and an uncertain future.

On the deck of the *Neva*, Lisyansky was joined by Alexander Baranov, eager to accept K'alyáan's surrender. It had been a hard-fought campaign. Now would come the tricky business of securing peace. Ideally, Baranov would have preferred to subjugate the Tlingit, as Grigory Shelikhov had done to the Alutiit in Kodiak. But there was no chance of imposing a conscription regime on the fiercely independent Tlingit. The governor was adamant, however, that the Kiks.ádi must relocate far away from Noow Tlein, to the south side of the Indian River, to reduce the threat of attack and minimize contact between the peoples. Any Tlingit caught violating the peace would be exiled to a work farm on Kodiak Island. Though Baranov intended to honor the terms of surrender and let bygones be bygones, he must have at least considered the advantages of reneging on the deal, and hanging the Kiks.ádi war chief instead.

Lisyansky stood by the *Neva*'s gunwale and frowned. The launch that he had sent to escort K'alyáan to the surrender ceremony was rowing back to the vessel in haste. "The natives have quitted the fort during the night," the cadet called up. Shís'gi Noow was deserted and the Tlingit had vanished.

The commander scanned the shoreline. There were no signs of life. He eyed the woods suspiciously. Baranov was incensed. Despite his disabled limb, he was ready to direct another war party back to the beachfront. But Lisyansky overruled. The Tlingit were likely hiding in the forest waiting to spring an ambush. Had the reinforcements arrived unnoticed? Lisyansky barked orders to his crew. All hands to high alert.

The day passed without incident. There were no signs of a Tlingit army lying in wait. Shís'gi Noow had indeed been abandoned. Lisyansky tried to make sense of the surprising turn. The protracted discussions with K'alyáan, he realized, were a subterfuge to disguise his real intentions. "It appears that they imagined we were capable of the same dishonesty and cruelty as they themselves were capable of; and if they had come out to us in open boats, as had been proposed, we would have fallen on them in revenge for their past behavior. Therefore, they preferred running into the woods." Lisyansky stared beyond the waterfront to Sitka's backdrop of forbidding forests and precipitous peaks. It was a desperate act.

⎯⎯∞⎯⎯

Columns of migrating pink salmon filed up the shallow creek, meandering through the estuary at Gájaa Héen. A dozen hungry bald eagles were perched in the surrounding trees, suspicious of the commotion below. Concealed just behind the shoreline brush, scores of Tlingit families were huddled on the ruins of Fort Saint Michael. The nighttime evacuation to the northern end of Sitka was completed. Grandparents, mothers, and children were greeting the fathers and sons, who arrived in the early morning. Dawn was approaching. Soon the Russians would discover that Shís'gi Noow was abandoned. These were the most fraught hours. If the Russian warships came hunting up the coast, the community would be exposed and defenseless.

The clan leaders hastily made the final preparations for the trek across the island. During the first twenty-four hours, the fear was that Russia's well-armed troops would organize a posse to track the Tlingit into the woods and finish them off. The headmen held council to reaffirm a commitment to hang together and vowed not to negotiate individual deals with the Russians.

This step was necessary because of the decentralized power structure and fluid nature of warfare in Tlingit society. The house leaders reelected K'alyáan as war leader.

Next, the headmen plotted an escape route. From G̲ájaa Héen, they would hike north-northeast to the wide coastal inlet (now known as Katlian Bay). Skirting the shoreline, they would traverse a narrow peninsula to Nakwasina Sound, a secluded spot more than thirty miles from Noow Tlein. Here the Tlingit households would regroup, replenish their food supply, and rest up before the difficult trek through the rugged interior. From the old stories, several clan elders knew of an ancient bear trail on the far side of Nakwasina. Finding the bear trail was their best hope for safe passage through the unexplored mountain forest. Their destination was Hanus Bay, along Peril Strait on the east side of the island. They knew that the Angoon Tlingit made a summer camp on the beachfront there, at the mouth of a stream where a glacial lake spilled into the bay. There was a chance that Hanus Bay would still be occupied by Angoon Tlingit, working the early autumn salmon run. If they missed this encounter, their prospects were dire, as the Peril Strait shoreline was remote and inhospitable.

Finally, the headmen organized a rear-guard defense of able warriors. With exacting care, K'alyáan distributed the last of the gunpowder to these elite fighters. The rear guard sent sharp-eyed lookouts up the harbor front mountains to monitor the Russian vessels on the sound. They were accompanied by the fastest runners, who were responsible for warning the marchers if Russian gunboats were on the move. The rear guard created a false trail to convince the Russians that the flight path was to the southeast, following the Indian River inland. They staked out positions at the edge of the woods for guerilla-style assaults, harassing any Russian or Alutiit who ventured too far away from the shoreline. Most importantly, the rear guard was instructed to come together as a single force to fend off any Russian force that dared to pursue the Tlingit into the forest.

As the Tlingit were breaking camp, a panting rear-guard runner arrived with a message from the mountain lookout. The Russians had descended on Shís'gi Noow, but there were no signs that they were organizing a search team. K'alyáan was encouraged. He delivered a final message of inspiration to the uprooted families. "The rear-guard warriors shall remain in action around Sitka for ten to twenty days before coming to join us. Take heart—no one is pursuing us, walk with a steady pace. This is our survival march."

—

Yury Lisyansky stepped out of the launch into the lapping surf and strode across the flats toward Shís'gi Noow. Over the past week, the commander had become obsessed with the impregnable fortress. He walked slowly along the front wall, noting the many divots his cannonballs had made and studying the unusual sloping design that had sent them careening harmlessly across the beach. He ordered the crewmen to gather the spent projectiles for reuse. He found the entrance to the fort in the back facing the woods. Stepping inside the compound, Lisyansky surveyed the effects of his siege. "From their haste, they left many things behind," he said.

So began the looting of Sitka. "We obtained a supply of provisions for our hunters and more than twenty large canoes," Lisyansky said. Baranov let his battalion run amok in search of anything of value that the owners had forsaken. Bentwood boxes containing bearskin blankets, iron knives, copper kettles, and serving plates were ransacked. The winter food stores of dried fish were uncovered and seized. These items were distributed among the Alutiiq hunters as war booty. The Tlingit also left behind three falconets and two small cannons, which were promptly transferred to Baranov's armory.

For Lisyansky, the deserted village was a cultural treasure trove. The amateur ethnographer took particular interest in the clan regalia of the elite families—raven-tail robes, ceremonial masks, war helmets, and suits of armor. Ellen Hope Hayes noted that "they couldn't take sacred objects with them. They could only take materials for survival." Lisyansky eagerly gathered up these cherished pieces as a prize package for the tsar, a sampling of the exotic wonders found at the far edge of His Majesty's realm. Indeed, the largest collection of early nineteenth-century Tlingit artifacts is found in the Peter the Great Museum of Anthropology, the Kunstkamera in St. Petersburg, courtesy of the commander of the *Neva*.

Stooping down to investigate one dugout dwelling, Lisyansky was startled to discover two old women and one young boy left behind. He ordered them to be taken to the *Neva* for questioning. Delving further, the naval commander was struck dumb as he came upon the dead body of an infant. "What anguish did I feel when I saw this massacre of an innocent." Lisyansky surmised that the Tlingit had killed the babe, whose crying would have alerted the Russians to the midnight escape. This conjecture was later supported by Tlingit elder Alex Andrews, who said that "while they were going along the Indian River a child cried out." The Tlingit feared that the cry would betray their location. "Kill him! They might find us by his voice." Lisyansky's sensationalist claim of infanticide, however, remains controversial among the Tlingit. "We don't know what is the truth on that," said Tlingit culture-bearer Mark Jacobs Jr.

——

The swift runners caught up to the Tlingit exodus north of Sitka near the shore of Katlian Bay. The headmen turned to their shaman to interpret the bits of information. "The Russians will not leave the safety of their ships to follow us into the deep woods." The harried marchers could rest. A makeshift camp was set up in a protected cove, with eight hundred people crammed into the tight quarters. For the rest of the day, the men fished salmon, flounder, and crab from the bay, while the women gathered berries and grasses from the woods. That evening, the Tlingit were nourished by the fruits of the sea and forest. But it was just a brief respite before the strenuous climb ahead. Late that night, the house leaders met to discuss the next phase.

The elders recalled the old stories of past Kiks.ádi migrations. "It is important for us to walk as families, but within reach of the house groups. We must avoid taking identical routes whenever possible. We must walk at a steady pace. And we must take advantage of all the food we find along the way." At Cedar Cove, on the north side of Katlian Bay, they would divide into three large parties to cross the peninsula to Nakwasina Sound. The house groups would employ fast runners to exchange information with one another in their search for the old bear trail that traversed the mountains. With the headmen in agreement, the council was about to conclude when a new dilemma arose.

Some of the wounded warriors declared that they were not going forward. Their injuries were too severe to make the arduous passage through the mountains. It was imperative for the exodus to reach Hanus Bay before the end of the salmon run. But their participation would only slow down the marchers and imperil the community. The men lobbied to stay behind at the campsite, insisting that there was enough food available to sustain them through the winter. A group of Tlingit elders joined the discussion. "We are old and it is not right for us to expect you to wait for us. We will stay here and winter with the wounded. There will be salmon in the streams until winter. Do not fear for us. We will be alright. Come and get us in the spring. We will be waiting."

K'alyáan was dismayed. He worried about the safety of these individuals and about the unity of the Sitka Tlingit. He argued against splitting up the community. But the war leader did not have the authority to reject the proposal. His reservations were overcome by the younger family members, who immediately went to work gathering firewood and building shelters for their disabled relatives. That evening the exiled Sitkans shared one last feast together with stories and songs. At dawn K'alyáan and the Point House family were the first to break camp, heading deeper into the rainforest than any of them had ever gone before.

For days, the migrants forged a path across the twelve-mile-wide peninsula. The scouts would double back to mark the trail for the families following behind. They followed the shore of Nakwasina Sound toward Fish Bay. They moved slowly through the muskeg foothills to intercept the deer coming down from the mountains for winter forage. They kept in close communication with the other parties, but no one had yet found the elusive passage through the mountains. The weather turned cold and snow was falling at the higher altitudes. Near Deadman Reach, another family informed K'alyáan that they were giving up the exodus. They turned off to look for an old hunting camp along the island's northern coastline. Again, K'alyáan tried to dissuade them, but to no avail. The effect was demoralizing. A panicky realization took hold that they were lost in the dense interior. The Kiks.ádi staggered on. Then a young warrior came running back up the path out of breath. The bear trail had at last been found, just as the elders described it.

"On October 8, the fate of Shís'gi Noow was decided. Mr. Baranov ordered the fort to be completely destroyed." Lisyansky received the command with misgivings. He had come to admire the Tlingit defensive wonder, analyzing, measuring, and sketching its layout. But Baranov was now confident of his victory and wished to eradicate this symbol of Tlingit defiance. A three-hundred-man demolition battalion with an armed naval escort was dispatched to Indian River point. A scavenger team was sent inside the compound to comb through the hovel dwellings one final time. "After everything that could be of use was removed, the fortress was burned to the ground."

The angled wooden barricade in front of the compound was dismantled. The sturdy spruce logs were towed by three-man baidarkas along the waterfront to Noow Tlein, where a building frenzy was underway. The Russian colony was resurrected and christened New Archangel, capital of Russian America. By the end of winter, it contained eight structures, including an imposing beachfront redoubt, cleared land for fifteen large garden plots, a bathhouse and brewery, and a barnyard with cows, sheep, and goats.

"With respect to the Sitkans who fled, we were wholly ignorant of what happened to them," Lisyansky said. "Our fishermen and hunters began to disperse almost everywhere." But the Russian occupation did not go unwatched. From the forest, the rear-guard warriors burned with rage, witnessing the foreigners despoil their homes. One afternoon, a baidarka ventured too far from the Russian gunboats and an Alutiiq hunter was shot and killed by a Tlingit sniper from the woods. Eventually eight more Alutiit turned up dead. Baranov fretted that a war party was still lurking behind the trees. "The enmity of the natives was unsubdued." He urged Lisyansky to mount a search-and-destroy campaign into the woods. But Lisyansky had no interest in sending his naval cadets on foot into the incomprehensible rainforest. Besides, Sitka was just a diversion. The captain of the *Neva* had an appointment with history as the first Russian to circumnavigate the globe.

The signs were heartening. The trail was now descending, the faint squawking of sea birds was heard, and shafts of daylight punctured the canopy. The Kiks.ádi youths ran ahead, racing each other. At last, the fastest boys broke through the foliage and gazed on the turbulent waters of Peril Strait. Go tell K'alyáan, we have made it to the far side. Excited runners ran back to announce the news to the beleaguered marchers. The Point House family hiked the four-mile pebbled beachfront of Hanus Bay, heading toward the summer campsite at the mouth of the salmon creek. They came upon a hunting bivouac, simple wooden shanties, fishing traps, drying racks, and ashen fire pits, but the camp was abandoned. The salmon run was over. No Angoon Tlingit were on site to greet them. Exhausted, hungry, and soaked, the Kiks.ádi were refugees in their own land.

October rains pelted the beachfront and impenetrable fog covered the bay. Straggler groups with tired grandparents and clinging children continued to arrive for another six days. Their disappointment could not be concealed. House leaders knew there would be more suffering and death if the community was forced to winter in this unforgiving environment. The best hope for survival was to reach their Angoon relatives on the other side of Peril Strait. The house leaders ordered the raising of a giant signal fire. The community collected and stacked wood for a blaze that could be seen from ten miles away. The boughs and branches were wet from incessant rains.

Taking a hatchet to three young hemlocks, an elder hacked a U-shaped cutout into the trunks and collected the slow-dripping tar pitch. The resinous goo was highly flammable so that even rain-drenched logs could be set aflame.

The gloomy atmosphere lasted for a week until the clouds parted. As dusk approached, the clan leaders rallied the households for the lighting of the great bonfire. The stack now reached twenty feet high and was drizzled in pitch. The Kiks.ádi shaman stepped forward, offered a prayer to the ancestors, and placed the first burning torch at the foot of the woodpile. The glowing orange tower warmed the beachfront and inspired the drummers. Stubby uprooted pine trees were placed to the side. As the flames climbed higher, the attendants lifted the pine shrubs on tall poles and dropped them on top of the stack, creating a spectacular exploding fireball in the night sky. The mood turned festive. The beach came alive with spontaneous singing and dancing.

Across the straits, the Angoon Tlingit sighted the distant bonfire. The next morning, canoes were dispatched to investigate. The Sitkans were saved. A council was convened at the Fortress of the Bears. K'alyáan chronicled the ordeals of the Battle of Indian River and the Survival March. The spellbound council offered the abandoned fort site at Chaatlk'aanoow as a residence for the Sitkans. Located at Point Craven on the southern tip of Chichagof Island, the Sitka Tlingit quickly erected a temporary home in the inner archipelago, less than ten miles from Angoon. Inside the cliffside sanctuary of Chaatlk'aanoow, the Kiks.ádi would heal their wounds and prepare for a new phase in their war with the Russian Empire.

The Survival March was a one-hundred-mile journey up rock-strewn creeks, through steep mountain passes, and along unnervingly exposed beaches. The trek claimed the lives of both wounded and elderly kinsmen. But faith in the enduring spirit of the clan was rewarded. As the Sitka Tlingit awaited rescue at Hanus Bay, K'alyáan and the headmen seized the moment to celebrate the epic feat. They carved their house crests into the trunk of a young hemlock on the edge of the bay.

The Point House elder paid tribute to the sons and daughters of the clan: "Always remember that you are the Sitka Kiks.ádi people. You carry the proud names of our noble ancestors in this battle and you have added glory to those names on this survival march. The clan will always remember that it was you who fought the hated Russians in defense of the Tlingit homeland, when no one came to our aid. It was you who spilled blood rather than disgrace your people and surrender to the Russians. It was you who knocked down Baranov and saw him carried off the battlefield. It was you who turned back the Russian attack and held Shís'gi Noow through many days of cannon fire. It was you who endured the long march from Shís'gi Noow to Hanus Bay in order for our tribe to survive with honor. We have much to do before we return to our ancient homeland in Sitka."

IN THE FOOTSTEPS OF SURVIVORS

Brothers Herb and Fred Hope grew up listening to their Kiks.ádi uncles tell about the Battle of Indian River and the Survival March: "A story of Tlingit courage, bravery, dedication, loyalty, honor and endurance in defense of the Kiks.ádi homeland." But they feared this Kiks.ádi perspective would be lost to their descendants unless it was accurately recorded. So in 1988, the brothers started a project to retrace and reenact the Survival March so they could "properly tell our story with pride and honor."

Concrete information about the Survival March was sparse. None of the Hopes' contemporaries knew the route (or routes) that the Kiks.ádi clan had followed. The available maps and charts did not provide sufficient detail of Baranoff Island's interior. But the brothers persevered, outlining all the possible ways from Sitka to Hanus Bay, which was across the strait from their final destination at Craven Point. Herb even built a scale model of the island, to get a better understanding of the terrain.

Starting in 1988, the Hope brothers set out to explore each of the possible routes to determine if it was a feasible journey for the beleaguered Kiks.ádi in 1804. Fred explained, "Our people . . . took several different paths. Some were over the steepest mountains and others were in the low hills. The amount of people we're talking about is said to be around 900. So when you have 900 people moving through the forest it's really a big deal."

Each year, Herb assembled a team and gathered the resources needed to undertake the multiday trek across Baranoff Island. Like their forebears, the Hopes had spent their childhood on the sea, not in the forest, so they had much to learn. "A lot of people learned how to go out in the woods and camp but we didn't do that . . . ," Fred admitted. "We had to learn how to light a fire with wet wood."

They planned their expeditions in the autumn to replicate the conditions their ancestors would have experienced in 1804. At this time of year, heavy rain and cloud cover were a constant, making navigation even more difficult. The challenges were many. One year—after climbing all day—the team reached a high-elevation lake that was surrounded by cliffs and impossible to get around. They were forced to turn back. On a different route, Herb remembered, "we ran into waterfall after waterfall. We pressed on, but it kept getting steeper and steeper. We ran into cliffs, landslides, heavy brush, and steep ridges. It was hard going. It rained without letup. We searched every possible trail or hint of a trail. We ran into more cliffs and steeper landslides."

After years of research and reconnaissance, Herb Hope accomplished his goal in 1996, successfully navigating a route from Sitka to Hanus Bay. A support vessel assisted the crossing to Craven Point. The outcome of Hope's effort is a detailed written account of the Survival March. Thanks to these efforts, his people will always know the courage and resourcefulness of their ancestors, "who endured the long march from Shís'gi Noow to Hanus Bay in order for our tribe to survive with honor."

PART THREE

CHAPTER 11
Season of the Moon

I n the summer of 1805 an emissary from New Archangel paddled a canoe through Peril Strait in search of the hidden fortress of Chaatlk'aanoow. Nearly a year had passed since the Battle of Indian River. From behind a rocky outcrop, Kiks.ádi canoes surged into the lane, encircling the trespasser. The calm Russian occupant spoke in Tlingit. He was looking for K'alyáan to deliver a message from Governor Alexander Baranov. The suspicious Kiks.ádi escorted the ambassador at gunpoint to Point Craven. They stopped alongside a sheer cliff. Behind this wall and out of sight from the strait was Chaatlk'aanoow. Respectful of Tlingit custom, the envoy waited patiently for an invitation to come ashore. Kiks.ádi guards along the high ridge stared down with contempt. Hours passed. No invitation came.

Refusing to abandon his errand, the messenger landed the canoe and found the steep path up to the Tlingit fortress. He went to the entrance of K'alyáan's house, listed his credentials, stated his business, and requested a parley. But K'alyáan refused a meeting. If negotiations between the Russians and Kiks.ádi were to take place, then protocol must be observed. It was a matter of honor and rank. K'alyáan was a leader of equal status to Baranov. If the Russian governor wanted a parley, he would have to negotiate it himself. After another lengthy delay, the envoy was told to go away.

Baranov's representative fumed. Undeterred, he remained outside the open doorway. In a loud voice, he addressed the clan elders inside: "Oh Great K'alyáan, Mighty War Chief of the Sitka Kiks.ádi people. The Lord

Baranov has sent me to carry his request to you. Your life and your presence are like the sunshine. Where you are there is bright sunshine. Without you there is no sunshine. Sitka is now a land without sunshine. The Great Baranov sends you this message. Return with your proud people to your ancient homeland. Return to Sitka. Let us live in peace. Let us live in sunshine."

K'alyáan called a council with the Kiks.ádi shaman and house leaders. The idea of giving up exile and returning home was tempting. The older headmen especially were open to Baranov's invitation. But the cost in reputation would be high. "The entire Tlingit nation will laugh at us," said one of the younger house leaders. "They will say that we have surrendered and have become the slaves of the Russians." The elders voted. The proposition was rejected.

K'alyáan chose a nephew to go outside and deliver the answer. "Let it be known that it is not the place of the Russians to invite the proud Kiks.ádi people to return to their homeland. Sitka still belongs to the Kiks.ádi. We will return to our homeland when we say the time is right. The sun rises each day in the east to bring warmth to the people and animals of the earth. But each evening it sets in the west to mark the end of the day. And then it is the time for the moon. For now, the sun has set in Sitka, and it is the season of the moon."

When the Kiks.ádi fled Sitka, Alexander Baranov basked in triumph. "The Tlingit were forced to leave the fort and the territory. They went really far, more than 150 versts." He kept on hand a company of a hundred Russian hunters and seven hundred Alutiiq workers to rebuild the colony. Russia now had the strategic advantage in the northwest over its British, American, and Spanish rivals. Baranov's bridgehead was within pouncing distance of both the teeming sea otter colonies of the inner archipelago and the sparsely populated coastline running down to Vancouver Island. Baranov was invigorated. "From October to spring, we had no more trouble with the Tlingit," he said. "Our hunters and workers wintered peacefully, and without boredom, since we had a supply of vodka. We were not very temperate."

Baranov's confidence was sustained by the looming silhouette of the *Neva* on Sitka Sound. Commander Yury Lisyansky had agreed to remain in the region to deter Tlingit counteroffensives. But his sailors needed somewhere to winter. "The mountains surrounding us are now covered in snow," Lisyansky said. "The cold is so strong that the thermometer does not rise above the freezing point. At night, we observe the northern lights." In November the *Neva* sailed to Kodiak, where stove-heated accommodations were available. To relieve the tedium, Lisyansky conducted a nature study of the island and organized winter games for the crew. "At Christmas, we constructed two immense ice hills, which the men could take a sledge to the top, climb in, and slide to the bottom. This was a common amusement in Russia, but the Alutiit came from all parts to enjoy the sight and partake in the sport."

In the spring the *Neva* returned to Sitka. "As soon as we lowered our sails, I had the pleasure of seeing Mr. Baranov, recovered from his wounded right arm." Baranov explained that his arm took five months to heal. It was disfigured and still ached when he performed clerical duties. Baranov escorted Lisyansky on a tour of the rebuilt colonial capital, New Archangel. "With great satisfaction, I saw the amazing fruits of Mr. Baranov's ceaseless diligence. During my short absence, he managed to construct eight buildings, which in appearance and size could be held beautiful, even in Europe." The commander of the *Neva* promised to remain in the governor's service through summer, but after that he must resume his round-the-world mission.

News of the Russians seizing Noow Tlein shot through the archipelago. The legend of Baranov was magnified. He had driven the Kiks.ádi from their homeland and had survived yet another deadly assault. Tlingit clans sent representatives to see for themselves and pay their respects to the new lord of Sitka. Even the Angoon Tlingit made sure to express their desire for peace with the Russians, knowing that they had abetted the Kiks.ádi escape and resettlement. Baranov's request to the clan leaders, however, to leave him with hostages as insurance were ignored. It nagged at Baranov that he was unable to secure K'alyáan's consent to a formal surrender.

Baranov was desperate to codify Russia's claim on Sitka. But attempts to engage the Kiks.ádi leaders at Chaatlk'aanoow were rebuffed. "It appeared they still held inimical feelings," Lisyansky noted. "Not one of their chiefs could be induced to come to our fort. Moreover, the other tribes near Sitka were busy fortifying their settlements. In a short time, our countrymen here will be surrounded by very formidable and dangerous neighbors."

Something was amiss in Sitka. The arrival of warm weather normally signaled the coming of visitors. As usual, Tlingit camps popped up around the sound to gather roe during the spring herring run, but the fishing parties completely ignored the Russian occupants. The reappearance of Kiks.ádi warriors, even if they were just fishing, rattled Russian nerves, at least until the *Neva* returned from Kodiak. Baranov also found it strange that throughout the summer no Tlingit trading parties approached Sitka to do business with the Russians. Moreover, foreign merchant ships seemed to bypass Sitka. Unbeknownst to the governor, the next phase in the Tlingit-Russian war was underway.

As Baranov and the Russians built up New Archangel, K'alyáan and the Kiks.ádi built up Chaatlk'aanoow. When they first arrived, the warriors bathed in the freezing waters to regain their strength. Tlingit culture-keeper Sally Hopkins explained that "they were getting ready for when the Russians would attack again." The site's abandoned longhouses were repaired with bark-strip roofing, canoes were fashioned from the abundant spruce, and defensive works were erected around the compound. Soon Chaatlk'aanoow was a viable fortress, snugly fit behind an impregnable rock wall. The area was bountiful with deer from the adjacent woods and fish from the shoreline reef.

After settling into their new home, the Sitka house leaders convened a war council. How could they battle the Russians from this place of exile? "Survival is not enough," a fiery headman said. "All the Tlingit must know that Sitka still belongs to the Kiks.ádi. We must blockade Peril Strait. No Tlingit must be allowed to trade in Sitka." The Kiks.ádi would wage economic warfare against the Russians.

The elders were dispatched throughout the archipelago to explain that the Kiks.ádi had not surrendered their homeland to the Russians. Sitka was still Tlingit territory. Those clans who had not answered the call to help defend Shís'gi Noow could contribute now by refusing to trade with the Russians. Kiks.ádi warriors were deployed around Peril Strait to enforce the economic blockade. When canoe parties carrying furs were spotted, the warriors intercepted them and warned: "Stay away from Sitka. The Kiks.ádi are still at war with the Russians. Trade canoes cannot pass. Sitka still belongs to the Kiks.ádi." As the summer went on, fewer and fewer canoes challenged the blockade.

The Tlingit also sought to isolate New Archangel from the British and Yankee traders, without disrupting their own prosperity. Under Shk'awulyeil, Sitka was a regular port of call for foreign merchants. After the establishment of Fort Saint Michael, the Boston men had found a reliable customer in the chronically undersupplied Russians, who traded surplus furs for food and rum. In the summer of 1805 foreign merchants heard the news of the Battle of Indian River from southern Tlingit and Haida people. They were informed of the trade boycott. The Anglo-American traders were never reconciled to Russian colonization in the region, so the blockade was a chance to squeeze their competitors. Shrewd Yankees established a new trading post on Catherine Island. Located directly across Peril Strait from Chaatlk'aanoow, the location was convenient for the Kiks.ádi as well as the half dozen Tlingit communities of the middle archipelago.

Meanwhile, Baranov was eager to take advantage of his new position in Sitka to exploit the archipelago's sea otter colonies. As soon as the weather turned warm, Baranov charged his trusted assistant Ivan Kuskov to lead a three-hundred-strong baidarka fleet onto the water. The return of Russian poachers to traditional hunting grounds roused Tlingit indignation. And this time, the Russians did not come with a gunboat escort. The Tlingit mustered resistance in a series of guerilla-style attacks. Canoe squads from Chaatlk'aanoow, Angoon, and Hoonah harassed and impeded the baidarka fleet. Ever the peacemaker, Kuskov retreated back to Sitka, rather than risk conflict. Baranov was in a quandary. The summer was passing, business was idle, and supplies ran low. The governor ordered the Alutiit back to Kodiak, where they could hunt in peace and work on the farms. The survival of New Archangel was in doubt.

Around the same time the Battle of Indian River was underway, a medium-sized merchantman set out from Bristol, Rhode Island, bound for southeast Alaska. The *Juno* was a handsome eighty-foot, three-masted vessel, featuring a likeness of its Roman goddess namesake as a figurehead on the bowsprit. At the helm was twenty-four-year-old John D'Wolf, making his debut as ship's captain.

The young D'Wolf was hardly an inexperienced sailor. He had been at sea from the age of thirteen, rising in status from cabin boy to boatswain to first mate. But his main qualification as captain of the *Juno* was that his uncle owned the ship. The D'Wolfs were major players in early America's East Coast merchantocracy. The family fortune was acquired in the slave trade, working the triangular route from West Africa to the

SEASON OF THE MOON

Caribbean to New England. In 1794 the US Congress forbade American ships from trafficking in human cargo. In 1797 Rhode Island slaver John Brown became the first American merchant tried in federal court for violating the law. That was warning enough for the D'Wolfs, who were forced to find something else to peddle. Hence the *Juno*'s foray into the Pacific fur trade.

For a sea captain, the lanky D'Wolf was more affable than imposing. Hauling a cargo of iron tools, cured meats, flour sacks, rum casks, tobacco leaves, guns, and gunpowder, D'Wolf's orders were to exchange these goods along the Northwest Coast for sea otter pelts, which in turn could be traded in Canton for porcelain, silk, tea, fireworks, and whatever else a prosperous New Englander might covet. The elder D'Wolf trusted their nephew with what seemed a straightforward assignment. But young D'Wolf had an adventurous streak. Before returning home, he made history for his dealings with Russian princes and Tlingit nobles, and for being the first American to traverse all of Russia on foot, from Kamchatka to St. Petersburg. Yet John D'Wolf is best known today for being the uncle and muse of author Herman Melville.

More than nine months after departing Narragansett Bay, the *Juno* sailed into Sitka Sound. The New England merchantman was a welcome sight to Governor Baranov. He sent out a pilot to guide the *Juno* through the tricky inner channel to an anchorage in front of Castle Hill, formerly Noow Tlein. The Yankee captain was hailed by the Russian governor, who laid out a lavish spread of local delicacies and spirits. "He ladled vodka with a gnarled hand from a bucket that was always at his side." D'Wolf brought his own cask of rum to the affair, and by the time dinner was over, the two sozzled traders had already agreed to a deal of "mutual advantage." Having been led to believe that the Russians were "little advanced from a savage state," D'Wolf was pleasantly surprised by his erudite and charming host. "From the kind treatment we received from the governor, I was induced to form a very favorable opinion of him."

Enjoying Baranov's warm hospitality and Sitka's prime location, D'Wolf decided to hang around through the end of summer. He went on trade jaunts up the coast, eventually accumulating more than a thousand furs. Hamstrung by the Tlingit boycott, Baranov was envious of D'Wolf's bartering skills. But Baranov liked D'Wolf's company, and even more so, he liked his barrels of food and rum. He haggled incessantly with the good-natured Yankee, until finally Baranov offered to buy the entire ship and its remaining supplies. Once D'Wolf realized the governor was serious, he negotiated a whopping price for the package. The *Juno* and cargo sold for $68,000, plus a seaworthy company vessel, completely rigged with two sets of sails, four cannons, and a hundred days' worth of provisions. The fee was paid partly in cash, partly in furs, and the rest in a promissory note drawn on the Russian Imperial Treasury. In a letter to the company directors, Baranov justified the expense: "If I had not purchased the *Juno*, more than five hundred people here would have become famine victims." D'Wolf, meanwhile, was triumphant: "The offer was accepted, and under a salute from the fort, I hoisted the stars and stripes over the *Yermak*, which became my property."

During his stay in Sitka, Captain D'Wolf was treated to many tales of K'alyáan and the Tlingit-Russian war. His curiosity was piqued. After concluding his business affairs, the young skipper "resolved to become more acquainted with the Sitka Indians who recently had been so roughly treated by the Russians." By this time, the Yankee trader had made friends with a German naturalist, Georg Heinrich von Langsdorff, lately arrived by ship from Russia, along with company director Nikolai Rezanov. Von Langsdorff too was keen to visit the Tlingit. Baranov tried to dissuade D'Wolff from the "perilous adventure to the other side of the island." But he cast aside his fears and provided D'Wolf and von Langsdorff with two large baidarkas, four Alutiiq chaperones, a Tlingit interpreter, and a pile of gifts. Thus, the thrill-seeking D'Wolf headed into the inner archipelago looking for the notorious K'alyáan.

After three days, the baidarkas pushed against the strong currents and winds of Peril Strait. "Suddenly, a great commotion arose on the shore. Some hundred naked Indians, armed with muskets, thronged to the water's edge." The baidarkas made landfall and were at once surrounded. John reckoned the worst was in store. "I expected nothing but an immediate and violent death." The visitors were shoved up the trail to Chaatlk'aanoow and left at the entrance of a longhouse. "Happily, our fears were groundless," D'Wolf said. As it turned out, the house leader was the father of the Tlingit interpreter. She explained that the visitors were guests of the Russians and that they wanted to meet the great Kiks.ádi people. They brought presents.

The next day D'Wolf and von Langsdorff were hosted by the "commandant of the fortress." More than a hundred inquisitive Tlingit gathered around the big house trying to glimpse the scene within. The daring foreigners endeared themselves to the clan leaders by distributing gifts of tea, sugar, tobacco, brandy, and wool. In exchange, the "most distinguished of the chiefs" presented a sea otter skin to D'Wolf and a beautiful sea otter tail to von Langsdorff. A delicious feast of fish and rice commenced for the guests, with an accompaniment of singing around the large fire pit. D'Wolf was alarmed at one point, when the flames caused the thin bark roof to catch fire. "But a boy ran like a mouse up the wall and extinguished it." After spending two busy days and nights in K'alyáan's village, D'Wolf and party returned to Sitka.

Baranov was anxious to debrief the Yankee captain about his Kiks.ádi antagonists. D'Wolf said that he personally was "received with much kindness." But he also learned that any Tlingit "who was friendly to the Russians would become an outcast to his own people." Moreover, he noted that the Tlingit had constructed a sophisticated defense of breastworks and palisades around their compound. An assault on Chaatlk'aanoow was all but impossible. These were not the answers that Baranov hoped to hear. Baranov realized that he must change strategies. Instead of conquest, the governor would seek coexistence.

Baranov knew that New Archangel would never prosper until peace was secured with the Kiks.ádi. The Russian governor sent an emissary to Chaatlk'aanoow to deliver a message of reconciliation and a request for negotiations. "They wanted to make payment for the fallen and persuade us to come back," Sally Hopkins said. "But as soon as they got to the beach, they were blasted back out." The war council assembled and debated the overture. The headmen were not ready to think about cohabitation with the Russians. Baranov's offer was refused.

Baranov was at the core a salesman, so he made another pitch. A second baidarka was dispatched into the archipelago. As the ambassador approached Point Craven, he raised a pole with dangling swan feathers—a gesture of peace. "Do you have Baranov's heart?" the suspicious Kiks.ádi pressed the envoy. While the lure of the homeland was strong, once more the offer was rejected. "Our interpreter returned from the Sitkans saying that the chiefs wanted further assurance of our good intentions before they would come to the fort," Lisyansky said. "The interpreter was sent back again with presents and a friendly invitation." This time Baranov's plea succeeded to sway several house leaders.

"The Russians came back again. And, finally, the third time, someone said 'Good, Let's go.'" Saiginakh was a Kiks.ádi elder. Before the 1802 uprising, Saiginakh had been on good terms with Governor Baranov. The ordeals of the Survival March and life in exile were hard on him. The Chaatlk'aanoow war council resolved that Saiginakh would accept Baranov's invitation and report back to the council whether the Russians were sincere.

A week later, Baranov's envoy returned to Sitka, accompanied by the Kiks.ádi elder. Saiginakh's retinue of five canoes paddled past Castle Hill and began to sing. "The embassy stopped when close to the beach and commenced dancing in their boats," Lisyansky said. "The chieftain himself jumped and capered in a whimsical manner, fanning himself with large feathers." Dressed in their finest, the Alutiit crowded the small beach, relishing the Tlingit show.

They answered the honored guest with their own song and dance performance. The scene went on for more than an hour, exhausting the patience of the unwitting Lisyansky. The elaborate call-and-response display was a social ritual known as the Deer Peace Dance, in which the sides signaled to one another an end to hostilities.

Baranov indulged the performance with good humor. The governor schemed to use this opportunity to stage a ceremonial handover of Sitka. He did not spare the pomp. Alutiiq attendants lifted Saiginakh out of his canoe and carried him high above their shoulders to a seat of honor in a pavilion set up on the beach. The master of ceremonies took over. Baranov delivered a gushing speech, lauding the nobleness of the Kiks.ádi, lamenting the death of so many brave warriors, and toasting the renewal of friendship between Tlingit and Russians. He bestowed a pile of luxurious gifts on the delighted Saiginakh, including a double-headed eagle crest, the imperial token that signified you belong to the tsar.

Baranov smiled and waved as a resounding cannon salute from the fort bid farewell to Saiginakh's party. The governor was pleased. The affair had gone well. Hopefully, Saiginakh would convince K'alyáan of Russia's good intentions. Back in Chaatlk'aanoow, the house leaders gathered to interrogate Saiginakh about the situation in Sitka. They closely examined the copper imperial crest that the governor had presented to him. "It is payment for the many who have perished," they were told.

In late July an ambassador from Chaatlk'aanoow paddled up to Castle Hill and delivered a package to Governor Baranov. It was a gleaming silver-gray fox fur coverlet, a gift from K'alyáan, announcing that he was ready for a summit. A week later, K'alyáan returned to Sitka to discuss the details for an armistice.

Baranov realized that the status-conscious headman would expect a show no less grand than Saiginakh had received. Unfortunately, he had already sent most of the Alutiit home to Kodiak. Accompanied by a dozen attendants, K'alyáan made a resplendent entrance. His dark hair was powdered and feathered, his face was painted red and black, and he sported a wispy beard. He wore a long blue gown under a woolen English overcoat with a black fox fur cap, whose bushy tail swished in the breeze. Even the reliably disparaging Lisyansky remarked that K'alyáan was "of an agreeable countenance." Only a few Alutiit were on hand, but the Tlingit company did not spare on ceremonial singing and dancing. Indeed, K'alyáan glowed with pride, saying that "he and his companions excelled in dancing beyond all of their countrymen."

The next order of business was the exchange of gifts. The Tlingit party brought sea otter pelts and larch tree cakes. Baranov presented K'alyáan with a great blue overcoat trimmed in ermine as well a silver medal and ribbon. He proudly sported the Russian badge on his chest for the rest of his life. Baranov spoke solemnly about the tragedy of the war. K'alyáan shared these sentiments. He assumed personal responsibility for leading the uprising against Fort Saint Michael, then "promised in the future to be a faithful friend."

Finally, Baranov and K'alyáan discussed the conditions for peace. Mostly, the governor wanted to affirm a territorial claim on Sitka. "The whole southeastern Alaska will belong to Russia. We will not mistreat you, and we will be kind to you. We will make peace with you." But K'alyáan countered with a more sparing offer. "This land does not belong to Russia. We will never make peace with you. We will annihilate you. The grounds of a peace treaty will be that everything still belongs to us, the land and the resources. Anything that you want, you will have to buy from us." Despite K'alyáan's unyielding stance, Baranov was fixed on ending the stalemate and he saw room for a deal. If the Kiks.ádi conceded that the Russians could stay in Sitka and have access to the land around Noow Tlein, then the Tlingit could return from exile without fear of reprisal and rebuild a village on the waterfront. A compromise was reached. The Tlingit and the Russians would share Sitka.

"From now on, we will be brothers," K'alyáan said. It was not an ideal outcome for either side, but it was preferable to protracted warfare. "It took more guts for K'alyáan to come back to Sitka than it did to fight the battle," Herb Hope said. "He moved back to Sitka and rebuilt the village right underneath the walls and cannons of the fort to reassert their right to be there."

At the end of summer, Lisyansky told Baranov that his tour in Alaska was concluded. By now the colonial governor had earned the naval captain's respect. "Before taking leave, Mr. Baranov kindly paid me a final visit," Lisyansky said. "I must observe, by his talents and patriotism, the Russian company could not have selected a better person. On September 1, we sailed out of the harbor at New Archangel."

A year later Lisyansky completed his historic voyage as Russia's first circumnavigation in the age of sail. "On August 4, we had a strong westerly breeze and in the morning cast anchor at Kronstadt. On our arrival, we were met by the commander-in-chief, the admiral, and all the officers with most ardent congratulations. As soon as the news reached Petersburg, persons of all ranks hastened to Kronstadt. So constant was the succession of new comers, so abundant their compliments, and so insatiable their desire to learn the details of our voyage that I was nearly exhausted by fatigue.

The emperor himself honored us with a visit, and expressed himself highly satisfied." The next day the Empress-mother Maria Feodorovna paid a call. Lisyansky had his sailors attired in fine new clothes purchased in Canton. The dandy outfits so impressed Her Highness that she gifted Lisyansky with a diamond ring, the officers with gold snuffboxes, and the crew with ten ducats each.

Lisyansky was promoted to full captain, knighted into the Order of Saint Vladimir, and endowed with an annual pension of three thousand rubles. "As to the *Neva*," Lisyansky said, "I shall be excused, if with the warmth of a sailor, I declare that there never sailed a more lovely vessel."

In Alaska, no sooner had the *Neva* weighed anchor and sailed off into the Pacific, the Tlingit took action. The New Russia settlement at Yakutat was a decade old. It grew from a small trading post to a fortified compound, housing as many as two hundred colonists. It was nearly overrun during the 1802 Tlingit uprising, but for the cool head of Ivan Kuskov. In 1804 Baranov used Yakutat as a base to launch his revenge tour through the archipelago. Over the next year, as New Archangel consumed Baranov's attention and resources, New Russia was neglected. By 1805 the settlement consisted of two forts, a dozen buildings, a shipyard, and sixty overworked colonists. The site was managed by Stepan Larionov, a trusted company veteran, who lived there with his Tlingit wife and Creole children. That summer not one Russian ship visited the settlement.

In early autumn Larionov was busy with the end of hunting season and the onset of winter preparations when a team of Chugach baidarkas stopped to rest on the long commute from Sitka to their home in Prince William Sound. The manager gave them food and lodging in exchange for labor. Company officer Ivan Repin later reported to Baranov: "In the morning, Larionov sent the Chugach out to the woods to pick berries. When they returned to the compound, nobody was alive. There were dead bodies lying all over the fort." The frightened men fled to their baidarkas on the beach. Taking to the water, gunshots from the backwoods whizzed around them, splashing the surface. "They paddled into the bay and were fired upon, but nobody was killed." Five days later, the exhausted Chugach party arrived at the Russian outpost on Nuchek Island, where they recounted the gruesome tale to Repin.

The assault on New Russia was led by Tanuk of the Teikweidí clan, in alliance with other clan leaders. Tanuk was well-known to the Russians and had many dealings with them. The compound was undermanned on the morning of the attack, its residents caught by surprise. "The fort was burned and the people knocked on the head," said Nikolai Rezanov, chief executive of the Russian-American Company. "The savages butchered all the Russians at Yakutat, numbering some forty people." Larionov was among the dead. Only the children were left alive. A dozen workers away from the fort managed to escape, only to end up as hostages in an Eyak camp, whose chief sold them back to the Russians for ransom. The New Russia settlement was destroyed. "Of all the buildings, not one log was left standing upon another. Ashes covered the whole village site."

A month later, the *Juno* arrived in Sitka from Kodiak, bringing the first news of the Yakutat tragedy to Baranov. The nightmare of Fort Saint Michael still haunted Baranov. His immediate impulse was to exact revenge. "The old man was inspired to make a new sacrifice for his country," said the naval officer Davydov. "He is starting on the ship *Rostislav*, taking four cannons and only twenty-five men. God help him, unless he can be talked out of it." But no Russian expeditionary force was ever sent to Yakutat. Without the *Neva*, Baranov's mighty armada was disbanded.

The Russian American colony was also vulnerable to its many dedicated opponents. "The Englishman [Henry] Barber found out about Yakutat and immediately sailed to Kodiak with the obvious aim of attacking the Russian settlement at the earliest opportunity. However, there was a company ship in the harbor, and he quickly left." After the Yakutat calamity, another friendly Tlingit leader turned hostile and led an assault against the Russian trade post on Nuchek Island. During the winter of 1805–1806, rumors swirled that a multiclan force of more than a thousand warriors from Angoon, Hoonah, Kuiu, and Ak'wa villages was massing in the northern archipelago. Things were no more promising in the opposite direction, where the Kake, Stikine, and Haida villages were located. "I have been assured," Rezanov said, "that the tribes lying to the southeast are numerous, and bear such determined hatred toward the conquering Baranov that a disastrous fate would await him and his followers if he should seek to establish a settlement further south."

In Sitka, meanwhile, the Tlingit and the Russians established a coexistence. Following the K'alyáan-Baranov summit, the Kiks.ádi gradually began returning to their ancestral homeland. The house leaders scoped out new sites to build along the hillside facing the sound and in the protected small bays. Still, resentment and distrust continued to permeate the two communities. The Russians walled themselves behind a tall stockade fence, adorned with watchtowers and cannons. Colonists slept with their guns primed and loaded. K'alyáan, however, kept his word. The Kiks.ádi did not resume hostilities against the Russians.

In the aftermath of the war, New Archangel was an unconvincing Russian enclave surrounded by an unwelcoming Tlingit nation. The prospects to expand the colony anywhere in the archipelago were naught. If a Russian America was to survive, Baranov needed to break out of this isolation. In desperation, the governor dispatched his Rhode Island comrade Captain D'Wolf on an emergency run to Spanish California to find food and supplies. When the *Juno* returned with stores of fresh provisions and reports of friendly Natives, Baranov had his answer.

APPROPRIATION AND REPATRIATION

By the time Yury Lisyansky sailed out of the New Archangel harbor in the summer of 1905, he had amassed an impressive collection of Indigenous art and artifacts. During his stopover in Alaska, he had admired the Tlingit handiwork. "The greatest art or craft of the local inhabitants may be considered carvings and drawings . . . You won't see a single toy—not a single tool or utensil—that is not adorned with many different images." He packed up his prizes—intricately carved shaman masks and rattles, combat daggers, boldly painted war helmets, and a complete set of wooden armor—and took them back to St. Petersburg.

Lisyansky was the first in a long line of amateur anthropologists (and later, professionals) who came to Alaska, studied the Native cultures, and acquired some cool souvenirs to take home.

Thanks to Lisyansky and his colleagues, the Kunstkamera museum in St. Petersburg has nearly 1,500 artifacts representing Indigenous groups in Alaska, including hundreds of Tlingit items.

This interest in "collecting" continued and escalated after the transfer of Alaska to the United States. By the late nineteenth century, it was accepted—even expected—that explorers would bring back exotic artifacts to study or just put on display. After twenty-five years in Alaska, US naval officer George Emmons sold thousands of cultural items to natural history museums back home. Ethnologist and linguist John R. Swanton spent several years recording Tlingit and Haida legends and histories and collecting hundreds of artifacts for the Smithsonian Institution.

The norm was to purchase items of interest from Native peoples, but there are several documented instances of more blatant pillaging. In 1899 the Harriman Alaska Expedition—lauded for its rigorous documentation of the territory's natural resources and Native cultures—stopped in the recently vacated Tlingit village of Cape Fox. There, they discovered Native homes, graves, totems, and other artifacts that had seemingly been abandoned. In fact, the residents had relocated due to a smallpox outbreak. But the village and the objects were nonetheless sacred to the former residents, as they believed they held the spirits of the ancestors who had lived there. Oblivious to the affront, the explorers loaded their

boat with several large totems and a Tlingit house, in addition to countless smaller artifacts. The objects ended up in museums throughout
the United States.

In a similar episode, George Emmons happened on the Tlingit village of Tuxecan, on Prince of Wales Island, after the Teeyneidí clan had
moved south. Clan leader Dave Jensen remarked that "[Emmons] loaded
up thousands of different articles of art and household goods—spoons
and bowls and boxes and paddles . . ." Most significantly, he took a
huge screen depicting a dog salmon—the Teeyneidí clan crest—that
was painted on twenty-three vertical planks and hung across the front
of a house in the village. "My great-uncle Henry Roberts used to pass
by Tuxecan every year on the way out to the fishing grounds," Jensen
recalled. "He would swing by and check on the house. And one year it
just wasn't there."

Fast forward a century, and the popular attitude about this type of
cultural appropriation has changed dramatically. The US government
enacted a series of laws that requires museums to return human
remains and cultural objects to Indigenous communities who request
them. The National Museum of the American Indian Act of 1989 applied
this requirement to the Smithsonian Institution, while the Native American Graves Protection and Repatriation Act of 1990 extended the mandate to any institution that receives federal funding. "A hundred years
ago, museums were interested primarily in enlarging their collections,"
observed Burke Museum curator Robin Wright, "whereas my primary
concern is building relations with native communities."

The National Museum of the American Indian (NMAI, part of the
Smithsonian) has returned some seventy-three items to the Tlingit
people. Repatriated items include a fifty-four-foot red cedar totem that
was returned to the descendants of the Cape Fox people and the dog
salmon screen that was returned to the Teeyneidí clan. Overseeing
the return of the items is "an absolute honor and privilege," said NMAI
repatriation manager Jaquetta Swift. "We are correcting an historical
wrong."

Museums are also finding other ways to make items in their collections more accessible to Native American peoples, such as lending them

for important events. For the historic Centennial Potlatch in 2004, four staff members from the Penn Museum hand-carried four ceremonial hats from Philadelphia to Sitka (for a total of eight airplane tickets).

In a particularly innovative example, the Smithsonian used 3-D technology to assist repatriation efforts, as in the case of one Kiks.ádi crest hat. The ceremonial wooden hat is in the form of a sculpin, or bullhead (the secondary crest of the Kiks.ádi). The hat—which had been in the institutional holdings since 1884—was badly damaged and too fragile to use in clan ceremonies. Instead of returning the original, clan leaders requested the Smithsonian to carve a new sculpin hat, using 3-D scanning and automated milling. According to Tlingit custom, such ceremonial items, or *at.óow*, must be created by the opposite moiety. In this case, someone from an Eagle clan had to craft the crest hat for the Raven-side Kiks.ádi. So, prior to construction, the Dakl'aweidí and Kaagwaantaan clans, both of Eagle lineage, adopted the two Smithsonian staff members who did the work. Upon completion, the new sculpin hat was dedicated during a moving ceremony, where Kiks.ádi clan leader Ray Wilson donned and danced the hat. "When you dance in it, you breathe life into it," he said, "and the hat comes alive."

Efforts at repatriation will undoubtedly continue for a long time to come. But the processes—and the results—have already demonstrated the Tlingit's irrepressible cultural resilience. "This repatriation helps us to study our history," said Eleanor Hadden, a Tlingit anthropologist, at one ceremony. "We do this for our ancestors and for our grandchildren . . . Thank you for being the caretakers of our objects."

CHAPTER 12

At the Edge of Empire

O n Christmas Day 1805 the Corps of Discovery christened Fort
Clatsop, named for the local Indigenous people, near the mouth of
the Columbia River. More shanty than stronghold, the rudimentary shelter
was the winter quarters of Lewis and Clark. The Americans had arrived
in the Pacific Northwest.

In the early nineteenth century an international competition arose over
the coastal territories between San Francisco and Vancouver. Because
Alexander Baranov was not able to overpower the Tlingit, his Russian
colony could not use its geo-strategic advantage to push southward. Until
now, Russia's main imperial rival in the region was Great Britain, moving
in pincer fashion over land from Canada and over sea from Hawaii. The
Spanish, meanwhile, refused to surrender their claim to the entire West
Coast, citing the pope's blessing as imperial entitlement. By this time the
French dropped out of the contest, selling their half-billion-acre stake in
North America to scrappy newcomers, the United States. Thomas Jefferson's
Louisiana Purchase directly impacted Baranov's predicament. Hemmed
in by K'alyáan's blockade, the Russian colony was in danger of collapse.
Baranov's solution was to go around the rainforest deathtrap and establish
an ocean lifeline.

In September 1808 a small schooner ventured forth from Sitka and
headed down the North American coast. The *Saint Nikolai* (née *Tamana*)
was earlier acquired by the Russian-American Company in unexpected

circumstances. In 1806 Baranov dispatched Pavel Slobodchikov to lead a team of Russian trappers aboard the American ship *O'Cain* to hunt sea otter in Southern California. The Yankee skipper became so irritated by the Russians' incessant bickering that he marooned the lot on the Baja peninsula. Desperate to get home, Slobodchikov traded 150 sea otter pelts to an American trader for the forty-five-foot *Tamana*, which he renamed the *Saint Nikolai*, after the patron saint of sailors. Back in Sitka, Baranov inspected the secondhand craft and deemed it fit for company service.

For the 1808 voyage, Baranov tapped navigator Nikolai Bulygin to command the vessel. A crew of twenty-two Russian and Alutiiq hunters was assembled, along with one additional passenger, eighteen-year-old Anna Petrovna, the captain's new bride. Baranov entrusted company stalwart Timofei Tarakanov with the expedition's main task—to stake out a territorial claim along the west coast to build a satellite settlement.

By early October, the *Saint Nikolai* was exploring the mouth of the Strait of Juan de Fuca between Vancouver Island and the Olympic Peninsula. Unbeknownst to Captain Bulygin, his craft was coasting next to the Columbia Bar, the graveyard of the Pacific. For four days the small ship drifted languidly toward the shoreline and then back out to sea, held in place by colliding westerly breezes and easterly currents. From shore, the vessel was appraised by the local Quileute people, the more daring of whom paddled out to make contact. Tarakanov expressed peaceful intentions, and traded some glass beads for a fresh halibut.

Without warning, the calm broke. A squall pounced out of the west. A strong gust snapped the foreyard, and the schooner could no longer tack into wind. The vessel reeled toward the shoreline, becoming trapped amid the hidden shoals. The captain proceeded slowly, tentatively, sending out sounding lines, hoping to find a channel. When darkness fell, Bulygin ordered all four anchors dropped, but during the night the cable lines were frayed and the ship lurched into the shallows. At daylight, an enormous swell delivered the coup: the *Saint Nikolai* was lifted, carried over the surf, and thrown onto a sandbank. Seawater gushed through the broken frame. The captain called to abandon ship.

It was fortunate that the crash occurred at low tide. The panicky crew slogged through the surf to the beach. But Tarakanov knew that the shore was no less dangerous than the sea. He ordered the company into formation to salvage the essentials—a cannon, powder kegs, and firearms—which were hoisted through the waist-high water to dry ground. Using ship sails, two canopy tents were raised, while crewmen with loaded rifles made a defensive perimeter. "We must be ready to beat off attacks by the natives, who we now need fear more than anything on earth," Tarakanov said. Shivering around the fire in their makeshift camp, the castaways did not have to wait long.

By midday, the resident Quileute people descended on the beach. One team seized the abandoned ship, pillaging the remaining stores, while a second team tested the camp's defenses, retreating after a cannon volley. The crew debated their options: find a defensible site to build winter quarters and hope to fend off the locals, or undertake a sixty-mile hike and hope to flag down the *Kodiak*, another Russian vessel exploring the coastland further south. Captain Bulygin endorsed the hike, and the company agreed: "We place ourselves in your hands."

The party stumbled into the evergreen maze, keeping within earshot of the sound of the surf. Each man was allotted two rifles, a pistol, and powder. Meanwhile, a Quileute posse harried the Russians all along the trek. "During the night a violent rain storm hit," Tarakanov recalled, "and we took shelter in a cave." The company was startled awake by a resounding crash. The Quileute had dislodged boulders from the cliffs above, trying to entomb the trespassers. The company clambered over the rocks and resumed their flight. At last, they were halted by an impassable, swift-running river. Reluctantly, they turned inward, deeper into the woods, to find safe crossing, fearing every tree and bush.

A Hoh woman greeted Tarakanov near the riverbank. Her companions had been monitoring the Russian party. She communicated her contempt for the Quileute who were chasing them, and offered passage across the river. Suppressing his doubts, Tarakanov agreed. By now, a large number of Hoh had converged on the opposite bank. Several canoes paddled over, the Russian party broke into small groups, and climbed in. At mid-river, the Hoh sprung their trap. The canoes were sabotaged with holes on the bottom that had been plugged. The Hoh escorts pulled out the plugs, jumped into the water, and swam away. Amid shouts of excitement, spears whizzed past as water poured in. The men stomped their boots over the holes to delay sinking, Tarakanov used his gunstock as a makeshift paddle. The current was in their favor, and the foundering craft made it to the bank. A battle between Russian firearms and Hoh arrows raged for the next several hours. When it was over, two Hoh warriors and two Russian hunters were dead and Anna Bulygin was taken prisoner.

The Russians regrouped and looked to their captain for orders. But Bulygin was overcome by grief. He conceded command to Tarakanov. The party headed upriver, choosing a protected cliffside perch to dig out a winter camp. For three months, they struggled against the Hoh and starvation. One morning a Hoh emissary called to negotiate the release of Anna. The Russians offered their warmest clothes, but the Hoh wanted four rifles and powder. The delirious Bulygin demanded the group accept the deal, but Tarakanov opposed the offer. "We knew this refusal would shock our distraught commander, but what else could we do?" The captain sank deeper into despair.

In February, Tarakanov's escape plan was ready. At dawn, the Russians crept from their shelter and huddled into two rough-carved dugout canoes. They braced for a wild ride through whitewater rapids, past hostile Hoh camps, and out to the seacoast. The party made it less than halfway before it was forced ashore at arrow-point. An entire Hoh village arrived at the riverbank to enjoy the commotion. Tarakanov made a desperate move. He drew a loaded pistol from his jacket and took three Hoh people hostage. The standoff lasted into the next day, until an old chief arrived with an enslaved woman. It was Anna Bulygin.

Elated to see his compatriot alive, Tarakanov immediately offered to swap prisoners. "But Mrs. Bulygin gave us an answer that struck like a thunder clap," Tarakanov said. "She was satisfied with her conditions and did not want to join us, and she advised us to surrender to her master, an upright and virtuous man." Captain Bulygin let the words sink in, then leapt to his feet and grabbed a rifle. Rushing forward, Bulygin aimed to shoot his wife. Instead, he collapsed in a sobbing heap. "It is better for me to die than to wander the forest with you," Anna said. "I scorn your threats."

Tarakanov gathered up Bulygin and returned to the Russian side, while the defiant Anna stood with Yutramaki and the Hoh people. A fateful decision had to be made. After consulting with his crew, Tarakanov handed over his rifle and submitted to the chief. The dazed Bulygin followed. But not everyone chose surrender. Yutramaki allowed those who refused to take their chances on the river. They were never heard from again. Yutramaki distributed the hostages among the Hoh chieftains. Anna and her husband were separated. For more than a year, Tarakanov lived with Yutramaki. The former Russian peasant impressed and endeared himself to his new master no less than he had done earlier to Baranov.

In May 1810 a two-masted sailing ship with United States colors appeared off the coast. "At long last," Tarakanov exalted, "merciful God heard our prayers." European hostages scored higher profits than sea otter pelts, and Yutramaki happily delivered his Russian prize to the ship commander. Captain John Brown would cash in later when he returned Tarakanov to New Archangel. After hearing Tarakanov's full account, the captain demanded that all the Russian hostages be rounded up and brought to the vessel. Negotiations and threats went back and forth for a week, before Captain Brown finally weighed anchor and sailed north to Sitka. Of the original company of twenty-two settlers, thirteen were rescued. Among the nine who died in captivity were the *Saint Nikolai*'s brokenhearted Captain Bulygin and his estranged wife Anna. There would be no Russian colony on the Columbia River.

The Indigenous Kashaya Pomo called their homeland Metini; the English sea dog Sir Francis Drake called it New Albion; and the Spanish called it Alta California. For the old European empires and the new United States, the most coveted prize along the Pacific was the coastline stretching from central California to Oregon. But who would get there first? "If the long-term plans of Peter the Great had been realized, then California never would have become a Spanish colony," Nikolai Rezanov bemoaned. After his failed mission to Japan, the count parted ways with the *Nadezhda* and hitched a ride to Sitka for a firsthand inspection of the Russian American colony.

The dream of Russian California was an old one. In April 1806 Count Rezanov was living that dream, as the *Juno* sailed through the Golden Gate into San Francisco Bay. The Russian colony's California gamble was forced by necessity. To survive, New Archangel needed to secure a sea-based lifeline to overcome the Tlingit land-based stranglehold. As the *Juno* entered the bay, a dirt cloud rose along the shoreline, stirred by twenty mounted troops from Castillo San Joaquin, where the Spanish had been waiting for the Russians for the past thirty years.

A premature fear of Russian expansion into Alta California had led the Spanish governor, in 1776, to build the Presidio, a barracks sentinel at the entrance to the bay. Now, the skittish guardsmen kept their rifles trained on the three-masted intruder, as their captain called out from atop his steed. Whence have you come? What is your business? The tension was prolonged because no one aboard the *Juno* could speak Spanish. Finally, the German naturalist Georg Heinrich von Langsdorff and a local Franciscan friar managed to get a dialogue going in Latin. "We have come from the Russian colony to the north. We seek rations and have furs to trade." The soldiers relaxed.

By the time the Russians arrived in Alta California, Spain had become more concerned about Great Britain, with whom they had been at war for the past decade. The *Juno* party was escorted to the Presidio for what became a six-week, wine-soaked sabbatical. The generosity of the Spanish hosts was boundless. By the time the *Juno* sailed back to Sitka, its empty hold was brimming with grain, its scurvy-ridden crew was revitalized, and its widower count was betrothed to the comandante's daughter.

Nikolai Rezanov was awestruck by the beauty and bounty of California. "There remains one last unoccupied stretch of coast whose resources we need very much. If we pass up this opportunity, what will posterity say?" Rezanov hurried back to Russia to petition the tsar. He envisioned a California colony that could feed all of Alaska as well as eastern Siberia. The settlement would grow rich and populous. The North Pacific would become a Russian pond. Succumbing to fever on route to St. Petersburg, Rezanov was not alive to witness the rise of Russian California. But the count's vision did not die with him. His petition won the approval of the Russian emperor, but that was only half the challenge. Avoiding the wrath of the Spanish emperor was the other half.

Baranov's fur hunters had already been testing the patience of the Spanish by poaching sea otter in California waters. But now the Russians risked open conflict by clearing a spot of land along the golden coast for settlement. Baranov delegated the task to cool-headed Ivan Kuskov, who was sent southward on reconnaissance aboard the *Kodiak*. Kuskov was lured by the raucous barking of sea lions to steer his vessel behind a red sandstone cliff, through a narrow channel, and into a shallow inlet. The lucky digression yielded more than a thousand sea otter and beaver furs. Bodega Bay became the future site of Russian California.

In March 1812 Kuskov returned to the sheltered cove with a hundred Russian and Alutiiq colonists. The company broke ground on a high ocean bluff with access to the bay and a nearby river (now the Russian River), a hundred miles north of San Francisco. The familiar accessories of Russian power—an armory and a church—went up first. Pastures, gardens, orchards, and wheat fields followed. Agriculture, rather than fur trapping, took precedence. In September Kuskov called the company to assembly and dedicated Fort Ross (short for *Rossiya*, or Fort Russia). Wearing a dress uniform and sporting an Order of Saint Vladimir ribbon for services rendered, Kuskov inspected the cannon mounts and defensive palisades. The new commander of Fort Ross wondered how long the colony could hold out before being evicted by either the Spanish or the Kashaya Pomo.

The Kashaya Pomo people had been foraging in this area for more than two thousand years. In the early 1800s they numbered roughly one thousand people, ranging twenty miles along the coast and about ten miles inland. And while Europeans had been sailing by the coast for more than a hundred years, it was not until Russia's Timofei Tarakanov stepped onto the beach in the early 1800s that first contact was made. The sight of Tarakanov's hunting party, sitting low in the water in baidarkas, led the Kashaya to give the intruders the name of "Undersea People." Now the Russians were back to stay. Baranov gave Kuskov explicit instructions: "You are strictly prohibited from even the slightest exploitation of the local natives. Do not insult or abuse them. You personally must make every effort to win their friendship and affection." Baranov was eager not to repeat the mistakes that had been made in his dealings with the Tlingit.

In a break with European colonizing norms, Kuskov never attempted to subjugate, dispossess, or convert the local Kashaya. The two peoples succeeded to coexist without major incident because they rarely interacted. "After the fort was built, they came to us very seldom," Kuskov said. Still, he was mindful of keeping good relations with local Kashaya leader Chugu-an, and was generous with gifts of clothes, axes, tools, and beads to his host. It helped, too, that the Kashaya Pomo and the Russians were not economic competitors. The Kashaya people survived from the forest, not the sea. Kuskov forbade the company from hunting in the woods, unless first receiving verbal permission from their hosts.

In 1817 Kuskov orchestrated the first and only peace treaty ever negotiated between imperialist Europeans and Indigenous Californians. The treaty was formalized with a grand ceremony and feast, attended by Kashaya chieftains and Russian officers. Even more remarkable, the Russians kept to the terms. Of course, Chu-gu-an recognized an advantage in having a Russian settlement in his domain. In particular, the long cannons were a useful hedge against the Spanish, who sometimes came north to capture Kashaya and Miwok people to replenish the labor supply on their mission estates in the south.

In 1812, on a routine inspection of the coast, Gabriel Moraga witnessed a Russian brig and a flurry of activity atop the cliffs near Bodega Bay. The lieutenant hurried back to San Francisco to tell the Presidio comandante, who in turn informed the colonial governor in Monterrey. The Spanish viceroy penned an official protest, demanding the Russians vacate the premises at once. The missive was hand delivered by Moraga to Kuskov, who devised a clever stall. "Your Excellency's letter I had the honor to receive," Kuskov wrote back, "but its contents remained unknown for the reason that I neither read nor write Spanish." Kuskov kept up the game for more than two years. Meanwhile, each Spanish vessel that arrived at Bodega Bay to deliver a threat became an opportunity for clandestine trading. At the edge of empire, the line between enemy and friend was frequently blurred.

In 1815 a new Spanish governor, Pablo Vincente de Solá, vowed to clear out the Russians from California. His aggressive campaign sought to disrupt Kuskov's operations, impound their crafts, and arrest trespassers. Spanish gunboats detained several Russian hunting parties. The Spanish were especially cruel toward the Alutiit, who suffered torture and even death in sadistic "conversion" rituals.

These provocations were beyond Kuskov's mandate and resources. Alexander Baranov intervened with a Russian show of force. He sent the battle-ready *Otkrytie* south to double down on his California claim. But while Spain and Russia's colonial agents were on the verge of conflict in the Americas, King Ferdinand and Tsar Alexander were on the best of terms in Europe, having just collaborated to defeat Napoleon. Governor Solá was ordered not to upset the peace. Begrudgingly, he opened negotiations with Baranov, leading to the release of the captives and de facto recognition of Fort Ross.

Alas, Count Rezanov's vision of an affluent Russian California never came to be. It took the company less than a decade to decimate the sea otter population along the California coast. The annual harvest fell from the thousands to the tens. The Fort Ross farmstead, meanwhile, produced many potatoes, but more were eaten by the gophers than were loaded onto ships. An outfit dedicated to trapping furs could not make the transition to tilling soil.

The Russian colony at Fort Ross was the scene of many California firsts—the first windmill, shipyard, and blacksmith. But after Kuskov departed in 1818, the settlement fell into deficit. In 1841 company directors in St. Petersburg were delighted to unload the property on Swiss émigré John Sutter, who was launching a settlement near Sacramento. Thus, Russia missed the gold rush by eight years. Well before these events, however, Baranov pondered an alternative site to expand the colony. In 1815 Baranov became fixed on the South Pacific to find a new jewel for the imperial crown.

The two-hundred-ton brigantine *Atahualpa* was launched from a Kennebunk shipyard in 1800 and commissioned for service in the China trade by Boston merchant Theodore Lyman. During its fourth Pacific run, the War of 1812 broke out. To avoid capture by British naval patrols, the skipper of the *Atahualpa*, James Bennett, made a deal with Russia's colonial governor, Alexander Baranov. For the steep price of twenty thousand sealskins, Russia would assume ownership of the vessel. Sailing under a neutral flag, Bennett remained captain, continued trading, and shared the profits with the Russian-American Company. Baranov insisted on a name change, so the *Atahualpa*, honoring the great Incan emperor, became the *Bering*, honoring the great Russian-Danish explorer.

Ever since Yury Lisyansky sailed the *Neva* into Waimea Bay and dined with the local chieftain, a friendship was born between Russia and Hawaii. In January 1815, more than a decade later, the *Bering* was swaying in the surf off the west coast of Kauai. Laying low in the water, the *Bering*'s hold was crammed with bales of sea otter and sealskins, a cache of tropical sandalwood, and a load of pigs, sweet potatoes, and rice for Baranov's hungry settlers. Captain Bennett was drinking tea with Chief Kaumuali'i, who was dictating his adorations to Governor Baranov. The chief's flattery had ulterior motives. The Russians would make a useful ally in his ongoing rivalry with King Kamehameha. Based on the Big Island, Kamehameha aspired to rule the entire Hawaiian archipelago. But the leeward island of Kauai remained out of his reach. Kamehameha and Kaumuali'i kept an uneasy truce, as neither possessed sufficient force to defeat the other.

Overnight a winter gale blew out of the north, broadsiding the *Bering* and crashing the brig onto the rocky beach. Trade was one thing—wrecks were another. Kaumuali'i immediately claimed salvage rights and seized the ship. Bennett was aghast, watching his furs, food, and hardwood get hauled away by Kaumuali'i's men. It was not until April that Bennett persuaded the Boston brig *Albatross* to take him back to Sitka. When Baranov learned of the outrage, he concocted a plan. No, he told Bennett, he would not send a warship. Instead, the governor enlisted his new acquaintance, Dr. Georg Schäffer, to cozy up to King Kamehameha. Baranov had designs for a Russian settlement on Hawaii.

A physician by trade and an adventurer by passion, Georg Anton Schäffer was born in Germany but moved to Russia, where prospects were brighter for a man of his roguish charm. He was accepted into the Russian officer corps and placed in charge of a futuristic squadron of hot-air balloonists. In 1813 he signed on as the ship's doctor for the *Suvorov*, embarking on a round-the-world voyage. Schäffer did not complete the journey, as the shipmaster of the *Suvorov* dumped the irksome doctor at Sitka. But the culture-starved Russian governor took an immediate liking to the well-educated German doctor. Hence, Schäffer's secret mission to Hawaii.

Baranov invented a far-fetched ruse in which Schäffer would pose as a naturalist, win the confidence of King Kamehameha, gain access to the lucrative sandalwood trade, and acquire property for a start-up Russian colony. Baranov would let the charismatic doctor work his diplomatic skills for a few months, then send in a ready-for-battle backup force. Schäffer was also charged with retrieving the *Bering's* seized cargo from Kuamualii on Kauai. "If he does not respond to peaceful negotiations," Baranov instructed. "Give him a military lesson. And if God will help you, the whole island of Kauai should be taken in the name of our Sovereign Emperor of all Russia."

In October 1815 Schäffer set out aboard the *Isabella* for Hawaii. Among his crew was adventure-loving Timofei Tarakanov and Alexander Baranov's Creole son Antipatr. By this time the War of 1812 had ended and Russia and the United States were back to being rivals. Approaching the Big Island from the north, Schäffer gazed at the rugged green summit of Mauna Kea and then spied flapping white sails and tall masts along the coastline. Hawaii had become the favorite port of call of the Boston men. King Kamehameha had been cooperating with the British since the 1790s, but these days the Americans were the most active traders. They had already secured an agreement with Kamehameha for exclusive export rights of sandalwood, a fragrant hardwood coveted by Chinese aristocrats.

The arrival of the oddball Bavarian from the Russian colony upset the kingdom's Anglo-American fraternity. The king's most trusted confidante was leathery British sailor John Young, who advised on all military and commercial matters. Young was suspicious of the slickster "scientist," who seemed more interested in politics and profits than in flora and fauna. He urged the king to expel the obnoxious poser. But Kamehameha was curious about Schäffer's hidden purposes and valued his medical skills. Instead, he assigned Georg to semi-exile on Oahu, where Schäffer stewed in isolation until springtime.

According to plan, Baranov dispatched the *Otkrytie* to Hawaii several months later. Kamehameha and the Boston men were dismayed to see the well-armed Russian sloop cruising the archipelago looking for Schäffer. By chance, a second Russian vessel, the *Ilmena*, arrived from Fort Ross at the same time. Now with a proper naval force to command, the puffed-up Schäffer left Honolulu and headed west to Kauai to confront the pillager of the *Bering*, Chief Kaumuali'i.

But the Kauai leader was as smooth an operator as the German doctor. Kaumuali'i startled Schäffer with a proposal for a strategic partnership. Schäffer seized the moment. After all, Baranov had given him sanction to improvise. "I will rely on your good sense not to pass up any opportunity to advance the interests of the Company and the Fatherland," the governor had instructed. So Schäffer jumped at the opportunity before him and negotiated a big deal for the empire: In exchange for exclusive trade rights and land concessions on Kauai, Russia would act as Kaumuali'i's muscle around the Hawaiian Islands.

The pair of schemers discussed future plans to launch an offensive against Kamehameha and divide up the archipelago spoils—Oahu, Maui, and Lanai. Kaumuali'i ordered his workers into the mountains to harvest sandalwood for the Russians. Schäffer gifted the king the *Ilmena* as the flagship of a new Kauai navy. In mid-summer, the *Otkrytie*'s main deck was swathed in pomp and ceremony for the treaty signing. Kaumuali'i was fitted with a Russian naval officer's coat, while Schäffer Řpreened in a royal Hawaiian feathered cape. The doctor bestowed a silver medal embossed with the imperial double-headed eagle on the chief, who signed an *X* to a hastily-prepared document, proclaiming Kauai's allegiance to the tsar. Tarakanov saluted as he watched Kaumuali'i attendant raise the Russian-American

Company flag over the royal palace. Schäffer was exuberant. "No power in the world has more right to these islands than Russia."

For the next eighteen months, Schäffer played the role of imperial viceroy of Russian Kauai. To Kaumuali'i's delight, he supervised the construction of a star-shaped fortress, built from red volcanic rocks and stocked with Russian artillery, next to the royal palace at Waimea Bay. Fort Elizabeth was named in honor of Tsar Alexander's wife, Elizabeth Alexeievna. The chief bequeathed a huge tract of fertile land for Russian settlement in the north along Hanalei Bay, where more fortifications and a vodka distillery were built. Schäffer commandeered several US merchant ships for his personal errands and put it on Baranov's tab. He cultivated cotton, tobacco, rice paddies, and a vineyard. In the evening, to enhance the mood of a Waimea Bay saffron sunset, Schäffer, in Fort Elizabeth, and Kaumuali'i, in the royal palace, traded cannon salutes. A new Russian colony was taking root in the South Pacific.

King Kamehameha was enraged by Schäffer's affront to his rule. The Boston men were incensed by his assault on their revenue. Yet they refrained from taking action, wary of a conflict with the Russian Empire. That is, until late 1816, when the fog of deception was lifted. The Russian settlement's floating bodyguard, the *Otkrytie*, was damaged in a storm and limped back to Sitka for repair. Meanwhile, another Russian naval brig, the *Rurik*, arrived in Hawaii, causing panic in Kamehameha's camp. But the captain of the *Rurik* assured the Hawaiian king that the Russian tsar had no plans to seize the archipelago. The *Rurik* departed without even stopping at Kauai. Schäffer's bluff was exposed.

The Boston men devised their own con to dislodge the Russians. Waiting until Schäffer was away in Hanalei, they arrived in force at the royal palace on Waimea Bay, spreading a rumor that the United States and Russia were at war and that US naval ships were on the way to Hawaii. Kaumuali'i did not hesitate to denounce his co-conspirator. When Schäffer returned to Waimea, his now ex-partner ordered him to leave the island at once.

Schäffer and a few comrades fled in the leaky *Ilmena*. Itching for a fight, he sailed to Oahu to pick up reinforcements from his small compound, but instead found the Americans celebrating the Fourth of July atop the charred ruins of the Russian blockhouse. Since the *Ilmena* was not fit for an open sea voyage, Schäffer was effectively under house arrest in the harbor.

The doctor was saved from harm by the arrival of the *Panther*. Its New England captain was sympathetic to the German physician, who had previously treated him for a malady on the Big Island. The captain sneaked Schäffer out of Honolulu, stopping at Waimea to pick up a few personal belongings. Poor Schäffer hid trembling in the hold, while Kaumuali'i's men searched the vessel for the fugitive. The *Panther* then sailed away to China, taking the deposed viceroy, but stranding a hundred Russian and Alutiiq colonists. Schäffer shrugged off the setback and waited for another chance at empire building. It came in Brazil, where the incessant schemer founded one of Germany's first South American colonies.

In the fall of 1815 Peter Corney stood at the rail of the *Columbia*, a British trade vessel moored at Sitka, and watched as Schäffer and company set sail to Hawaii. "It is their intention to gain a footing in there," Corney wrote. "The Sandwich (Hawaiian) Islands, so conveniently near, would serve as the West India Islands do for America. I am of the opinion that they will possess them in time." So too dreamed Governor Baranov. For roughly a year and half, the Russian Empire extended to the Hawaiian Islands. Before the gambit was foiled, Baranov's secret agent had run up a two-hundred-thousand-ruble debt, antagonized the rising United States, and fomented lasting ill will in the island kingdom. The tumultuous episode of Russian Hawaii was yet another blow to Baranov's exhausted American colony at the edge of empire.

A TALE OF TWO FORTS

From the ventures of the Russian-American Company outside of Alaska, two forts remain—in very different states.

Of the three forts built in Kauai, the only one that is still in existence—somewhat—is Fort Elizabeth, near Waimea. In reality, this fort flew the Russian flag on only a few occasions, as Dr. Georg Anton Schäffer and the Russian-American Company were expelled even before construction was complete. It was better known as the site of King Kaumuali'i's residential compound, which was just outside the walls.

Hawaiian chiefs and soldiers continued to occupy the fort for nearly forty years after Kaumuali'i's death, referring to the site as Pā'ula'ula, which means "red walls." They used it as a residence, a prison, and a burial ground. The fort gradually fell into disuse and was abandoned in the 1860s.

More than a century later, in 1972, the fort ruins and surrounding property opened as Russian Fort Elizabeth State Historical Park. It was, perhaps, an odd choice of name considering the Russians' short and rather tenuous connection to the site. Nowadays, the exterior walls are mostly intact, but only the foundations of some interior buildings remain. The state is hesitant to do any restoration, since it is also a gravesite.

In 2021 park officials unveiled a new bronze statue of King Kaumuali'i, and the following year, the state officially changed the park's name to Pā'ula'ula State Historic Site. The change was lamented by the Russian community, but lauded by others as an important and overdue measure to preserve and promote the native Hawaiian connection to the site.

By contrast, Fort Ross in Northern California was occupied by Russians and their descendants for nearly thirty years, from its founding in 1812 until its sale in 1841. The state of California purchased the fort for preservation and restoration in 1903. Nowadays, Fort Ross is a California State Historic Park, while the nonprofit Fort Ross Conservancy supports activities and programming at the site and in the surrounding parklands. The Fort Ross Conservancy also maintains a library and archives, collaborates with researchers, and undertakes archeological investigations on the site.

The fort contains the restored Rotchev House (original from the Russian period) as well as half a dozen other buildings that have been re-created based on archeological findings and archival research.

The story of Fort Ross is not only a Russian story but also one of Native Alaskans (Unangan) who lived there and Californians (Kashia Pomo) who inhabited the surrounding land. The Fort Ross Cultural Trail explores the site history from the perspective of all these peoples, using the voices of their descendants to tell their stories.

The Kashia Band of Pomo Indians were the original inhabitants of this area, which they called Metini. After the departure of the Russians in the nineteenth century, the US government forced the Kashia to move inland to a reservation. They lost all but forty acres of their homeland and—most devastating—they lost access to the coast.

But in 2015, after 150 years, the Kashia Band reclaimed nearly seven hundred acres of coastal land just north of Fort Ross—a piece of land with "dense redwood forest, towering coastal bluffs and waterfalls, and expansive views of the Pacific Ocean." In a groundbreaking deal, California landowners sold the one-mile strip to the Trust for Public Land, who then restored ownership to the Indigenous group in the form of the Kashia Coastal Reserve. The Kashia Pomo, for their part, pledged to maintain the land as a demonstration forest, protecting it from development. They have also agreed to allow the California Coastal Trail to cut through the property, granting public access to the stunning coastline.

"This is not just a piece of land to us," said one Kashia Band member. "It's family. If you don't know your cultural history, your language, your land, you lose your identity. This property brings us back home."

CHAPTER 13
On the Brink of Extinction

W hat sustains a nation? Wealth and arms, but not only those. The vitality of a nation, of a people, requires more. It requires a viable homeland, an environment that provides sustenance, shelter, and sense of belonging. It requires good health—vigorous individuals who regenerate the collective body. And, it requires a deep-rooted culture, a shared sense of identity, and sanctity of beliefs that connects the individual to the larger group. A sustainable nation is an organic whole.

The encounters between imperialist Europe and Indigenous America played out in a familiar fashion across the continent. The cohesiveness and vitality of an Indigenous people were worn down by a cascade of crises, which undermined the environmental, physical, and spiritual supports of the community. Even the nations that waged robust resistance campaigns against colonization eventually succumbed to the relentless assaults of coercion and disease. Displaced, dispirited, and disoriented, Indigenous peoples and their cultures were decimated across North America. In the early 1800s the Tlingit battled the Russians to a stalemate and tenuous coexistence. But in the ensuing years, this same cascade of crises threatened the sustainability of the Tlingit, too, pushing the nation to the brink of extinction.

In 1829 the Russian brig *Baikal* sailed into Sitka Sound, returning from an extended hunt and trade mission along the California coast. The crew unloaded barrels of grain, kegs of salt, and one bundle of sixty-three sea otter pelts. Four hundred fewer skins than the *Baikal* had delivered two years earlier, and 4,500 fewer than the *O'Cain* brought back from California two decades earlier. The soft gold rush was over.

It took three quarters of a century for human predation to push the sea otter to the edge of extinction. In the mid-eighteenth century this marine mammal thrived all along the semicircular perimeter of the North Pacific. But after the survivors of Vitus Bering's expedition returned to Russia in 1742, a hunting frenzy ensued. By the 1760s, the sea otter was systematically annihilated in the Far East, on the Kuril Islands, the Kamchatka Peninsula, and the Commander Islands. Russian hunters then turned eastward. By the 1790s, Russian subjugation of Aleut and Alutiiq baidarka hunters hastened the demise of the sea otter colonies of the Aleutian Islands and the Gulf of Alaska. At this point, the publication of Captain Cook's travelogues set off a tsunami of British and American fortune seekers, directly competing with Russian trappers in the North Pacific. The abundant sea otter colonies of the northwest archipelago were wasted in less than two decades. Before 1820, the last of the big hunts were conducted by Russian-American joint ventures down the California coastline.

The sea otters were defenseless against the onslaught. Mature females and young pups were easy targets, leaving behind small rafts of otters insufficient to regenerate the colonies. A witness to the hunts, Russian naval officer Gavril Davydov, described a favorite tactic: "The females love their pups dearly. They carry the little ones on their backs and fetch seaweed and shellfish for them from the seabed. When hunters see a female with her pup, they try to catch the latter. At first the mother dives, but after she swims to the baidarka and looks pityingly at the taken pup. Then she is killed too."

Between 1743 and 1823 Russian ships recorded the sale of over two hundred thousand sea otter skins. American, British, and French fur traders added another six hundred thousand pelts in recorded transactions, more than half of which were sold in Canton. In some locations, such as Haida Gwaii and Baja California, sea otters became extinct. During the heyday of the global fur trade, more than a million sea otters were culled from the waters of the North Pacific.

As the sea otter declined, Russian fur traders wreaked havoc on other species. The sleek hide of the northern fur seal was coveted almost as much as the sea otter. Between 1799 and 1829 the Russian-American Company collected more than seven hundred thousand fur seal skins from clubbing raids on remote island rookeries. More than two million northern fur seals were slaughtered before the mid-nineteenth century. By 1821, the company had traded over one hundred thousand fox furs, ninety thousand beavers and beaver tails, and sixty thousand pounds of walrus tusks. The decimation of the herds eventually prompted Russian efforts to regulate hunting in hope of reviving the marine mammal bounty. In 1823 the colonial governor in Sitka imposed a ban on sea otter hunting in the inner archipelago, and in 1834 another ban was enacted on fur seal hunting in the Pribilof Islands. Meanwhile, ever-resourceful merchants found another commodity to swap in Canton. Gentlemen Brits and pious New Englanders became the main suppliers of the illicit opium trade, grown in India and Turkey. The staunch resistance of the Chinese emperor to Anglo-American opium smuggling incited a series of disastrous wars for the ill-fated Qing dynasty.

The Pacific fur trade undermined the Tlingit nation, beginning with the environment. The sea otter is a "keystone" species. The relentless pursuit of sea otter eroded the coastal ecosystem, causing the deterioration of the kelp forests in and around the archipelago. The dispersal of sea mammals, shellfish, and rockfish made hunting more difficult and dangerous for the Tlingit, who were forced to travel further distances on open water in search of prey. Like the Indigenous nations of the American hinterland, the Tlingit were forced to endure the intrusion of outsiders, who transformed their environment. American westward expansion ravaged the vast bison herds of the plains on a scale comparable to the devastation of the sea otter colonies of the North Pacific. Unlike the Comanche and the Sioux, however, the Tlingit did not depend on the sea otter for subsistence. The staple food of the Tlingit was salmon. And despite the degradation of the kelp forests, the annual salmon migrations and harvests were not disrupted.

The global fur trade also transformed the Tlingit economy. By the 1790s, rarely a month went by without the arrival of at least one tall ship cruising for fur. The goods offered in exchange, especially guns and clothing, became high-status consumables. The Tlingit came to expect these trade visits and adjusted their routines accordingly. Previously, sea otter hunting was a low priority task. An individual would go out with bow and arrow, conceal himself in a blind or behind rocks, and wait for an otter to come ashore. The skinned and dressed pelt was likely used as an adornment on clothing or a warm coverlet. But with the arrival of the foreign traders, hunting took on greater significance. It became a more organized and intensive endeavor, traveling in boats on extended outings across the archipelago. The Tlingit adopted the Aleut team-hunting tactic of encircling their quarry in open water. Hunting skills evolved from dexterity with arrows and spears to marksmanship with a rifle. The motive was no longer personal consumption, but rather surplus accumulation.

The maritime fur trade upset the balance between collective and individual property rights in Tlingit villages. Salmon fishing, for example, was always a collective enterprise. The village as a whole participated in the labor-intensive gathering and drying tasks, then subsisted on the shared bounty during the winter months. It reflected a collective survival strategy, shaped over time by the natural environment. Fur hunting and processing, by contrast, was an individual activity. The dressed pelt was a personal accessory, and the property of an individual member of a household. Traditionally, the ownership rights of fur had little effect on inter-household relations. Within a village, the status of a household was based on its size and its clan ancestry. Social differences were kept in check by the potlatch gift-exchange economy.

But the onset of the fur trade impacted the traditional social order. Collectivist norms gradually weakened, and individual wealth became a source of rank and power. Russian monk Veniaminov observed that "one chieftain's son began to trade with just several beaver skins, and in the course of three to four years obtained eight slaves, an excellent boat, a wife, several guns, and numerous other items. In a word, he became a rich man." Because of the fur trade, Tlingit villages became more stratified by wealth and hierarchy. The new opportunities for personal reward clashed with social customs, kin relations, and clan cohesion.

With the end of the global fur trade, in the latter half of the nineteenth century, these social and economic changes impelled many Tlingit to abandon the traditional economy and seek employment as individual laborers for mining operations, steamships, and fish canneries. Village sustainability and collectivist survival strategies passed out of existence across the Tlingit homeland.

In the clash between imperial Europe and Indigenous America, the most decisive factor was not the Old World's weapons, wits, or gods, but its germs. The comingling of long-isolated peoples caused an intercontinental transfer of infectious disease. In the so-called Columbian Exchange, the Americas received smallpox, measles, and the flu, while Europe received a lasting case of syphilis. Early Spanish encounters with Mesoamerica were followed by devastating outbreaks of smallpox. Prosperous and powerful civilizations were infiltrated by bacteria and viruses of pandemic proportion, undermining their physical capacity to repel conquistador assaults. Similarly, in North America, a smallpox plague decimated coastal communities in southern New England, creating the opportunity for English religious separatists to found a small colony, which would later launch an ethnic-cleansing crusade against its Native hosts. For the next two centuries, the pattern was replicated again and again, as sodbusters and freebooters moved west, depopulating and dispossessing the Native residents they met along the way.

In 1786 Grigory Shelikhov remarked on the hardiness of the Alutiiq people: "They do not have the common diseases. They have not ever had smallpox. The people are basically of strong constitution and live to the age of 100 years." As Russian fur trappers moved eastward, they brought the "common" diseases with them, including smallpox, to all the peoples of the Aleutians and southern Alaska. In the Tlingit homeland, however, the pathway of lethal infection was from the south. It was not the Russians, but the Spanish who introduced smallpox to the Tlingit, during the 1770s epidemic that ravaged Native communities from Tillamook to Sitka.

In August 1787 HMS *King George* sailed passed Mount Edgecumbe into Sitka Sound. Commander Nathaniel Portlock, a veteran of Captain Cook's third voyage, entertained boatloads of curious Tlingit with ship tours and spruce beer, while accumulating a stash of sea otter skins. The curious captain accepted an invitation to travel upriver to visit a Tlingit village. "I went in the whaleboat with one of the young Indians. We arrived at the habitation about noon. On the beach was a large boat, capable of holding thirty persons, and three more of smaller size. I expected to see a numerous tribe, but was quite surprised to find that there were only three men, three women, five girls and boys, and two infants." The lack of occupants, Portlock learned, was due to smallpox.

"I observed the oldest of the men to be very much marked with the smallpox, as was a girl about fourteen years old," Portlock said. "The old man described the excessive torments he endured and gave me to understand that it had happened some years ago. The distemper had carried off great numbers of the inhabitants and he himself had lost ten children, marked by ten strokes tattooed on his arm. I did not observe any of the children under twelve that were scarred. Therefore, I have reason to suppose that the disorder raged little more than that number of years ago. As the Spaniards were on this part of the coast in 1775, it is very probable that it was from them that these poor wretches caught the fatal infection." As the *King George* sailed on, Portlock's supposition was confirmed: "A number of Indians who visited us from the east were marked with the smallpox, but none from the west had the least traces of it."

By the time Alexander Baranov established a Russian colony at Sitka in 1799, the Tlingit had recovered. Good health, no doubt, was a crucial factor in explaining how the resilient Sitka clans fought the Russians to a stalemate in their three-year war. Still, the Tlingit were knowledgeable and fearful of the disease. Saiginakh remembered when he was "a small child an epidemic of smallpox that spread from Stikine to Sitka (the 1770s epidemic) and left only one or two persons in each family." The Tlingit avoided another outbreak for more than a half century. In the early 1830s, Dr. Eduard Blaschke, the Russian colony's chief medical officer, observed that "the Tlingit are toughened by their continuous outdoor existence in the fresh air and repeated bathing in the sea. They rarely fall victim to illness, but are robust and healthy, often living to advanced age."

In November 1835, two weeks after a British trader weighed anchor, several people in the Tlingit settlement fell ill. It started with a headache and fatigue, followed by a fever and body aches. Hot tea made from devil's club was served. After a few days, an abnormal red spot was observed on the mouth. Within twenty-four hours, more spots appeared on the face and arms. Alarm spread through the village. A crimson rash, an unrelenting itch, and burning pain spread over the entire body. Bathing lotion made from highbush cranberry was applied. The red spots turned into clear blisters, then oozing pustules, then withered scabs, gouging the skin with pockmarks. The dread had returned.

In the late 1830s, a second smallpox plague descended over the Northwest Coast, from the Columbia River to the Yukon. The busy port of New

Archangel was hit hard. Traditional remedies and medicinal plants were applied, but the virus was indomitable. In Sitka as many as four hundred villagers perished by the end of spring in 1836—almost half the population of the settlement next to the fort. The scourge spread through the archipelago. It nearly annihilated the Tlingit community at Khutsnov. It moved up the coast, striking the Alutiiq and Aleut peoples in the north. The virus waned in the summer months, when families dispersed, and waxed in the winter, when they congregated in big houses. For five years, the "Great Death" stalked the Indigenous people of southeast Alaska.

"This illness was brought to us by the raven as a punishment for our endless wars," Saiginakh said of the 1770s epidemic. It was presumed that a disease so pitiless must emanate from malicious intent. The shaman was summoned. Not so much to heal, but to determine the source of the misery and foretell the fate of the stricken. Clan elders and family heads gathered around the seer, who pointed to the Russian fort. In fact, the disease first appeared among the inhabitants of New Archangel, where fourteen Creoles fell ill and died, following the visit of the British trader.

Living in close proximity to the Russian compound, the Tlingit witnessed the disease's impact on the other side of the stockade. Smallpox caused fewer deaths among the Russians and Creoles, who were either unaffected or recovered quickly. Russia was at the forefront of European public health efforts to eradicate smallpox, after Catherine the Great launched an empire-wide vaccination campaign. By the 1830s, most of the Russians and some of the Creoles were vaccinated. The Russian colony had a full-time medical doctor on site, supplied with a stock of smallpox vaccine. The colonial governor made a genuine effort to share the vaccine with the Tlingit, but the level of distrust was high. Only a small minority of Sitka Tlingit submitted to the Russian cure.

The everyday routines that sustain a healthy community were neglected—food gathering and preparation, fertility and child-rearing, socializing and trading. The deaths occurred over a half decade, but the impact was long lasting. At the beginning of the 1830s, the Tlingit population of southeast Alaska was estimated at 10,000 people. The smallpox scourge slashed the population by forty percent, to roughly 6,000 people. A generation later, in 1860, the community was estimated at roughly 7,500 people, having regained less than half of its losses.

The epidemic's toll weighed heaviest on elders, including headmen and shamans. The elders were the authorities in community affairs and the keepers of accumulated knowledge. The sudden demise of this cohort created a void in the life of the clans. The legitimacy of Tlingit social order was shaken, as the vitality of Tlingit nation was diminished.

⚭

"I commend to you and your workers, the Archpriest Ioasaph and his monks, chosen by Her Majesty to preach God's word in America," Grigory Shelikhov informed his company director on Kodiak Island. To gain royal backing, Shelikhov pitched Catherine the Great with the notion that his venture was not just about gathering furs but also about gathering souls. The tsarina responded by issuing to the colony a dual mandate to pursue both commerce and conversion. Given the makeup of the colonists, these twin tasks were not easily reconciled.

In 1793 Empress Catherine instructed the abbot of the Valaam Monastery to recruit eight clerics for missionary work in Alaska. Led by the future bishop of America, Father Ioasaph, the holy octet arrived a year later at the settlement on Kodiak, now under the care of Alexander Baranov. The monk and the merchant clashed immediately. "I am concerned about the French spirit of freedom that agitates here," the archpriest frothed. "Not only are the barracks full of loose women, but they have gatherings and games and dancing all night long. This goes on every Sunday. And Baranov calls himself a Christian!" Accustomed to the starchy deference of aristocratic Russia, Ioasaph was appalled by the bawdy manners of the frontier. He placed the blame squarely on the company director, and tried to wheedle his dismissal. "Baranov's men are not ashamed. They ridicule the rules of the church, and they curse and argue with me. I suggest you send someone else here with managerial skills. Afterwards, with God's help, I may be able to restore order."

It was true that Baranov was not a religious man. His limited resources went into the business, not the mission. When the Valaam monks arrived in Kodiak, there was no church building, as had been promised. "I have seen nothing done to carry out your good intentions," Ioasaph complained to Shelikhov. "I asked Alexander Andreevich to give us some canvas for a tent to have a travelling church, but he would not do it." Pressed to respond to these charges, Baranov wryly noted that "when the Father Priest arrived, he found at my place his favorite sweet brandy."

In October 1799, having just been elevated to the rank of bishop, Father Ioasaph boarded the *Phoenix* in Okhotsk for a triumphant return to Kodiak. The vessel never arrived. Upon the spring tides, crates of church candles, ecclesiastical vestments, and leather-bound bibles washed up on the island's western shore. Father Ioasaph and retinue had perished, and the Russian Orthodox mission in America was curtailed. The same year, Baranov relocated the colonial capital to Sitka. His attention remained focused on profits. The Russians had their priests and the Tlingit had their shamans. Baranov did not care to upset the balance.

In a Tlingit worldview, the material and spirit worlds are interwoven and interactive. Everything in the material world, animate and inanimate, has a spirit. The shaman's role was to serve as mediator between the two realms. It was a male-dominated, family-inherited occupation, the secrets of the spirit realm passed down from fathers to sons. A novice underwent a long apprenticeship, enduring isolation and deprivation, deep in the rainforest. The trainee learned to commune with the spiritual forces that animated throughout the natural world and capture their essential qualities with ceremonial regalia, such as a bear-claw necklace or an otter-tongue amulet.

Shamans never cut their hair, which was a source of their mystic power. Every Tlingit clan had a shaman as spiritual counselor to foresee future occurrences, detect unseen spirits, and uncover their motives. Respected and feared as much as the warrior elite, shamans were consulted by clan leaders on the most crucial matters.

The 1830s smallpox epidemic tested the authority of the shaman. They attended the sick and performed cleansing rituals, but could not stop the disease from spreading. The shamans were directly exposed to the virus and put into mortal danger themselves. As the disease persisted, the Tlingit gradually became more accepting of Russian medicine. For a people long certain of their cultural superiority, the epidemic effectively weakened the spiritual underpinnings of Tlingit society. Coinciding with the smallpox plague, the Russians launched a new conversion campaign. This time led by a most remarkable evangelist.

Father Veniaminov was a native Siberian and first in his class at the Russian Orthodox seminary in Irkutsk. In 1824 the bright young deacon answered the call to bring the Divine Liturgy to the people of Alaska. Veniaminov spent the next ten years spreading the Russian Orthodox faith to Russian settlers and Indigenous people, traveling by baidarka throughout the Aleutian Islands and Kodiak. He immersed himself in the local cultures and languages, winning many converts along the way. In 1834 Veniaminov was reassigned to the parish of New Archangel, where piety was in short supply. He got to work on a new church, Saint Michael's Cathedral, which became the first Russian Orthodox cathedral in the New World.

By all accounts, Veniaminov was a charismatic personality, captivating storyteller, and persuasive orator. He did not wield power or pretense to win friends and influence people, but rather he showed an interest in who they were and what they thought. In Sitka Veniaminov studied Tlingit language and customs, traveled around the archipelago, and conducted a census of the nation. His reputation grew in America and in Russia. He was ordained the bishop of Kamchatka, the Kuril Islands, and Russian America, taking the name Innokenty. Eventually, he was promoted to the center of ecclesiastical power as metropolitan of Moscow. Almost a hundred years after his death, he was canonized by the Russian Orthodox Church—Saint Innokenty, the Apostle of America.

By the end of the 1830s, Veniaminov was encouraged that the social and institutional conditions were in place for Russian Orthodoxy to take root among the Tlingit. He did not boast high conversion numbers to impress Russian officialdom. He knew that most previous baptismal ceremonies in Sitka had less to do with embracing Christianity and more to do with receiving gifts. But he earned the trust of some clan elders, who granted him the unusual privilege of an open invitation to their homes. "The intelligent conversations with the Tlingit at confession were always a comfort and joy for me." The Tlingit were wary of religious conversion, Veniaminov said, because they rightly associated Russian Orthodoxy with submission to Russian authority. "The Tlingit are independent and fearless. They believe that the Alutiit were once just as independent as they are, but baptism turned them into Russian slaves."

When he was called back to Russia, Veniaminov provided a summary of his work with the Sitka Tlingit. "At present there are only twenty baptized Tlingit, yet they fulfill their Church duties very well. They go to church whenever they are able, they fast, and they willingly listen to sermons. Not one of them has returned to the rites of his former belief." Notably, this select group included several young nephews, in line to become the future headmen in the elite family households. Veniaminov's optimism about the long-term prospects of conversion were not misplaced. By the time of his death in 1879, Russian Orthodox baptisms had become common.

Paradoxically, it was not until after the Russians ceded Alaska to the United States that the Tlingit turned to Russian Orthodoxy in greater numbers. Perhaps it was a reaction against the heavy-handed efforts of the proselytizing Presbyterian newcomers. Or perhaps it was the influence of Father Donskoi, a young Russian Orthodox priest who arrived in the

1880s. Donskoi tolerated hybrid adaptations of Russian Orthodox practice and Tlingit sensibility. He participated in Tlingit memorial feasts and traditional ceremonies, which was considered a show of honor and respect. He utilized holy water, crosses, and icons to bless and heal believers—a comforting practice for a people who attributed value and power to sacred items. He even incorporated songs and prayers in the Tlingit language into the church services. Anthropologist Sergei Kan explained, "In contrast to the Presbyterians, the Russian clergy was not only somewhat more tolerant of the 'old customs' but also simply too weak politically and too small in numbers to do much about them, except occasionally voicing its disapproval of the most blatant manifestations of 'heathenism.'" By the end of the nineteenth century, traditional shamanism among the Tlingit had become a minority faith.

Similar to the experience of other Indigenous peoples in North America, foreign invaders systematically undermined the environment, health, and spirituality of Tlingit nation. But Tlingit resistance remained formidable, and Russian pressure was not as direct or as intense as what many other Native American peoples encountered. As such, while the Tlingit way of life was under strain, traditional survival strategies, social relations, and cultural practices endured well past the midpoint of the nineteenth century. Ultimately, it was not the Russians who pushed the Tlingit to the brink of extinction. Rather, it was Russia's most tenacious rival in the Pacific Northwest, the United States, who brought more resources, purpose, and acrimony to the challenge of breaking Tlingit nation.

THE LEGACY OF LOUIS SHOTRIDGE

In the early twentieth century, the Tlingit and other Native American groups struggled to hang on to their culture and at the same time adapt to a changing world. Nobody was more aware of this challenge than Louis Shotridge, son of a prestigious Tlingit family, who went on to become an accomplished anthropologist. Louis belonged to the Killer Whale Fin House of the Kaagwaantaan clan, while his father was house leader of the powerful Whale House in the Gaanaxteidí clan. He married Florence Skundoo, daughter of a prominent shaman from Lukaax.ádi clan. He was a practicing Christian and a student at the Wharton School. But he recognized that his own culture—his birthright—was in grave danger of disappearing, not only from active practice but also from the historical record. In 1923 he wrote, "It is clear now that unless someone goes to work to record our history in the English language and place these old things as evidence, the noble idea of our forefathers shall be entirely lost." So he set out to do just that.

Louis Shotridge ended up working for the University of Pennsylvania Museum of Archaeology and Anthropology (now the Penn Museum). Initially, his main role was to assess new pieces for acquisition by the museum. Eventually, he organized expeditions to Alaska to study the Native cultures and to acquire additional items for the museum collection.

Over the course of two decades, Shotridge procured hundreds of utilitarian and ceremonial objects, most of which were of Tlingit origin. He purchased items from families who had converted to Christianity and/or moved to the city, so they no longer used them. He purchased items from clan elders who feared the younger generation would not care for them, and he purchased items from families who were desperate for money. In all cases, he promised to safeguard the items at the museum. And so he did, packing up and shipping out some 570 objects from Alaska back to Philadelphia.

After his father's death, Shotridge even tried to acquire artifacts from the Whale House, arguing that they would "stand as evidence of the Tlingit claim of a place in primitive culture." But his uncle refused his offer and Shotridge's insistence caused a rift in the relationship.

Shotridge was a controversial figure in the Tlingit community, to say the least, considering he facilitated the removal of so much cultural heritage from his homeland. Yet he did so with the goal of preserving the objects and the culture. To this end, Shotridge also took hundreds of photographs of daily life and did extensive research on the origins of Tlingit peoples and clan names. This was all in preparation for a comprehensive book on Tlingit culture—which he never completed due to his unexpected dismissal from the museum and unfortunate early death.

In 2011 the Penn Museum launched the Louis Shotridge Digital Archive, which includes all of the scholar's publications, notes, photographs, and recordings, as well as images of the objects that he acquired for the museum. This is one of the most extensive and best-documented Tlingit collections in the world—now available for students and scholars as well as the Tlingit community.

Shotridge's methods were controversial, no doubt, but his motives were pure. And, arguably, the digital archive goes a long way toward fulfilling his goal—preserving this valuable history for future generations of scholars and Tlingit culture-keepers.

CHAPTER 14

Once and Future Rivals

"The colonies have told England goodbye forever," the empress beamed. Holding court in her glittering Winter Palace in St. Petersburg, Catherine the Great received the news of Jefferson's Declaration of Independence. She could not conceal her delight—a blow against Britain was a boost for Russia.

As King George III fumbled to put down the American mutineer ingrates, he sought help from his fellow monarchs divine. It was reasonable for George to assume that Catherine would want to supply him twenty thousand infantry troops to fight alongside his redcoat regulars. She was, after all, an unabashed autocrat and staunch opponent of revolution. Meanwhile, General George Washington hoped that the Russian empress might favor the American cause. Catherine was a proud patron of the freethinking philosophes, and always eager to show off her enlightened side. The Continental Congress dispatched diplomat Francis Dana to St. Petersburg, seeking Russian support for their independence bid. Mostly, the empress was befuddled by the conflict, which she blamed on British mismanagement. "I wish with all my heart that my friends the English would get along with their colonies."

In the end, Catherine disappointed both Georges. She came up with excuses to decline the king's request for a regiment or two, saying that her army was too exhausted from its recent string of battlefield victories against the Turks. "I am only now beginning to enjoy the peace, and Your Majesty

will know that my empire needs repose." Meanwhile, the tsarina was careful
not to confer diplomatic status on any American until a proper peace was
concluded. She kept would-be ambassador Dana waiting for an audience
for two years before he finally took the hint and went home.

Instead, Catherine famously declared that Russia was neutral. Accordingly, nonaligned ships freely traded with either of the belligerents, as long
as they were not trafficking war materials. Holland, Denmark, and Sweden
liked the idea, and joined with the empress to form a neutrality league. By
not choosing sides, Catherine was indirectly supporting the Americans.
"We are not just a little pleased," said George Washington, "to find that
the solicitations of the Court of Great Britain to the Empress of Russia
have been rejected with disdain." Catherine's declaration of neutrality,
Washington said, "humbled the pride and power of the British navy."

The empress, however, was not completely sold on the American political
experiment. She withheld recognition of American statehood and forbade
the dissemination of the Declaration of Independence in her realm. Nonetheless, its author, Thomas Jefferson, still described Russia as "the power
most friendly to America." Russian society was intrigued by American
events and personalities who had so boldly stood up to Great Britain. The
best-known American was Benjamin Franklin, who—as scientist-inventor,
master raconteur, and incorrigible flirt—set aflutter the European salon
scene in the 1780s. One highbrow Russian gazette predicted that Poor
Richard "will be revered as a god in several centuries. While electricity is
transforming all physics, the English colonies are transforming all politics."
In 1789 Franklin was the first American elected to membership in the
Russian Academy of Science.

The United States and Imperial Russia did not establish formal relations
until the reign of Alexander I, Catherine's charmer grandson, who was even
more of a flirt than Franklin. In 1809 the American brig *Horace* arrived
in St. Petersburg, carrying the young republic's first official envoy, John
Quincy Adams, along with his wife Louisa and two-year-old son Charles

Frances. "I am so glad that you are here," the tsar greeted Adams. The frugal Yankee was forever flustered by Russia's over-the-top aristocrats. Keeping up with the pomp almost consumed the Adams family fortune. Still, John Quincy and Tsar Alexander struck up a warm acquaintanceship, in French, the language of the Russian gentry. In the evenings, the pair could be seen strolling the banks of the Neva in cordial conversation. Britain's jealous foreign minister, Lord Castlereagh, sniped that "the Emperor of Russia is half an American."

The main issue in Russian-American relations at this time was commerce. In the ambassador's first year, more than two hundred American ships called in Russian ports. Russia grew so dependent on American shipping that the tsar issued a special decree welcoming Yankee traders in defiance of Napoleon's attempt to blockade the continent. When Russia went to war against the bellicose Bonaparte, the United States returned Catherine's favor by declaring itself neutral in the conflict. At the turn of the nineteenth century, Russia and the United States were on good terms from the perspective of high politics, but relations were less amicable from the vantage point of the Pacific Northwest.

—⁂—

It was "the dawn of bright prospects," John Ledyard said. The Connecticut-born sea rover had figured out how a Yankee merchant could get rich in the Pacific fur trade. Ledyard served as a marine with Captain James Cook aboard the HMS *Resolution*. When he returned home in 1783, Ledyard began chatting up investors for an American venture to the North Pacific. But his scheme to exchange Native-gathered furs for Chinese-made goods frightened Wall Street's cautious traders. The persistent Ledyard finally got a sniff from Robert Morris, the Philadelphia financier and signee to the Declaration of Independence.

Ledyard brimmed with optimism. "The Honourable Robert Morris has disposed to give me a ship to go to the North Pacific Ocean. He instantly took to my ideas, and I am now drawing up the details of a plan for the greatest commercial enterprise that has ever been embarked on in this country. If the affair is concluded, as I expect it will be, then I will set off for New England to procure a crew of Yankee sailors." Alas, Ledyard would not lead America's first trade mission to the Pacific. With too many debts to juggle, Morris passed on the project. Frustrated by the short-sightedness and stinginess of his countrymen, Ledyard departed for Paris and new adventures, though not before sharing his idea with some Bay State businessmen.

The protagonists of rebellion, Boston's merchants had much to celebrate, having won their liberty from the insufferable King George. Unfortunately, political gain came with economic loss. The once well-to-do entrepreneurs were now shut out of their old trade markets in the West Indies and United Kingdom. With the end of wartime privateering, the shops aligning Merchant Row were quiet, while the sloops clinging to Long Wharf were idle. But if Ledyard was right, then prosperity beckoned on the other side of the world.

New England shipyards turned out trim sailing crafts with copper-plated hulls that could swiftly cross vast stretches of open ocean and could safely maneuver the narrow passages of the northwest archipelago. More daring and desperate than their New York counterparts, Massachusetts traders were "distinguished by a lively imagination and a general spirit of adventure," according to historian Samuel Eliot Morison. The "Boston Men" would expand the limits of American enterprise into the North Pacific, a harbinger of the empire to come.

Amid the lush gardens of his Summer Street mansion, Boston merchant Joseph Barrell was studying a newly published memoir just arrived from London. Captain Cook's *A Voyage to the Pacific Ocean* was a late eighteenth-century bestseller on both sides of the Atlantic. Everything Ledyard had been spouting about the fur trade was confirmed. Barrell was ready to invest. He enticed fourteen backers, at $3,500 per share, including famed architect Charles Bulfinch, Revolutionary War veteran Captain Robert Gray, Boston Tea Party accomplice John Kendrick, and an expert furrier. He bought and refitted two vessels, the three-masted square-rig *Columbia* as flagship and the sloop *Lady Washington* as tender. In September 1787 the historic voyage departed Boston Harbor.

Two years later the Yankee traders reached the Pacific Northwest and encountered the Tlingit. For two months they engaged the coastal villages, trading blankets, knives, and iron bars for sea otter, fur seal, and beaver pelts. Captain Gray then headed west to Canton, where his lush cargo was exchanged for Chinese tea. In August 1790 the *Columbia* issued a thirteen-cannon salute, announcing its return to Boston Harbor. John Ledyard's far-fetched Pacific project had been realized. The *Columbia*'s homecoming marked the first American circumnavigation of the globe and the dawn of a new era in maritime trade.

At the same time that the *Columbia* was en route to Alaska, Ledyard found himself embroiled in troubles of his own making. Ledyard's next big idea turned out to be an overland journey of discovery, traversing the Eurasian and North American interiors. The ambitious adventure seemed ludicrous to Empress Catherine, who suspected that Ledyard was a French spy. Having departed St. Petersburg without Her Majesty's permission, Ledyard was apprehended a year later in the middle of Siberia and deported back to Poland. "My ardent hopes are once more blasted," he wailed. It would not be the last time that impudent New Englanders provoked the empress.

"Coats of arms should be made and hung from the trees along the shores to show the people disembarking from vessels that these parts belong to the Empire of Her Majesty," protested Nikita Panin, Empress Catherine's foreign minister. When Russia first settled in North America, England

and Spain posed the greatest threat to the undertaking. But it was not long before the independent United States provided the colony's most nettlesome callers.

Even before the Tlingit annihilated Fort Saint Michael, the Russians were alarmed by the New Englanders' readiness to swap guns for furs. "I have told the Americans many times that they should not sell firearms and powder to the natives," Alexander Baranov said. "This trade is dangerous for them, but more harmful for us who have settled here. I told them but they paid no attention." Baranov's appeals to moral principle and personal safety were lost on those whose fortunes were built on slaving and smuggling. So rich were the returns from the Pacific fur trade—as much as 500 percent on the investment—that the Boston men rebuffed the governor's warnings. "We are traders, sailing fifteen thousand nautical miles in search of profits," they scoffed. "No one has told us that such trading is prohibited." The flouting of Russian claims incensed Empress Catherine, who ordered her envoy in Paris to take up the matter with Benjamin Franklin.

The Russians were convinced that the Boston men were to blame for setting the Tlingit on their rampage in 1802. Ivan Kuskov reported to Baranov shortly after the attack on Fort Saint Michael. "Chief Tykin at Khootsnov village distributed lots of powder, ammunition, and several big cannons to the other chieftains. He received arms from the English and the Republican Americans who have been trading along the coast. Men from an American vessel wintered at the Khootsnov village. They told the natives that unless they destroyed our fort and our hunting party, the Tlingit would become the losers in the fur trade. These traders are very greedy." And Nikolai Rezanov insisted that "The Tlingit are armed by the Bostonians with the very best guns and pistols, and have falconets too. We are in great anxiety as to the safety of our hunting parties."

Later, when Russia and the United States established diplomatic relations, the Boston men were at the top of the agenda. Tsar Alexander instructed his first ambassador to the United States, Andrei Dashkov, "to use arguments based on law and friendship" to impress upon the president that the "safety of the subjects of His Imperial Majesty was being threatened" by a willful disregard for Russian sovereignty. Specifically, he insisted that the New England merchants must trade with the Russian American colony, rather than the Tlingit. The assignment proved more difficult than Alexander supposed. "The freedom of commerce in the United States is almost unlimited," Dashkov wrote to the tsar. "The Americans load their ships with forbidden military goods and announce their destination as they wish." Moreover, whenever Dashkov raised the issue, the US response was to suggest fixing a boundary between Russian and American territorial claims along the Northwest Coast. Alexander, however, was reluctant to endorse any agreement that restrained Russia's southward advance. The tsar still hoped to fulfill Peter the Great's vision of a Russian empire in Northern California.

It was not the case that the Russian American colony wished to expel the Yankee traders. The New Englanders brought valuable goods and food to the neglected settlement and their ships provided reliable transportation. More importantly, the Americans were licensed to do business in Canton, and the Russians were not. Rather, Russia's goal was to force the Boston men to recognize the tsar's sovereignty in the region and conduct business through the colony. If only New Archangel could be transformed into a maritime commercial hub, Nikolai Rezanov said, the problem would be solved. "When we have more shipyards and ships and warehouses, our fur trade will increase and the Bostonians will have fewer opportunities to trade with the natives. Now they are harmful to us, but when they can no longer trade with the natives, they will be obliged to engage us in trade. When our company becomes stronger, the Bostonians will come here willingly to avoid the risks of long sea voyages, savages, and pirates."

Rezanov's hope that Yankee traders would become more cooperative with the Russian American colony occurred sooner than expected. In

1812 both Russia and the United States were at war. In Europe, Napoleon marched his Grande Armée all the way across the continent to Moscow; while in North America, Great Britain sought to avenge its humiliating loss to the upstart Americans. The Wars of 1812 brought Russia and America into geopolitical alignment.

———

War fever gripped the United States. Still chafing from defeat, the British bullied American commerce at sea and blocked western expansion on the continent. In June Congress voted to commence hostilities. President James Madison signed on, and Secretary of State James Monroe delivered the proclamation to the British ambassador. Gather the forces, harness the horses, America was going to war.

The news found Captain David Porter, commander of the naval frigate USS *Essex*, on the wrong side of a British blockade. Fearing capture, Porter decided "to pursue the course that seemed to me best calculated to injure the enemy." Tacking southward, the *Essex* launched a one-ship crusade against British commerce. The coy commander deceived his prey by pretending to be a wayward merchantman and running up British flags before unveiling his deadly cannons at close-range. The strategy was surprisingly effective. The *Essex* captured ten prizes before rounding Cape Horn, with the thirty-six-gun frigate HMS *Phoebe* and sloop of war HMS *Cherub* in pursuit.

Porter evaded capture for more than a year, as he wreaked havoc on British whalers in the Pacific. Finally, in March 1814, desperate for supplies, the *Essex* slipped into Valparaiso, Chile. While at anchor, the *Phoebe* and the *Cherub* cruised in and blocked its retreat. The outgunned skipper tried to fight his way out to sea. More than half of the 250 crew were killed before the surrender flag was raised. Porter was eventually given safe passage back to the United States, while the *Essex* was seized and turned into a prison ship for Irish rebels. The exploits of the *Essex* may have thrilled American patriots back east, but they terrified American merchants out west. The British navy had arrived in the Pacific, and Yankee traders were the prey.

Meanwhile, the Russian American colony had never seemed so isolated. Baranov's plan to expand the settlement by sea was a flop, not the least because of a lack of transport. His Alaskan shipyards produced vessels of dubious design, poor workmanship, and too few nails. The leaky crafts were no match for the petulant Pacific. The relationship between the Boston men and Russian settlers was never fixed. Agents of different realms, competitors for the same resources, they were inherently suspicious of one another. Sometimes rivals, sometimes allies, their rapport depended on circumstances. Now, circumstances dictated cooperation.

The Americans wanted to trade but needed protection; the Russians wanted to trade but needed ships. The solution was to form joint ventures. The vessels still operated with American captains, but sailed under a neutral Russian flag. The ships would collect furs and commodities from around the Pacific and conduct business in Canton. The profits would be split. American ships also shuttled the colony's Alutiiq hunters down the California coastline. Boston-based Captain Thomas Meek was able to cram fifty-two baidarkas aboard the *Amethyst* on one such expedition that returned over seven hundred sea otter pelts.

Russia and America shared an interest in keeping Great Britain out of the North Pacific, which created further prospects for cooperation. By the 1810s, British traders had opened a new overland front in the fur trade, when the Hudson's Bay Company crossed the Canadian Rockies and pushed toward the coast. At the same time, a fierce American competitor moved up the Columbia River from the south. German immigrant John Jacob Astor was America's first multimillionaire. In 1808 he persuaded Thomas Jefferson to grant permission to his American Fur Company to establish a network of trading posts west of the Mississippi all the way to the Pacific. To secure claim over this coveted patch of wilderness, Astor surmised that Alexander Baranov might prove a useful ally. He sent an agent to New Archangel "with a proposition to the governor for the purpose of friendly intercourse and mutual benefit in trade."

Astor suggested that the two companies form an alliance with the aim of "removing all outsiders from commercial operations." The American Fur Company wanted to establish a trade post, Fort Astoria, at the mouth of the Columbia River. He promised not to encroach on Russian-claimed territories to the north and not to trade weapons with the Natives. Astor's company would provide New Archangel with food and manufactured goods as well as the means to sell Russian furs in Canton. In exchange, Astor wanted to be the exclusive American trader to the Russian colony and to gain entry into Russia's protected domestic fur market. He specifically asked for the right to sell "up to two thousand skins of bear, badger, and polecat free of duty" in Russia annually.

Baranov loved the idea. And, except for Astor's bid to access the Russian market, the tsar's ministers loved it too. "The combined efforts of the Russians and the Americans could remove from the seaboard all these undesirable neighbors." A flurry of high-level negotiations followed. Alas, Astor's vision of a Russian-American duopoly in the Pacific Northwest was not to be. The conspiracies of frontier merchant companies were no match for His Majesty's Royal Navy. Once the War of 1812 spilled into the Pacific, the British war sloop HMS *Racoon* chased the American Fur Company out of Fort Astoria. John Jacob had little choice but to cut his losses and sell his investment at a loss to the British.

Trying to balance relations between the two Anglo-speaking belligerents put Russia in an awkward position. Tsar Alexander made an earnest effort to mediate the conflict. The United States had started the war, hoping to gain in trade and territory, but after two years, neither goal was in sight. Meanwhile, Napoleon's defeat freed up Britain's vast military resources for redeployment to North America, which is why the tsar's offer to broker a peace suddenly appealed to the Americans. "Russia is the only power in Europe that commands respect from both France and England, and at this moment is at its zenith," President Madison said. "We are encouraged by the friendship of Emperor Alexander to render a favorable interposition." King George, however, demurred, and insisted on direct negotiations. The resulting Treaty of Ghent, signed on December 24, 1814, returned things to the prewar status quo, both in the Atlantic and the Pacific. The Boston men resumed their role as antagonist to the Russian American colony.

"The entire northwest coast of America from the Bering Strait to the fifty-first latitude is exclusively granted to Russian subjects. It is therefore prohibited to all foreign vessels not only to land on the coasts and islands belonging to Russia, but to approach them within less than a hundred Italian miles, subject to the confiscation of the transgressor's vessel and cargo," Tsar Alexander declared in September 1821. The imperial decree was as bold a claim as Russia had yet made on the American continent. And to show that he was serious, an American ship, the *Pearl*, was seized off the coast of Sitka a few months later.

When news of the emperor's edict reached the east coast, the reaction was swift and shrill. Captain William Sturgis, among the richest of Yankee merchants from the northwest fur trade, expressed the animus of New England's profit-driven patriots. "The claim to Russian sovereignty over the North Pacific and pretense of making it a closed sea is more unwarrantable than her other territorial usurpations. Nearly all of the sea otter skins are procured north of the 51st latitude. It will give Russia control of the China market. The august Emperor Alexander may choose next to annex California for his extensive dominions. He already has a considerable settlement at Port Bodega." Congressman Charles Ingersoll of Pennsylvania called Alexander's decree "an outrage," and urged President James Monroe to abandon "the policy of good understanding with Russia" and evict them "by force" from the northwest.

The task of crafting a reply fell on Secretary of State John Quincy Adams. Twelve years had passed since Adams served as ambassador to Tsar Alexander in St. Petersburg. And while Adams still valued Russia as a global friend, he too was jealous of American prerogative in the Western Hemisphere. "What right has Russia to any colonial footing in North America?" he said. "We should contest their right to any territories on the continent." Rather than enflame the dispute, Adams encouraged negotiations, believing that a mutually acceptable compromise could be found. He urged President Monroe to make a definitive public statement, which came in the 1823 State of the Union address.

"The occasion is proper for asserting a principle involving the rights and interests of the United States, that the American continents are henceforth not to be considered as subjects for future colonization by any European powers." The Monroe Doctrine is well-known as an assertion of hemispheric hegemony by the United States. What is less known is that the Monroe Doctrine was provoked by the threat of Russian territorial claims on the North American West Coast. Of course, both Russia and the United States were intent to restrain Great Britain as well. The flummoxed British Foreign Secretary George Canning reported to his government that "this apparently extravagant American doctrine is principally, if not specifically, directed against the no less extravagant doctrine of the Russian Ukase of 1821."

———

At the edge of empire, the world's two rising continental powers were on a collision course. Alas, diplomacy prevailed. In 1824 Russia and the United States signed a treaty in St. Petersburg, fixing the northwest border at the 54-40 line of latitude. In the interest of keeping the peace, the treaty made no mention of Fort Ross in California. The reserves of goodwill and mutual respect between Russia and the United States ran deep at this time. Tsar Alexander had once told Thomas Jefferson that "your nation has made its

independence most noble, by giving a wise constitution that assures the hap-
piness of all." Jefferson, in turn, praised Alexander, saying "a more virtuous
man does not exist." Adams was no less gushing, referring to the tsar as "the
Titus of our age and darling of the human race." Despite their outstanding
contrasts, Russia and the United States remained faithful allies throughout
the nineteenth century. Not until the twentieth century, when tsarist autoc-
racy fell to revolutionary socialism, did Russia and America become avowed
archenemies. The entrenched acrimony continues to this day.

Before relations between the two great powers turned inimical, the col-
lusions of Russia and the United States would have a profound effect on the
Tlingit nation. For more than half a century, the Tlingit had successfully
defied the predations of mighty tsarist Russia on their homeland and lifestyle. But in the second half of the nineteenth century, with the arrival of
the United States, the Tlingit would face a more implacable imperial foe.

ALASKA NATIVE BROTHERHOOD AND SISTERHOOD

After the legalistic United States gained control of Alaska, the Tlingit were systematically denied political, cultural, and economic rights under the new colonial regime. In 1912 the Alaska Native civil rights movement was born. A dozen individuals from various Indigenous tribes in Southeast Alaska—Tlingit, Haida, and Tsimshian—joined forces to form the Alaska Native Brotherhood (ANB), an activist organization with the aim of protecting Native rights and promoting Native solidarity. In 1914 they built the Alaska Native Brotherhood Hall on the Sitka waterfront, and in 1915 the counterpart Alaska Native Sisterhood (ANS) was formed. The main goal was to claim the rights of citizenship promised in the US Constitution and long-denied to Alaskan Natives.

The founding group were all graduates of the Sheldon Jackson School, a missionary school for the education and acculturation of Indigenous boys in Sitka. As such, the ANB founders were well-read, well-bred, and—significantly—members and leaders in their Presbyterian congregations. They worked to abolish "the old ways"—that is, Native culture and customs that their white teachers considered "uncivilized"— namely, their Native languages and the tradition of potlatch.

Around 1920, a change of leadership at the ANB inspired a shift in priorities. William Paul was Alaska's first Native American (Tlingit) attorney, and he recognized that the ANB could be a powerful tool for pursuing Native interests. Under his direction, the ANB began to advocate for change within the legal system, targeting specific policies that were impacting their members. Instead of promoting education in general, the ANB took a stand against the segregated "two-school system" in Alaska. They protested against the use of fishing traps by commercial fisheries—a practice that was ravaging the salmon stock. They continued to advocate for full citizenship for Indigenous Alaskans, which was granted by the Indian Citizenship Act of 1924. During this time, the ANB also changed its official stance toward traditional Native practices.

Native languages and potlatch ceremonies were no longer discouraged—a change that attracted many new members and allowed the organization to expand. By the 1930s, the ANB had representation in every Native village in Alaska.

In the following years, the Alaskan Native Brotherhood and Sisterhood led an anti-discrimination campaign across the state. They started by boycotting restaurants and theaters that restricted admission for Natives. Tlingit leaders Roy and Elizabeth Peratrovich (grand presidents of the ANB and ANS, respectively) introduced an anti-discrimination bill to the Alaska Senate. In 1945—nearly two decades before the federal Civil Rights Act of 1964—the legislature passed the Alaska Equal Rights Act, thanks in part to Elizabeth Peratrovich's impassioned testimony on the Senate floor.

As early as 1929, the ANB began supporting Native land claims—an effort that eventually (after statehood was granted in 1959) resulted in federal recognition of the Tlingit and Haida tribal claim to their homeland. Arguably, that landmark decision led to the Alaska Native Claims Settlement Act of 1971, which defines Alaska today.

In recent decades, the ANB has perhaps taken a back seat to other organizations, such as the Alaskan Federation of Natives. But the ANB's early activism was critical for defining and protecting the rights of Indigenous people in Alaska within the United States. "There can be no accounting of all the Alaska Natives that helped in the fight to protect aboriginal claims," according to historian Peter Metcalfe, "but no one person or group of loosely affiliated Alaska Natives could have exerted the influence of the ANB."

CHAPTER 15

Heirs of K'alyáan

A llow me the temerity, Mighty Sovereign, to fall at your feet, I beg you to be lenient," Governor Alexander Baranov addressed Tsar Alexander. "I express my sorrow that my health, weakened by advanced years and many trials, does not allow me to continue to labor for Your Grace. My strength is exhausted and I am forced to seek retirement." Since the battle to retake Sitka, Baranov implored his superiors to relieve him from duty. His fortitude was worn down by never-ending Native resistance, foreign intrigue, worker discontent, and chilling rain.

Twice the company recruited successors, and twice ill fate intervened. One would-be replacement died in Kamchatka just before embarking on the final leg of the journey to Alaska, while the other was lost at sea in a shipwreck less than one day out from Sitka. Baranov might well have concluded that the position was cursed. But the main reason his entreaties were ignored was because he was good at his job. For the company's high-end investors, Baranov reliably produced profits. And, for the empire's geopolitical schemers, he zealously defended Russia's North American foothold. He did so with scant support from St. Petersburg and little to show for himself, except a hereditary title and a merit badge. Instead of acquiescing to his pleas, Baranov's bosses served him more directives, sprinkled with encouragements. "Pray that God will strengthen you in health and force so that these instructions may be carried out." Moved by steadfast loyalty and patriotic pride, Baranov soldiered on.

In November 1817 the Russian vessel *Kutuzov* arrived in Sitka. Baranov saluted Captain-Lieutenant Leonty Hagemeister for the consignment of goods and grain. But the naval commander was bringing more than supplies. Hagemeister also delivered a surreal message to the governor. The company board of directors in St. Petersburg have agreed to release you from service. Baranov was stunned—more offended than relieved. A culture clash long existed between the Russian Admiralty and the Russian-American Company. The noble-bred high command looked down on the middle-class merchants, who controlled this prized imperial asset. Henceforth, only naval officers would serve as governors in Russian America. The settlement would run more orderly, but less profitably.

Captain Hagemeister assumed control of the colony's business operations, a task he immediately delegated to Kirill Khlebnikov, the supercargo aboard the *Kutuzov*. Baranov was at a loss. The suddenly ex-governor did not know what to do or where to go. He had spent a quarter of a century in Alaska. He had lost touch with his scattered Russian family. There was a brother, he thought, somewhere in Siberia. Declining health compelled Baranov to seek warmer climes, and he considered settling in Hawaii, where King Kamehameha had once promised him a plantation. But Captain Hagemeister urged Baranov to return to St. Petersburg, so he could advise the company's board of directors on colonial affairs. Ever the dutiful servant, Baranov consented. In the meantime, he took under his wing the young bookkeeper Khlebnikov, explaining the fiscal accounts and expounding on frontier adventures.

Anna Baranova, Alexander's Native wife, did not want to leave Alaska. Fully assimilated to Russian colonial culture, Anna went to live at the Russian Orthodox monastery on Kodiak. With a recommendation from Hagemeister, Alexander's twenty-one-year-old son Antipatr was enrolled as a cadet at the Imperial Naval Academy in St. Petersburg. The *Kutuzov* also brought life changes for Baranov's fifteen-year-old daughter Irina. After just two months ashore, the ship's second-in-command, thirty-year-old Simeon Yanovsky, married her. When Hagemeister departed New Archangel, he named Lieutenant Yanovsky as the new governor of Russian America, thus keeping the post in the Baranov family for another two years.

In the autumn of 1818 the *Kutuzov* was ready to transport Baranov home to Russia. His new son-in-law made certain that the settlement's patriarch was given a proper send-off. Atop Castle Hill, the colonists gathered to pay tribute. "Many of his colleagues were gray-haired and old like himself," Khlebnikov said. "He was godfather to many and had taught most of the younger ones. Those who had shared his adventures and hardships, and followed him boldly into danger now sobbed like children as they parted forever with their beloved leader."

Baranov's farewell was an event not to be missed, even by his devoted antagonists. "The Tlingit said goodbye with a mixture of joy and sadness," Khlebnikov said. Known to the Tlingit as Wa-nanok, Baranov was the stuff of legend for his death-defying exploits. Now the same chieftains who so bitterly fought against the Russian settlement came to say goodbye to their old nemesis. "There was much feasting and speech-making."

Baranov used the occasion to reveal the secret behind his invincible aura. He showed off the chain-mail suit that he wore in battle under his clothes and that protected him many times from the blows of his enemies. To the delight of the partygoers, Baranov presented the chain-mail as a gift to his former foe, Naawushkeitl. The occasion inspired such good feeling that Baranov vowed to create a lasting symbol of Tlingit-Russian coexistence in Sitka. He ordered from a Siberian factory a Tlingit-style ceremonial hat, made out of brass and decorated with beads and sea lion whiskers. The Baranov Peace Hat, as it came to be called, was gifted to the Kiks.ádi Point House in Sitka.

In November 1818 the *Kutuzov* weighed anchor and headed out to sea. A lone figure stood by the gunwale. Huddled inside a frayed woolen overcoat was the man who had fulfilled Peter the Great's dream to expand the Russian Empire all the way to California. Alexander gazed on Sitka Sound and Mount Edgecumbe for the last time. In December the *Kutuzov* bypassed Hawaii and sailed westward. Baranov grew despondent. In January they encountered tropical storms in the West Pacific. Baranov took ill. In March the *Kutuzov* anchored in Batavia. Baranov became feverish. In April the *Kutuzov* passed through the Sunda Strait and entered the Indian Ocean. Baranov died in his cabin. "The following day, off Prince Island, a funeral service was held and his body was lowered over the side. The waters of the ocean closed forever over the last earthly remains of Alexander Baranov."

K'alyáan's reaction to the news of Baranov's death is not known. The two men had been acquainted for nearly twenty years, first as tactical allies, then as deadly enemies, and finally as reconciled peers. The old warrior was a guest of honor at the governor's farewell feast. Khlebnikov observed: "The famed Chief K'alyáan, who had harmed Baranov more than anyone else, arrived to make his peace. Baranov respected K'alyáan for his intelligence and bravery, while K'alyáan admired Baranov's bold and decisive spirit." He cut a stylish figure in a white tunic and leggings with deerskin trimmings, an exquisitely patterned raven-tail cloak, soft Athabaskan leather boots, and an ornate conical spruce hat. Around K'alyáan's neck was the silver medal that Alexander had bestowed on him as a 'Friend of Russia' at the end of the war."

The truce that sustained Tlingit-Russian cohabitation in Sitka had as much to do with K'alyáan as it did with Baranov. Only weeks after Baranov was replaced by Captain Hagemeister the tenuous peace was nearly shattered. Two Russian hunters ventured beyond the safety of the fort into Tlingit woods and were shot and killed. Hagemeister immediately blamed K'alyáan and mustered an armed crew, who came in three boats to arrest the revered leader in a dawn raid. But Kiks.ádi warriors were quick to the threat. Taking up rifles and launching a canoe, they confronted the Russians on the water. A standoff ensued with Russians aiming a cannon at the Kiks.ádi craft, and the Kiks.ádi aiming rifles at the sailors holding the fuse. K'alyáan stood defiantly in the bow and challenged the new governor. "If you have come to kill me then you had better take this medal you gave me from my chest, and then kill me." Hagemeister backed down and requested a parley. K'alyáan knew about the killings and that the Kaagwaantaan clan was to blame. But he advised Hagemeister not to provoke a fight, as the Kaagwaantaan had ten cannons and plenty of gunpowder inside their compound. The new governor let the matter drop.

By this time, K'alyáan was perhaps the most influential powerbroker and peacekeeper on Sitka as well as a local celebrity. Visitors to the island were hopeful to meet the Kiks.ádi war commander, who had defied the Russian Empire. K'alyáan obliged the curious with colorful accounts of his bloody deeds. One such person was Vasily Golovnin, who arrived in Sitka on a navy inspection tour in the summer of 1818. The Russian commander found K'alyáan at once contemptible and compelling.

"We received a full-dress visit by K'alyáan, the elder of the Sitka chieftains, along with eight of his nephews and their wives. The oldest nephew directed the ceremony and led the songs. K'alyáan shook a rattle. When the singing finished, K'alyáan got up, put on a special pointed hat, and made a speech. He said that he wanted to live in peace with the Russians. I treated them to biscuits and molasses, and vodka. But these people are very dangerous. Chief K'alyáan took part in the extermination of the first Russian settlers here, and he does not deny it." Before leaving, Golovnin commissioned portraits of K'alyáan and his wife. "They are very good likenesses, true to the originals, the very faces revealing their cunning and brutality."

K'alyáan lived for at least twenty years after Baranov's exit. Father Veniaminov makes reference to conversations with the venerable Kiks.ádi leader in the late 1830s. There is no consensus in Tlingit history on the circumstances of K'alyáan's death. One perspective is told by Kiks.ádi elder Al Perkins, a descendant of K'alyáan, who led the project to raise the K'alyáan pole on the site of Shís'gi Noow. Perkins said that K'alyáan fell victim to Russian revenge. "We fought with the Russians many times, not just the one big battle. We fought many times in between. No one today mentions how Chief K'alyáan died. He was shot in the back at Old Sitka. Not too many people make reference to that. But I know, it was passed down to me." While this account is not common in Tlingit narratives about K'alyáan, it is a familiar scenario in Native American history. A proud warrior chief resists would-be conquerors and negotiates a separate peace, only later to be murdered by vindictive enemies in an act of duplicity and cowardice. This was the fate of the Lakota leaders Sitting Bull and Crazy Horse as well as Apache chief Mangas Coloradas.

A second perspective comes from Alex Andrews, who as a child in the late nineteenth century listened to accounts of K'alyáan, only one generation removed. "K'alyáan, the man who battled the Russians, was taken by the sea in Silver Bay. The box containing the raven helmet and the blacksmith hammer was all that was found at the entrance of Silver Bay. But K'alyáan was not found. He was killed by the sea." The implication that K'alyáan drowned in the deep-water channel south of Shís'gi Noow is less sinister than murder, but no less mysterious. Andrews's account takes on a legendary quality. "K'alyáan put his box up high above the current and the blood flowed down the cliff into the sea, so that his box could be seen. That is why they brought back the box by canoe and broke it open."

K'alyáan's raven helmet and blacksmith hammer are among the most sacred relics of the Sitka Kiks.ádi. Such items are known as *at.óow*, or cultural property, that is imbued with the spirit of the clan ancestors. They are cultural artifacts that animate an enduring sense of autonomy and resistance in Tlingit collective identity. As expressed in one retelling of the Battle of Indian River, "K'alyáan waited until the Russians started coming ashore and then exited the fort. A cannon ball grazed his head and he fell. *Ha—the attackers said—K'alyáan has finally fallen.* So they came around him and were going to chop off his head. But he jumped up and made the sound of a Raven, then started hitting them with his hammer." K'alyáan's war helmet and hammer were passed down to his nephews, in a tradition similar to the way a crown and scepter are passed down in a ruling dynasty.

The heirs of K'alyáan would keep alive the story of the war against the Russians, a memory burned into the collective consciousness. Foreign invaders had tried to defeat the Tlingit and evict them from their homeland, but they failed. During the period of Russian colonization, the Tlingit maintained their political independence and social order. Tlingit relations with the Russians became a mix of strategic cooperation and passive resistance, with occasional violent flare-ups.

Then, in the 1850s, a newly appointed Russian governor disrupted the norms of coexistence by instituting unfavorable terms of trade and imposing restrictions on liberties of his Tlingit neighbors. Tensions built amid a renewal of hostilities. In March 1855, the Sitka Tlingit launched an assault on the New Archangel settlement. Scores of young warriors breached the palisade walls of the Russian compound, targeting the gunners whose deadly cannons were aimed at the adjacent Tlingit longhouses. After a desperate two-hour battle, the defenders withstood the onslaught. Thirty Russian soldiers and colonists were wounded and five were dead. As many as sixty young Tlingit men fell victim to Russian firepower in the short-lived revolt.

For the heirs of K'alyáan, it was a final act of armed defiance to oust the foreigners from their homeland. But while New Archangel survived the attack, the colony's masters in St. Petersburg conducted a grim reassessment of the future of Russian America. Soon after, the Russians would give up their claim to Sitka, but under circumstances that did not restore Tlingit sovereignty.

"His Majesty the Emperor of all the Russias agrees to cede to the United States all the territory and dominion possessed by said Majesty on the continent of America and adjacent islands, and in consideration thereof, the United States agrees to pay to the diplomatic representative of His Majesty seven-million-two-hundred-thousand dollars in gold."

For nearly a century, the Russian Empire had been the great power of the Pacific Northwest. But in the late 1860s, Tsar Alexander II was persuaded to give up on Russian America. The costs of empire exceeded the returns. In retrospect, at two cents per acre, the deal was a steal for the United States, especially accounting for the future discoveries of gold and oil. At the time, however, Alexander's empire was overextended. Having been trounced by industrial-primed Great Britain in the Crimean War, the emperor marshalled his dwindling resources for an ambitious modernization program at home. The American colony was an extravagance that the reforming tsar could no longer afford. Besides, New Archangel was vulnerable to predation by the Russophobic Brits, whose Dominion of Canada encroached on the colony's southern border. Better to sell the enterprise to his American friends than to lose it to his English enemies.

In the late afternoon on October 18, 1867, a parade of soldiers tramped around Castle Hill. In front of the two-story headquarters of Russian America, the assembly halted and formed two columns—the Russian Siberian Line Battalion on one side and the US 9th Infantry Regiment on the other side. Into the gauntlet strode Captain Alexei Peshchurov and Brigadier General Lovell Rousseau. They stopped at the base of the flagpole for a ritual exchange of the modern state's version of sacred crests. To a rolling drumbeat, an honor guard lowered the Russian-American colonial flag, and with a resounding cannon burst, Rousseau's teenage son raised the American flag to the top of the pole. With the formalities concluded, Civil War Union General Jefferson C. Davis (no relation to the Confederate president) moved into Alexander Baranov's old house and assumed the role of US territorial governor in Alaska.

The flag exchange was witnessed by hundreds of spectators, bobbing atop the waves on Sitka Sound. The American naval sloops of war the *Ossipee* and the *Jamestown* along with the new steamer, the *Resaca*, exercised their long nines to show approval. Amid the Yankee gunboats, dozens of Tlingit spruce wood canoes crammed the shoreline for a closer look at the hilltop ceremony. The occupants gazed from afar at the familiar promontory, Noow Tlein, burnished in the autumn sun. No Tlingit leaders were invited to the service. In the negotiations over the 1867 Treaty of Cession, neither Tsar Alexander II nor President Andrew Johnson was bothered by the notion that they were trading in stolen property.

"Ill feelings exist with several of the tribes," General Davis acknowledged. "They frequently express dislike at having not been consulted about the transfer of territory and do not like the idea of whites settling in their midst." To the Sitka headmen, their objection was obvious: you cannot sell something that does not belong to you. "Dissatisfaction with the sale arose from the fact that their fathers had originally owned all the country, but allowed the Russians to occupy it for mutual benefit," a US Treasury agent reported. "The right of the Russians to sell the country, except with the intention of giving them the proceeds, is denied." The Americans had a ready legal response. According to the bill of sale, "the inhabitants of the territory may return to Russia within three years; or, should they prefer to remain in the ceded territory, may be admitted as citizens of the United States with free enjoyment of liberty, property, and religion, *with the exception of the uncivilized native tribes*." Thus, with the stroke of a pen and the flash of a gun, a new army of occupiers moved into the Tlingit homeland.

It was not Manifest Destiny that the United States should rule over North America. Neither the British and their Canadian legatees, nor the French and their Quebecois legatees, nor the Spanish and their Mexican legatees could be driven off the continent. Likewise, it was not inevitable that Russia should give up its North American colonial possessions. In the early nineteenth century, the Russian Empire was on the rise. Its armies defeated Napoleon and occupied Paris. Its global ambitions were boundless. If a network of coastal forts between Kodiak and California had been built, as Grigory Shelikhov advocated, or if Sitka had become a commercial maritime hub, as Nikolai Rezanov advocated, then Russia might have consolidated an enduring presence in the Western Hemisphere. Russian colonizers had moved unimpeded through the Aleutian Islands and the Gulf of Alaska, until reaching the northwest coastal rainforest. Here, at Sitka, Russian expansion was finally stopped by a resolute coalition of Tlingit bands.

Unlike Spain's conquest of Mesoamerica, Britain's capture of the Atlantic coast, and the United States' relentless push on the western frontier, Russia's encroachments and conflicts with Native America are mostly unknown. This, even though these experiences include the horrific massacre against the Alutiiq people and the virtual enserfment of the Aleut people. But it was Russia's encounters with the Tlingit that proved to be the most extraordinary. Arguably, the three-year war and protracted stalemate represent the most successful Indigenous resistance movement waged in North America against European imperialism.

"The Battle of Sitka, in 1804, showed the rest of the world that the Russian forces in Alaska were too weak to conquer the Tlingit people," Herb Hope said. This story of defiance was preserved and passed down by the heirs of K'alyáan: how the charismatic young commander rallied the Kiks.ádi clan in a quixotic campaign to expel the Russians from their homeland—and nearly succeeded. "The Sitka Kiks.ádi were the last of the Tlingit people to send their warriors into a full-scale battle against the white intruders from Europe."

The Tlingit-Russian conflict marks the only time that Russia has ever been at war in North America. In this contest, Russia could not defeat the Tlingit. As consequence, the Russians could never gain a secure foothold on the continent and the dream of a West Coast Russian-American empire was dashed. Over the generations, Tlingit culture-bearers have ensured that the Battle of Sitka is not forgotten. The epic struggle of their ancestors is a defining feature of contemporary Tlingit identity, a sustaining source of pride, bitterness, and survival. "Today Baranov is gone. The *Neva* is gone. The *Anooshee* roughnecks are gone. The Aleut hunters are gone. And the Sitka Kiks.ádi still live in their ancient homeland."

THE RAVEN HELMET

At.óow. This Tlingit word translates as "property" but it refers to a clan's most prized possessions—not only meaningful objects but also sacred sites, formative stories, clan crests, and timeless traditions. *At.óow* embodies the spirits of ancestors, so it must always be treated with great respect.

The Raven Helmet—worn by the warrior K'alyáan in the Battles of 1802 and 1804—is one of the most important pieces of *at.óow* for the Kiks.ádi clan. Clan elder Andrew Johnson recounted how his house, prior to the battles, "asked the southern people—the Kiks.ádi's grandparents—for a war bonnet. The people of the south made a war bonnet, a Raven head made out of cedar gnarl. When it was brought to us, we recognized the emblem of our grandparents. They wanted us to go to war in their emblem." As such, K'alyáan carried with him the spirit and blessing of his ancestors when he fought against the Russians. After K'alyáan's death, the helmet was entrusted to a "son of Kaagwaantaan," also known as K'alyáan, for he was named after the great hero warrior.

The story takes a strange twist in the early twentieth century, when the Tlingit community was under enormous pressure from the Presbyterian Church and from local politicians to abandon their traditional customs and adopt Christianity and adapt to the modern American lifestyle. Governor John Brady, a former missionary, had previously founded the Sheldon Jackson School to train and convert Alaska Natives. Now he was at the forefront of the efforts to get the Tlingit to change their ways.

Around this time, the younger K'alyáan turned over the cherished Raven Helmet to the Sheldon Jackson School. According to school records, he gave the helmet directly to Sheldon Jackson teachers, vowing, "As I give this, I give up my past life, my old superstitions and my sin; all envy, strife, malice, witchcraft and all selfishness, and take the American flag for my emblem and the Lord Jesus Christ as my Guide and Savior." In another account, K'alyáan brought the helmet to Governor Brady, who turned it over to the school.

Clan elder Alex Andrews offered a different interpretation of the incident, saying that "the preachers talked him out of it. They made a promise: 'When you die, a marble grave marker will be put over you.' This was why he released it to the . . . Presbyterian museum. When he died, this didn't happen. Yes, these ministers lied."

Nowadays, the Raven Helmet is on display at the Sheldon Jackson Museum (successor to the now-closed school). The museum is the guardian of this precious artifact, but the Kiks.ádi clan still use it for ceremonial purposes, such as the 2004 bicentennial of the Battle of Sitka. Steve Henrikson, curator of collections at the Alaska State Museums, explains that "even when resting in institutions . . . these venerable objects remain the *at.óow* of Tlingit clans and symbolic of their skillful and vigorous endurance in the face of momentous change." Moreover, the helmet retains the spirit of the warrior K'alyáan and other ancestors who crafted it and wore it through the generations.

EPILOGUE
Reconciling the Present

C oncealed in a tall Sitka spruce, a raven spied on the flurry of human
activity in a forest clearing below. It was early autumn. The cruise
ship season was past, and the national park was usually quiet at this time.
Yet on this morning the peace was disturbed by clanging metal poles and
pounding wooden mallets. A work team was erecting a large tent on the
mossy green that marked the site of Shís'g̲i Noow. The tent was arranged
in front of the K'alyáan pole, memorializing the Battle of Indian River,
the climactic episode of the Tlingit-Russian war. The suspicious raven kept
watch as a broad-striped white and blue canvas was unfurled and raised on
the posts. A drizzling rain collected on the canopy.

The anniversary of the battle was long observed by the Kiks.ádi in Sitka.
"It seemed like it was always there," Fred Hope said. "They used to invite
different people to meet in the park for a sort of Memorial Day, talking
about the people that were their relatives who had gotten killed in that
battle." The practice fell into abeyance in the mid-twentieth century, but
was revived by a later generation of Tlingit tradition-bearers, culminating
in the raising of the K'alyáan pole in 1999. Now, five years on, the sacred
ground of Shís'g̲i Noow would again host a special gathering to commemo-
rate the 200th anniversary of the Battle of Sitka. To mark the bicentennial,
Kiks.ádi clan leaders were moved to devise something extraordinary.

"What we are doing with this event," said Tom Gamble of the Clay
House, "is coming out with some of the history and some of the background

the way that we've known it. But not the way that many other people have known it." The ceremony would be unlike any other previously organized by the Tlingit. It would include the Kiks.ádi and their clan relatives but also descendants of Russian and Alutiiq participants. "The big goal is that we will be able to reconcile any hard feelings," Gamble said. "And more important, we will give recognition to those people who fought against a whole other nation." The bicentennial would bring resolution to all the descendants of the epic clash.

Tracing the lineage of the New Archangel colonists eight generations past required serious detective work. Clan leaders solicited help from the genealogy specialists at the Library of Congress and eventually came up with the address of Irina Afrosina. The Moscow resident was at first startled by the inquiry. Who wanted to know? Yes, she was the great-great-granddaughter of Alexander and Anna Baranov, a direct descendant of their Creole offspring who moved to Russia in the nineteenth century. In the early 2000s the brightly lit Russian capital was a stark contrast to the fog-shrouded coastal settlements of the Pacific Northwest. But these worlds would soon be connected again, for the first time in nearly 140 years, in the hope of reconciling the past to the present.

"The way our ancestors stood up for us, we will now stand up for them," said Al Duncan, leader of the Kiks.ádi Clay House. On Saturday morning, October 2, the Battle of Indian River bicentennial got underway. A Tlingit crying ceremony was held in front of the K'alyáan pole on the site of Shís'gi Noow. The ceremony was a kind of traditional Tlingit wake, a time to vent grief for a personal loss and mourn ancestors in the company of others. "The only way this event will have any meaning in the future is if other clans acknowledge it," Tom Gamble said. Huddled under the striped tent were several hundred people, wearing Chilkat robes, spruce hats, painted faces, and crest regalia. They were the members of the Tlingit clan houses involved in the battle, along with a sprinkling of representatives of the Russian and Alutiiq communities. "Some people are under the impression that after the battle in 1804, the Russians won and the Tlingit left," Gamble asserted. "But had we really lost that battle, then you would not see the descendants of the Kiks.ádi here today."

For generations of Tlingit, the Battle of Indian River has been a source of mental anguish. The crying ceremony was a collective catharsis. "Pain is like a knot within you, only with ceremony can it end," said Nora Marks Dauenhauer of the L'uknax̱.ádi clan. "You've been holding the pain for so long, now release it." Each of the house leaders spoke about how their families were affected by the Tlingit-Russian war. Kaagwaantaan leader Anaaxoots reassured his counterpart-clan relatives that "the wolf screen will protect you and the wolf blanket will catch your tears." The solemnities lasted all morning and into the afternoon. Toward the end, some Kiks.ádi participants wiped the black paint off their faces, symbolizing that their grief was leaving them.

On Sunday, the location and mood shifted. The Kiks.ádi hosted a celebratory potlatch feast at Centennial Hall on the Sitka waterfront. At center stage were the three most revered Kiks.ádi clan relics together for the first time—K'alyáan's war helmet, K'alyáan's blacksmith hammer, and Baranov's peace hat. The pride of the Kiks.ádi clan elders could not be contained.

The theme of the potlatch was reconciliation with Russia. The potlatch "will be valuable in building bridges," said Steve Johnson of Point House. "There are many ties from that era between our country and theirs." The Sunday potlatch included a traditional naming ceremony. Kiks.ádi elder Tom McFarquhar of the Strong House received a new Tlingit name—K'alyáan. In so doing, the bicentennial would personalize the resolution of the Tlingit-Russian war, with the heirs of both K'alyáan and Baranov, the principal antagonists in the Battle of Indian River, standing together.

Finally, the guest of honor from Moscow came forward to speak. Irina Afrosina took the microphone from the Kiks.ádi host. Her black dress and flower-print scarf stood in relief to the clan regalia motif throughout the hall. She added her own gifts to the relics on the front table—a stone-carved double-headed eagle crest and an icon of Russia's protector-saint, Alexander Nevsky. Then Irina spoke: "I would like to pay tribute to the courage and wisdom of the local Tlingit community in honoring this sad event from the past, but also in attempting to put the tragedy and sadness behind you. I applaud you for being broadminded and forgiving enough to involve the descendants of your former enemies in this beautiful ceremony. Your culture has not only survived, but blossomed, despite the many attempts to destroy it or assimilate it. Today, when so much of the world is filled with war and intolerance, you were able to put together a celebration of peace and reconciliation."

Kiks.ádi elders made the most of Afrosina's short visit to Sitka. Irina and her husband Sergei were led through the rain on a tour of the small park on top of the bluff overlooking Sitka Sound. This memorial site is the former location of Shk'awulyeil's longhouse of Noow Tlein and Baranov's headquarters of Castle Hill. The Russian guests were also on hand for the unveiling of a new feature to the national park. Away from Shís'gi Noow, across the Indian River, they witnessed an Orthodox priest bless a stone marker, dedicated to "the memory of the Russian sailors and Aleut hunters killed in the battle with the Kiks.ádi clan in 1804."

In a few days, the tent came down. Autumn rustlings filtered through the park. A bald eagle alighted on a protruding driftwood limb in the shallows of the Indian River, awaiting a late-arriving coho. A black raven skipped atop the rippled mudflats, foraging for mussels and clams. Nearby, through a stand of moss-brushed spruce, K'alyáan's pole kept vigil over Shís'gi Noow. A soft rain fell.

Acknowledgments

We are grateful to the Tlingit people and honored to share this consequential but little-known history with a wider audience. We are especially thankful to Ray Aanyaanáx Wilson, Lorrie Gax̲.áan.sán Heagy and Joanne Wiita Gamble for reading and providing feedback on our manuscript. Ernestine Hayes, Tommy Joseph, Theresa Dewitt and Lisa Edenshaw-Krieger offered insights on Tlingit culture and lore, while Lance X'unei Twitchell was our expert advisor on the Lingít language. We also appreciate the support we received from Kaawóotk Ghuwakaa (Harold Jacobs) and Ben Didrickson.

We are also indebted to other Indigenous peoples of Alaska, especially the Sugpiaq (Alutiiq), who were the victims of the massacre at Awa'uq, as described in chapter 4. Dehrich Schmidt-Chya provided invaluable feedback on this chapter; Sven Haakanson was also helpful.

Our research benefited from the assistance of many individuals and institutions, including: Alaska State Library Historical Collections; Alaska State Museum in Juneau; Alutiiq Museum, especially Amanda Lancaster; Beineke Rare Book and Manuscript Library at Yale University; Kodiak History Museum, especially Margaret Greutart; Penn Museum, especially Lucy Fowler; Rasmuson Library at University of Alaska Fairbanks; Sealaska Heritage, especially Emily Pastore; Sheldon Jackson Museum, especially Jacqueline Fernandez-Hamberg; Sitka Historical Museum; Sitka National Historical Park, especially Jessica

Perkins and Tracy Laqua; Sitka Public Library; Sitka Sentinel, especially James Poulson; Sitka Tribe of Alaska, especially Lisa Gassman and Jessica Perkins (again); University of Alaska Southeast (Ketchikan) Library, especially Kathy Bolling; Wrangell Museum.

Thanks to Julie Witmer for her impeccable cartography skills and Ray Troll for his creative interpretations of all things Alaska. We are always grateful for the ardent support of Jill Marr at Sandra Dijkstra Agency and Jessica Case at Pegasus Books. We appreciate Zora O'Neill and Lauren Hammer for offering their astute feedback on our proposal and manuscript.

The Last Stand of the Raven Clan recounts a tale of ambition and greed, of courage and defiance, and of resilience and survival. This history belongs not to us, but to the Tlingit people. But it is also a history that should inspire indigenous and colonized people across the continent and around the world. We all have something to learn from this compelling tale. And we are so grateful and honored that we have the opportunity share it. *Gunalchéesh.*

Notes

Glossary

p. ix   In consultation with Lance X̱'unei Twitchell, associate professor of Alaska Native Languages at the University of Alaska Southeast in Juneau.

Prologue: Raising the Past

p. xv   On the day's events and participants, see *Sitka Daily Sentinel*, September 15, 1999, 1.

p. xvi   "Ever since . . ." (Perkins quote), *Sitka Daily Sentinel*, September 15, 1999, 1.

p. xvi   On the decline of the Shís'gi Noow memorial day tradition, see Louise Brady interview, December 22, 1998.

p. xvi   On Tlingit social organization, see Emmons and de Laguna, *Tlingit Indians*, chaps. 2 and 3, and Krause, *Tlingit Indians*, chaps. 3 and 4.

p. xvii "Al, you will never . . ." Al Perkins interview, February 23, 1999.

p. xvii Perkins on statue . . . *Sitka Daily Sentinel*, September 15, 1999, 1; Al Perkins interview, February 23, 1999.

p. xviii On US assimilation policy toward the Tlingit, including boarding school, see Bolton, "Why a Wrangell Boarding School Plan Stirs Bad Memories."

p. xviii "the biggest . . ." Tommy Joseph interview, August 23, 2022.

p. xviii "the way . . ." (Perkins quote), *Sitka Daily Sentinel*, September 1, 1999.

p. xix   "Ignorance of . . ." Tommy Joseph interview, November 17, 1999, Project Jukebox, https://jukebox.uaf.edu/interviews/3318.

p. xx   Perkins quotes . . . *Sitka Daily Sentinel*, September 15, 1999, 1.

Chapter 1: Raven Makes the World

p. 3   Physical description of Noow Tlein . . . taken from ink and watercolor drawing of Sitka waterfront in 1793 by Sigismund Bacstrom, ship's doctor aboard the HMS *Butterworth*. Reproduced in Dauenhauer, Dauenhauer, and Black, *Russians in Tlingit America*, plate 2.

p. 3   Archaeological evidence of Tlingit in the Pacific Northwest. William J. Hunt Jr., "Tlingit Archeology, Legends, and Oral History at Sitka National Historical Park," National Park Service, https://www.nps.gov/articles/aps-v10-i1-c10.htm.

p. 4   Moieties or phraeties as social organization. Raven and Eagle (sometimes called Wolf). On Tlingit clan structure, see Emmons and de Laguna, *Tlingit Indians*, chap. 2.

p. 5   *Potlatch* is a Chinook word that is commonly applied to all the Northwest
        people. The Tlingit word is k̲u.éex'. The potlatch described here does not
        represent a specific event from history. Rather, it is a composite sketch based
        on nineteenth-century eyewitness accounts, included to give readers an
        understanding of the purpose and rituals and rules of the Tlingit potlatch.
        See Beck, *Potlatch*, 5–11, and Kan, "19th-Century Tlingit Potlatch,"
        191–212.

p. 5   Background on Shk̲'awulyeil, see Dauenhauer, Dauenhauer, and Black,
        Russians in Tlingit America, xxix.

p. 7   How raven stole the stars, moon, and sun is found in Swanton, *Tlingit Myths
        and Texts*, 3–21. John R. Swanton transcribed this collection of stories from
        interviews with Tlingit elders in Sitka and Wrangell in 1904. The rendering
        cited here is from Swanton's Sitka interviews.

p. 9   "When we were first born . . ." Swanton, *Tlingit Myths and Texts*, 295. John R.
        Swanton recorded this particular version of the origins of the Kiks.ádi from
        K'alyáan in Sitka in 1905.

p. 9   On the Kiks.ádi migration, see Thornton, "Know Your Place," 290, 295–307.

p. 9   "They came down the Stikine River . . ." Al Perkins interview, February 23,
        1999, part 3.

p. 9   "A man and his wife . . ." Swanton, *Tlingit Myths and Texts*, 224. John R.
        Swanton recorded the story of how the Kiks.ádi obtained the Frog Crest from
        interviews with Sitka Kiks.ádi elders in 1904.

p. 10   "The Kiks.ádi people were . . ." Al Perkins interview, February 23, 1999,
        parts 3, 4.

p. 12   On slavery in Tlingit society, see Donald, *Aboriginal Slavery on the Northwest
        Coast of North America*; Landfield, Woebler, and Baxter, "Sah Quah."

p. 13   For a list of slave trade values, see Mitchell, "Predatory Warfare, Social
        Status, and the North Pacific Slave Trade," 40, table 1.

p. 13   "The petitioner . . ." From Landfield, Woebler, and Baxter, "Sah Quah."

p. 13   On potlatch executions, see Kan, "19th-Century Tlingit Potlatch," 207.

p. 15   On the Last Potlatch (sidebar), Jacobs, *Resilience: War on Tradition,
        Commemorating the "Last Potlatch"*; Preucel and Williams, "Centennial
        Potlatch," 10–15.

Chapter 2: The Great Northern Expedition

p. 17   On young Peter I, see Massie, *Peter the Great*, chap. 3.

p. 18   On Bering's appointment and quotes from Bering's journal, see Frost, *Bering*,
        30–31.

p. 19   "Sail along . . ." Frost, *Bering*, 34.

p. 20   "It is better to return . . ." Frost, *Bering*, 55.

p. 20   "We, your humble servants, will be sailing . . ." Frost, "Vitus Bering
        Resurrected," 96.

p. 21   "They are like . . ." Frost, *Bering*, 145.

p. 22   "The wind charged . . ." Frost, *Bering*, 205.

p. 23   "When Captain-Commander Bering . . ." Steller, *Journal of a Voyage with Bering*, 49.

p. 23   "They deluded themselves . . ." Steller, *Journal of a Voyage with Bering*, 57.

p. 23   On relations between Steller and crew, see Frost, *Bering*, 124.

p. 23   "Have you been there . . ." Steller, *Journal of a Voyage with Bering*, 63.

p. 24   "Get your butt . . ." Steller, *Journal of a Voyage with Bering*, 71.

p. 25   "exceptionally good smelling . . ." Steller, *Journal of a Voyage with Bering*, 163.

p. 26   "In case of separation . . ." Divin, *Great Russian Navigator*, 139.

p. 26   Background on Chirikov, Frost, *Bering*, 31–32.

p. 26   "A number of ducks and gulls . . ." Divin, *Great Russian Navigator*, 155–56.

p. 27   "If you see . . ." Divin, *Great Russian Navigator*, 159–60.

p. 27   "Over the next twenty-four hours . . ." Golder, *Bering's Voyages*, 294.

p. 28   "We thought we saw . . ." Golder, *Bering's Voyages*, 296.

p. 31   On Bering's Bones (sidebar), "Russian Doctor Presents Bust of Bering to
         Alaska"; Lind, "Archaeologists and Vitus Bering's Grave," 297–328.

Chapter 3: To the Face of the Clouds

p. 33   On Lituya Bay in Tlingit lore, see Dauenhauer, Dauenhauer, and Black,
         Russians in Tlingit America, 28.

p. 33   "The boats had traveled . . ." Charles White interview, "First Russians," in
         Haa Shuká, Our Ancestors, ed. Dauenhauer and Dauenhauer, 295–97.

p. 34   "Such is the beauty . . ." Love, *Sea Otters*, 37.

p. 34   "This is why the Russians . . ." Jennie White interview, "Raven Boat," in *Haa
         Shuká, Our Ancestors*, ed. Dauenhauer and Dauenhauer, 299.

p. 35   Background on Siberian fur trade, Fisher, *Russian Fur Trade*, chaps. 2–4.

p. 35   "They covered the shore . . ." Love, *Sea Otters*, 36–37.

p. 35   "We were living . . ." Steller, *Journal of a Voyage with Bering*, 143–44.

p. 36   "At first . . ." Love, *Sea Otters*, 36.

p. 36   "we killed more . . ." Steller, *Journal of a Voyage with Bering*, 145.

p. 36   On Basov's expedition, see Ravalli, *Sea Otters*, 6.

p. 37   On Russian fur trade, see Gibson, *Feeding the Russian Fur Trade*.

p. 37   "Is it not natural . . ." Ravalli, *Sea Otters*, 30.

p. 38   "On 16th August . . ." Quotes from Bodega y Quadras expedition are from
         journal of ship's officer Mourelle. Barrington, *Miscellanies*, 504–5.

p. 39   "A great many canoes . . ." Ravalli, *Sea Otters*, 51.

p. 39   "There is no doubt . . ." Gibson, *Otter Skins*, 22.

p. 39   "The *Sea Otter* is arrived . . ." From London newspaper (1786) cited in "James
         Hanna (trader)."

p. 39   On French first encounter, see Emmons, "Native Account of the Meeting
         between La Perouse and the Tlingit," 294–98.

p. 39   "We perceived an inlet . . ." La Pérouse, *Voyage around the World*, 364–66.

p. 40   "The people seemed pleased . . ." Dixon, *Voyage around the World in the Years
         1785–1788*, 168–69.

p. 41   "If our success . . ." Dixon, *Voyage around the World in the Years 1785–1788*, 191.

p. 41   "Colored glass beads . . ." Marchand, *Voyage Round the World Performed in the Years 1790–1792*, 284–85.

p. 41   "prefer coats and trousers . . ." Ostenstad, *Impact of Fur Trade*, 39.

p. 41   "These cunning . . ." Gibson, *Otter Skins, Boston Ships, and China Goods*, 119–20.

p. 41   "They examined . . ." Marchand, *Voyage Round the World Performed in the Years 1790–1792*, 285–89.

p. 42   "in all our commercial . . ." Gibson, *Otter Skins, Boston Ships, and China Goods*, 120.

p. 42   "Coo-coo . . ." Beresford quote from Dixon, *Voyage around the World*, 189.

p. 42   "Hard-and-Sharp . . ." Gibson, *Otter Skins, Boston Ships, and China Goods*, 120.

p. 42   "If the Europeans . . ." Marchand, *Voyage Round the World Performed in the Years 1790–1792*, 283.

p. 44   "A party . . ." Ross, *Pioneering Conservation in Alaska*, 10.

p. 45   On Save the Sea Otters (sidebar), "Sea Otters and Kelp Forests"; "Northern Sea Otter"; Preston, "Far-Reaching Influence of Alaska's Sea Otters."

Chapter 4: Massacre at Refuge Rock

p. 47   "I was a boy . . ." Holmberg, *Ethnographic Sketches*, 57.

p. 47   "only a few . . ." Holmberg, *Ethnographic Sketches*, 52, 61.

p. 48   "We will search . . ." Grinev, *Russian Colonization of Alaska*, 148.

p. 49   "War is for them . . ." Black, "Warriors of Kodiak," 142.

p. 49   "These savage-thinking people . . ." Grinev, *Russian Colonization of Alaska*, 119.

p. 49   "Upon a signal . . ." Holmberg, *Ethnographic Sketches*, 57–59.

p. 50   "In the year 1783 . . ." Shelikhov, *Voyage of Gregory Shelikhof from His Journal*, 1–2.

p. 50   "was drawn from . . ." Matthews, *Glorious Misadventures*, 72.

p. 51   "I was aboard . . ." All quotes from Shelikhov, *Voyage of Gregory Shelikhof from His Journal*, 2.

p. 51   "The local inhabitants . . ." Quotes from Zaikov in Shelikhov, *Voyage of Gregory Shelikhof from His Journal*, 40–42.

p. 52   On Qaspeq allying with the Russians, see Holmberg, *Ethnographic Sketches*, 59, and Knecht, Haakanson, and Dickson, "Awa'uq," 178.

p. 53   "I am master . . ." Report of Britukov, in Shelikhov, *Voyage to America*, 123.

p. 53   "I presented them . . ." Shelikhov, *Voyage to America*, 38.

p. 54   "Having no idea . . ." Shelikhov, *Voyage to America*, 38.

p. 54   "I disregarded . . ." Shelikhov, *Voyage to America*, 41.

p. 54   On the Alutiiq response, see Black, "Warriors of Kodiak," 146.

p. 54   "The Alutiit were expecting . . ." Quote from Report by Shelikhov, November 18, 1786, in *Russian Penetration of the North Pacific Ocean*, ed. Dmitryshin, Crownhart-Vaughn, and Vaughn, 300.

p. 55   "Attempt to persuade . . ." Shelikhov, *Voyage to America*, 38.

p. 55   "Qaspeq had relatives . . ." Holmberg, *Ethnographic Sketches*, 59.

p. 55   "A multitude . . ." Shelikhov, *Voyage to America*, 39, and *Russian Penetration of the North Pacific Ocean*, ed. Dmitryshin, Crownhart-Vaughn, and Vaughn, 299.

p. 55   "If you return . . ." Holmberg, *Ethnographic Sketches*, 59.

p. 56   "Leave these shores . . ." Quote in *Russian Penetration of the North Pacific Ocean*, ed. Dmitryshin, Crownhart-Vaughn, and Vaughn, 299.

p. 56   Description of the Refuge Rock compound in Knecht, Haakanson, and Dickson, "Awa'uq."

p. 56   "The likelihood . . ." Shelikhov, *Voyage to America*, 39.

p. 57   Description of the Russian charge, Shelikhov, *Voyage to America*, 115.

p. 58   "was boldly the first . . ." Shelikhov, *Voyage to America*, 115.

p. 58   Description of the violence, from archaeological findings in Knecht, Haakanson, and Dickson, "Awa'uq."

p. 58   "This experience was . . ." Dmitryshin, Crownhart-Vaughn, and Vaughn, *Russian Penetration of the North Pacific Ocean*, 301.

p. 59   "The Alutiit felt . . ." Dmitryshin, Crownhart-Vaughn, and Vaughn, *Russian Penetration of the North Pacific Ocean*, 302.

p. 59   "If it had not been . . ." Dmitryshin, Crownhart-Vaughn, and Vaughn, *Russian Penetration of the North Pacific Ocean*, 301.

p. 59   "They assembled in great numbers . . ." Shelikhov quote in *Russian Penetration of the North Pacific Ocean*, ed. Dmitryshin, Crownhart-Vaughn, and Vaughn, 301.

p. 59   On execution of male prisoners, quote from Britukov report in *Russian Penetration of the North Pacific Ocean*, ed. Dmitryshin, Crownhart-Vaughn, and Vaughn, 380; confirmed in testimony of Izmailov, in *Russian Penetration of the North Pacific Ocean*, ed. Dmitryshin, Crownhart-Vaughn, and Vaughn, 370.

p. 60   "I took advantage of . . ." Shelikhov, *Voyage to America*, 42.

p. 60   "After the massacre . . ." Holmberg, *Ethnographic Sketches*, 59.

p. 60   Description of Shelikhov's coercive campaigns, from testimony of Britiukov in *Russian Penetration of the North Pacific Ocean*, ed. Dmitryshin, Crownhart-Vaughn, and Vaughn, 376.

p. 61   "pillaging, cruelty . . ." Decree of Empress Catherine to Governor-General of Siberia, in *Russian Penetration of the North Pacific Ocean*, ed. Dmitryshin, Crownhart-Vaughn, and Vaughn, 336.

p. 61   "kindly treatment and trust . . ." Quote from petition in Shelikhov, *Voyage to America*, 121.

p. 61   "new locations for Russian settlements . . ." Shelikhov quote in Grinev, *Russian Colonization of Alaska*, 157.

p. 62   "the proposal of a man . . ." Matthews, *Glorious Misadventures*, 73.

p. 62   "suffering from a long . . ." Quote in Owens, *Empire Maker*, 113.

p. 62   "Most Gracious Sovereign . . ." Quote in Black and Petrov, *Natalya Shelikhova*, 51–52.

p. 63   On Shelikhov's monument, see Shelikhov, *Voyage to America*, 137.

p. 63   "master robber . . ." Quote in Grinev, *Russian Colonization of Alaska*, 151.

p. 64   "the darkest period . . ." Pullar, Knecht, and Haakanson, "Archaeology and the Sugpiaq Renaissance," 80.

p. 64   "When our people revisited . . ." Aminak quote in Holmberg, *Ethnographic Sketches*, 59.

p. 64   On the whale bone cairn monument, see Knecht, Haakanson, and Dickson, "Awa'uq," 189–90.

p. 64   "I made every effort . . ." Shelikhov, *Voyage to America*, 40.

p. 64   "between 2,500 and 3,000 people perished." The estimate from "Afognak Alutiiq People," 1–2.

p. 64   "the Russians went to the settlement . . . 300 Alutiit were shot." Aminak quote in Holmberg, *Ethnographic Sketches*, 59.

p. 65   "armed men murdered about 500 people . . ." Britukov quote in Shelikhov, *Voyage to America*, 124.

p. 65   Schmidt-Chya, "When the Russians Arrived."

p. 65   Quotes in Enders, "Archaeologists May Have Found Site of Alaska Massacre."

p. 67   On Refuge Rock Rediscovered (sidebar), Knecht, Haakanson, and Dickson, "Awa'uq," 183, 188–90.

Chapter 5: Into the Land of the Raven

p. 69   "During the darkest hours . . ." Letter from Baranov to Shelikhov, July 24, 1793, in Tikhmenev, *History of the Russian-American Company*, 2:29.

p. 69   "God shielded me . . ." Tikhmenev, *History of the Russian-American Company*, 2:30.

p. 70   On Baranov early life, see Khlebnikov, *Baranov*, chap. 1.

p. 70   On Baranov's responsibilities and contract, see secret letters from Okhotsk commandant I. G. Kokh to Baranov, August 14 and 16, 1790, in Tikhmenev, *History of the Russian-American Company*, 2:23–27; Owens, *Empire Maker*, 52–55.

p. 70   "the great state of boredom . . ." Khlebnikov, *Baranov*, 3.

p. 71   "My first steps . . ." Khlebnikov, *Baranov*, 6.

p. 72   "It may seem unnecessary . . ." Khlebnikov, *Baranov*, 4–5.

p. 72   "We noticed that . . ." Letter, Egor Purtov to Baranov, August 9, 1794, in Tikhmenev, *History of the Russian-American Company*, 2:50.

p. 72   On Kuskov, see Watrous, "Ivan Kuskov and the Founding of Fort Ross," 4–5.

p. 73   On Anna Grigorievna, see Chevigny, *Lord of Alaska*, 69–70.

p. 73   "In the year 1788 . . ." Dauenhauer, Dauenhauer, and Black, *Russians in Tlingit America*, 45.

p. 74   "with great joy . . ." Dauenhauer, Dauenhauer, and Black, *Russians in Tlingit America*, p. 46.

p. 74   "is inhabited by . . ." Barratt, "Battle of Sitka," 20.

p. 74   "All without exception . . ." Dauenhauer, Dauenhauer, and Black, *Russians in Tlingit America*, 42.

p. 75   "The chief was . . ." de Laguna, *Under Mount Saint Elias*, 145.

p. 75   On the conflict and quotes, see Interview with Chief Kashitan by John R. Swanton (Wrangell, 1904), in Swanton, *Tlingit Myths and Texts*, 161–65.

p. 75   "an extraordinary helmet . . ." de Laguna, *Under Mount Saint Elias*, 145.

p. 76   "the raven is moving . . ." Swanton, *Tlingit Myths and Texts*, 161–65.

p. 76   "He exerted his . . ." Deur et al., *Yakutat Tlingit*, 108.

p. 77   "Russia wanted friendship . . ." Letter from Purtov to Baranov, August 9, 1794, in Tikhmenev, *History of the Russian-American Company*, 2:50.

p. 77   "the Tlingit were . . ." Deur et al., *Yakutat Tlingit*, 110.

p. 77   "I am seriously grieved . . ." Letter from Baranov to Polomoshny, April 28, 1798, in Tikhmenev, *History of the Russian-American Company*, 2:93.

p. 78   "They are abusing . . ." Deur et al., *Yakutat Tlingit*, 112.

p. 78   "The benefits and advantages . . ." Tikhmenev, *History of the Russian-American Company*, 1:54.

p. 79   "I was compelled . . ." Khlebnikov, *Baranov*, 25

p. 79   "If you should happen . . ." Tikhmenev, *History of the Russian-American Company*, 1:44.

p. 79   Sally Hopkins interview, "Battle of Sitka," in Dauenhauer, Dauenhauer, and Black, *Russians in Tlingit America*, 356.

p. 79   "They did not train him . . ." Andrew Johnson interview, "Battle of 1804: Part Two," in Dauenhauer, Dauenhauer, and Black, *Russians in Tlingit America*, 257–58.

p. 81   "Despite our weaknesses . . ." Khlebnikov, *Baranov*, 25

p. 81   "This place is G̲ájaa Héen. . ." Andrew Johnson interview, "Battle of 1802: Part One," in Dauenhauer, Dauenhauer, and Black, *Russians in Tlingit America*, 158.

p. 81   "I have been busy . . ." Letter from Baranov to Larionov, July 24, 1800, in Tikhmenev, *History of the Russian-American Company*, 2:108.

p. 82   "supply him with . . ." Dauenhauer, Dauenhauer, and Black, *Russians in Tlingit America*, 144.

p. 82   "It was not . . ." Letter from Baranov to Rodionov, May 14, 1800, in Tikhmenev, *History of the Russian-American Company*, 2:102; Dauenhauer, Dauenhauer, and Black, *Russians in Tlingit America*, 134.

p. 82   "They did not expect . . ." Letter from Baranov to Larionov, July 24, 1800, in Tikhmenev, *History of the Russian-American Company*, 2:113.

p. 82   "This fort created . . ." Dauenhauer, Dauenhauer, and Black, *Russians in Tlingit America*, 126.

p. 83   On the removal of the Baranov statue (sidebar), Hannon, "Alaskan City Relocates Russian Colonist Statue to a Museum"; Rose, "Sitka's Baranov Statue Will Come Down but It's Not Going Far"; Rose and McKinstry, "Sitkans Gather to Demand Relocation of Controversial Baranov Statue."

Part Two
**Chapters 6–10 chronicle the events of the Tlingit-Russian war. The Tlingit perspective is compiled mainly from oral histories, based on the recitations of the original participants in the battle that were told to their direct descendants. Each subsequent generation had its own designated tradition-bearers and culture-keepers, who were entrusted with responsibility to learn the history and to pass down the knowledge down to their kin. While oral histories generally agree on the broad themes and interpretations, there is no single Tlingit historical narrative for any particular major event—rather, there is a degree of variation in the retelling from clan to clan and from house to house. In the twentieth century, these narrative accounts were recorded in oral interviews and transcribed in written form. The context and quotations used to construct the narrative in these chapters come mostly from culture-keepers Sally Hopkins, Andrew P. Johnson, Alex Andrews, and Herb Hope (see bibliography for more detail).

Chapter 6: Fortress of the Bears

p. 87   "Circumstances do not permit . . ." Letter from Baranov to Medvednikov, April 19, 1800, in Dauenhauer, Dauenhauer, and Black, *Russians in Tlingit America*, 147–54.

p. 88   "The woman interpreter . . ." Letter from Baranov to Larionov, July 24, 1800, in Tikhmenev, *History of the Russian-American Company*, 2:113–14.

p. 89   "These people have enjoyed . . ." Letter from Baranov to Medvednikov, April 19, 1800, in Dauenhauer, Dauenhauer, and Black, *Russians in Tlingit America*, 147.

p. 89   "Punish anyone . . ." Letter from Baranov to Medvednikov, April 19, 1800, in Dauenhauer, Dauenhauer, and Black, *Russians in Tlingit America*, 148.

p. 90   "The Russians must keep . . ." Letter from Baranov to Medvednikov, April 19, 1800, in Dauenhauer, Dauenhauer, and Black, *Russians in Tlingit America*, 147.

p. 91   "Two died . . ." Letter from Baranov to Rodionov, May 14, 1800, in Dauenhauer, Dauenhauer, and Black, *Russians in Tlingit America*, 135.

p. 91   On the Kochesov brothers, Interview of Fillipp Kachevarov by K. T. Khlebnikov, June 10, 1822, in Dauenhauer, Dauenhauer, and Black, *Russians in Tlingit America*, 97.

p. 91   "The behavior of the Russians . . ." Davydov, *Two Voyages to Russian America*, 189.

p. 91   "The Russian were very cruel . . ." Andrew Johnson interview, "Battle of 1802: Part One," in Dauenhauer, Dauenhauer, and Black, *Russians in Tlingit America*, 158.

p. 92   On Russian killings and Kochesov's implication, see Alex Andrews interview, "Battle of Indian River," in Dauenhauer, Dauenhauer, and Black, *Russians in Tlingit America*, 337; Letter from Khlebnikov to Baroness von Wrangell, June 21, 1831, in Dauenhauer, Dauenhauer, and Black, *Russians in Tlingit America*, 176; and testimony of Boston-based sea captain William Sturgis, cited by Grinev in *Tlingit Indians in Russian America*, 124.

p. 92   "The Russian officials made promises . . ." Andrew Johnson interview, "Battle
          of 1802: Part One," in Dauenhauer, Dauenhauer, and Black, *Russians in
          Tlingit America*, 158.
p. 92   "The hunters started . . ." Davydov, *Two Voyages to Russian America*, 189.
p. 92   "When the Tlingit walked . . ." Andrew Johnson interview, "Battle of 1802:
          Part One," in Dauenhauer, Dauenhauer, and Black, *Russians in Tlingit
          America*, 158–59.
p. 93   Stoonook's story and accompanying quotes are from Sally Hopkins interview,
          "Battle of Sitka," in Dauenhauer, Dauenhauer, and Black, *Russians in Tlingit
          America*, 358–59; Andrew Johnson interview, "Battle of 1802: Part One,"
          in Dauenhauer, Dauenhauer, and Black, *Russians in Tlingit America*, 159;
          and Alex Andrews interview, "Battle of Indian River," in Dauenhauer,
          Dauenhauer, and Black, *Russians in Tlingit America*, 330.
p. 95   "No one comes . . ." George Ramos interview, September 18, 1999; "Alaska
          Native Collections: Sharing Knowledge," Smithsonian Learning Lab, https
          ://learninglab.si.edu/resources/view/5734.
p. 96   "What will happen . . ." Davydov, *Two Voyages to Russian America*, 189.
p. 96   "The Russians act kindly . . ." Quote from Ivan Kuskov in Letter from
          Khlebnikov to Baroness von Wrangell, June 21, 1831, in Dauenhauer,
          Dauenhauer, and Black, *Russians in Tlingit America*, 181.
p. 96   On Kanyagit and the pro-war argument, see Hope, "Kiks.ádi Survival March
          of 1804," 274.
p. 97   "It was agreed . . ." Letter from Kuskov to Baranov, July 1, 1802, in
          Dauenhauer, Dauenhauer, and Black, *Russians in Tlingit America*, 198.
p. 98   "Throughout the winter . . ." Letter from Kuskov to Baranov, July 1, 1802, in
          Dauenhauer, Dauenhauer, and Black, *Russians in Tlingit America*, 199.
p. 98   "badly equipped . . ." Davydov, *Two Voyages to Russian America*, 189.
p. 98   "When a Tlingit . . ." Andrew Johnson interview, "Battle of 1802: Part One,"
          in Dauenhauer, Dauenhauer, and Black, *Russians in Tlingit America*, 164.
p. 99   On the bombing of Angoon (sidebar), Kiffer, "Navy Bombed Angoon 125
          Years Ago." Morris, "Sacred Carving Returned to Tribe"; "Shelling of the
          Alaskan Native American Village of Angoon."

Chapter 7: Retaliation
p. 101   "During the night . . ." Andrew Johnson interview, "The Saint Michael Battle,
          1802: Part Three," in Dauenhauer, Dauenhauer, and Black, *Russians in Tlingit
          America*, 167–68.
p. 101   On Tlingit warfare, see Emmons and de Laguna, *Tlingit Indians*, 324–51.
p. 103   "Bind up twenty bundles . . ." Alex Andrews interview, "The Battle at
          Indian River," in Dauenhauer, Dauenhauer, and Black, *Russians in Tlingit
          America*, 331; Sally Hopkins interview, "The Battle of Sitka," in Dauenhauer,
          Dauenhauer, and Black, *Russians in Tlingit America*, 360.
p. 103   Description of Tlingit weapons, see Joseph, "Constructing Tlingit Armor,
          Tommy Joseph at TEDxSitka."

p. 103   "Hand it over . . ." Sally Hopkins interview, "The Battle of Sitka," in
          Dauenhauer, Dauenhauer, and Black, *Russians in Tlingit America*, 355.

p. 104   "The ermine pelts . . ." All quotes from Letter from Ivan Kuskov to Baranov,
          July 1, 1802, in Dauenhauer, Dauenhauer, and Black, *Russians in Tlingit
          America*, 192–95.

p. 105   On Plotnikov's account, see Deposition, Abrosim Plotnikov (Yakutat), in
          Tikhmenev, *History of the Russian-American Company*, 2:134.

p. 106   "They killed this man . . ." Andrew Johnson interview, "The Battle of 1802:
          Part One," in Dauenhauer, Dauenhauer, and Black, *Russians in Tlingit
          America*, 161.

p. 106   "Trouble . . ." Deposition, Ekaterina Pinniun (Yakutat), in Tikhmenev,
          History of the Russian-American Company, 2:137.

p. 106   "The Tlingit were stabbing . . ." All quotes from Depositions of Plotnikov and
          Pinniun, in Tikhmenev, *History of Russian American Company*, 2:134, 138

p. 106   "When K'alyáan charged . . ." Alex Andrews interview, "The Battle at Indian
          River," in Dauenhauer, Dauenhauer, and Black, *Russians in Tlingit America*, 335.

p. 107   "the Russians defended . . ." Deposition, Ekaterina Pinniun (Yakutat), in
          Tikhmenev, *History of the Russian-American Company*, 2:137.

p. 107   "A son of . . ." All quotes from Andrew Johnson interview, "The Battle of
          1802: Part One," in Dauenhauer, Dauenhauer, and Black, *Russians in Tlingit
          America*, 161.

p. 107   On the old veterans and the fire at the fort, all quotes from Andrew Johnson
          interview, "The Battle of 1802: Part One," in Dauenhauer, Dauenhauer, and
          Black, *Russians in Tlingit America*, 161–62; Sally Hopkins interview, "The
          Battle of Sitka," in Dauenhauer, Dauenhauer, and Black, *Russians in Tlingit
          America*, 363.

p. 108   "From my hiding place . . ." Deposition, Abrosim Plotnikov (Yakutat), in
          Tikhmenev, *History of the Russian-American Company*, 2:134.

p. 108   Total number of furs seized, Grinev, *Tlingit Indians in Russian America*, 121.

p. 108   On the fate of the women, see Andrew Johnson interview, "The Battle of
          1802: Part One," in Dauenhauer, Dauenhauer, and Black, *Russians in Tlingit
          America*, 162; Deposition, Ekaterina Pinniun (Yakutat), in Tikhmenev,
          History of the Russian-American Company, 2:138.

p. 109   "I went to look . . ." Deposition, Abrosim Plotnikov (Yakutat), in Tikhmenev,
          History of the Russian-American Company, 2:134.

p. 109   The capture of Gidák and all quotes from Letter from Khlebnikov to
          Baroness von Wrangel, in Dauenhauer, Dauenhauer, and Black, *Russians in
          Tlingit America*, 178; Andrew Johnson interview, "The Battle of 1802: Part
          One," in Dauenhauer, Dauenhauer, and Black, *Russians in Tlingit America*,
          162–63; and Sally Hopkins interview, "The Battle of Sitka," in Dauenhauer,
          Dauenhauer, and Black, *Russians in Tlingit America*, 364–65.

p. 110   On Urbanov's hunting party, see Letter from Khlebnikov to Baroness von
          Wrangel, in Dauenhauer, Dauenhauer, and Black, *Russians in Tlingit America*,
          179–80; Barratt, "Battle of Sitka," 51.

p. 111   All quotes from Letter from Ivan Kuskov to Baranov, July 1, 1802, in
          Dauenhauer, Dauenhauer, and Black, *Russians in Tlingit America*, 196;
          Barratt, "Battle of Sitka," 59.

p. 111   "On the last day . . ." Deposition, Abrosim Plotnikov (Yakutat), in
          Tikhmenev, *History of the Russian-American Company*, 2:135.

p. 111   "I arrived on the sound . . ." Excerpt from Barber's log, in Barratt, "Battle of
          Sitka," 204.

p. 112   "a melancholy account . . ." Excerpt from Barber's log, in Barratt, "Battle of
          Sitka," 204.

p. 112   "We were very glad . . ." Deposition, Abrosim Plotnikov (Yakutat), in
          Tikhmenev, *History of the Russian-American Company*, 2:136.

p. 113   "In the morning . . ." Excerpt from Barber's log, in Barratt, "Battle of Sitka,"
          206.

p. 113   "The commander released . . ." Deposition, Abrosim Plotnikov (Yakutat), in
          Tikhmenev, *History of the Russian-American Company*, 2:136–37.

p. 113   "From humane motives . . ." Barratt, "Battle of Sitka," 66.

p. 115   On the Rainforest Warriors and Tlingit armor in contemporary art (sidebar)
          Haakanson and Steffian, "Impact of the Rasmuson Art Acquisition Fund
          on Alaskan Museums," 42; Henrikson, "Armored Warriors of the Northern
          Northwest Coast"; Joseph, "Constructing Tlingit Armor."

Chapter 8: Voyage of the *Neva*

p. 117   On Tlingit mourning song and warrior death rituals, see Emmons and de
          Laguna, *Tlingit Indians*, 270–73, 281–89.

p. 118   "A funeral pyre . . ." Alex Andrews interview, "The Battle at Indian River," in
          Dauenhauer, Dauenhauer, and Black, *Russians in Tlingit America*, 337.

p. 119   On Gidák's rifle, see quote from Alex Andrews interview, "The Battle at
          Indian River," in Dauenhauer, Dauenhauer, and Black, *Russians in Tlingit
          America*, 337; and, on Gidák's body dumped in the sound, see Andrew
          Johnson interview, "The Battle of 1802: Part One," in Dauenhauer,
          Dauenhauer, and Black, *Russians in Tlingit America*, 164–65.

p. 119   Shaman's prophecy "a huge schooner . . ." Alex Andrews interview, "The
          Battle at Indian River," in Dauenhauer, Dauenhauer, and Black, *Russians in
          Tlingit America*, 339.

p. 119   On the preparations for Russia's first circumnavigation, see Matthews,
          Glorious Misadventures, 129–41, and Tikhmenev, *History of the Russian-
          American Company*, 1:69–73.

p. 121   On Baranov's reaction and the company's fortunes, see Tikhmenev, *History of
          the Russian-American Company*, 1:68, and Klebnikov, *Baranov*, 40–41.

p. 123   "From Noow Tlein . . ." Alex Andrews interview, "The Battle at Indian River,"
          in Dauenhauer, Dauenhauer, and Black, *Russians in Tlingit America*, 339.

p. 123   On the seasonal cycle of gathering winter stocks, see Oberg, *Social Economy
          of the Tlingit Indians*, 65–78, and Rokfar, "Managing Mountain Goats
          Traditional Purposes by Indigenous User Groups," 37–41.

270 NOTES

p. 124 On Tlingit stick gambling game, see Emmons and de Laguna, *Tlingit Indians*, 413–14.

p. 124 "The Russians are coming . . ." Sally Hopkins interview, "The Battle of Sitka," in Dauenhauer, Dauenhauer, and Black, *Russians in Tlingit America*, 365.

p. 125 "The wind was favorable . . ." Kruzenshtern, *Voyage Round the World*, 37.

p. 125 On the early phase of the voyage, see Barratt, "Battle of Sitka," 101.

p. 126 "The same day . . ." Kruzenshtern, *Voyage Round the World*, 37.

p. 126 On the voyage through South Atlantic, around Cape Horn, and into South Pacific, see Matthews, *Glorious Misadventures*, 159–63.

p. 126 "an old man's . . ." Kruzenshtern, *Voyage Round the World*, 192–93.

p. 127 On Lisyansky's meeting with Kaumuali'i, see Barratt, "Battle of Sitka," 104.

p. 128 On Shís'gi Noow and quotes, see Alex Andrews interview, "The Battle at Indian River," in Dauenhauer, Dauenhauer, and Black, *Russians in Tlingit America*, 339; Andrew Johnson interview, "The Battle of 1804: Part Two," in Dauenhauer, Dauenhauer, and Black, *Russians in Tlingit America*, 257.

p. 128 On Baranov's mission into the archipelago and quotes, see Barratt, "Battle of Sitka," 81–84, and Lisyansky, *Voyage Round the World*, 149.

p. 130 "We met with . . ." Lisyansky, *Voyage Round the World*, 141.

p. 130 The *Neva*'s arrival in Kodiak and quotes, Lisyansky, *Voyage Round the World*, 142–43.

p. 130 The *Neva*'s arrival in Sitka and quotes, Lisyansky, *Voyage Round the World*, 145–51.

p. 131 "The Sitka natives . . ." Letter from Baranov to Kulikalov, April 29, 1805, in Tikhmenev, *History of Russian America*, 2:141.

p. 133 On the Wreck of the *Neva* (sidebar), "Archaeologists Piece Together How Crew Survived 1813 Shipwreck in Alaska"; McMahan and Thompson, "American-Russian Investigation of the NEVA Wreck and Survivor Camp"; McMahan, "200-Year-Old Russian Wreck Found on Kruzof Island Near Sitka"; Rosen, "Archaeologists Say They've Found the Campsite Used by Survivors of Legendary 'Doomed' Ship"; Dunham, "Archaeologists Believe They've Found Artifacts from Alaska's 'Cursed' Warship."

Chapter 9: Battle of Indian River

p. 135 "He was a real strong leader . . ." Bill Brady interview, in *Portraits of Leadership*, 6.

p. 136 Baranov quotes from Lisyansky, *Voyage Round the World*, 156.

p. 136 "By noontime . . ." Eyewitness account, Yury Lisyansky, "Battle of 1804," in Dauenhauer, Dauenhauer, and Black, *Russians in Tlingit America*, 230.

p. 137 "They were feeling . . ." Letter from Baranov to Kulikalov, April 29, 1805, in Tikhmenev, *History of Russian America*, 2:142.

p. 137 "retired in military order." Quote by Lisyansky in Barratt, "Battle of Sitka," 128.

p. 137 "When it begins . . ." Quote from Alex Andrews interview, "The Battle at Indian River," in Dauenhauer, Dauenhauer, and Black, *Russians in Tlingit America*, 340.

p. 137   "Let's go now . . ." Quote from Andrew Johnson interview, "Battle of 1804: Part Two," in Dauenhauer, Dauenhauer, and Black, *Russians in Tlingit America*, 267.

p. 138   "Shall we start back . . ." Quotes from Andrew Johnson interview, "Battle of 1804: Part Two," in Dauenhauer, Dauenhauer, and Black, *Russians in Tlingit America*, 260.

p. 138   "Our launch . . ." Lisyansky, *Voyage Round the World*, 155.

p. 138   "My nephews . . ." Quote from Alex Andrews interview, "The Battle at Indian River," in Dauenhauer, Dauenhauer, and Black, *Russians in Tlingit America*, 340.

p. 138   On the exploding gunpowder keg and quote, see Alex Andrews interview, "The Battle at Indian River," in Dauenhauer, Dauenhauer, and Black, *Russians in Tlingit America*, 341, and Andrew Johnson interview, "Battle of 1804: Part Two," in Dauenhauer, Dauenhauer, and Black, *Russians in Tlingit America*, 261.

p. 139   "With great difficulty . . ." Quotes from Lisyansky, *Voyage Round the World*, 155, and Barratt, "Battle of Sitka," 124.

p. 139   "Later he was taken . . ." Andrew Johnson interview, "Battle of 1804: Part Two," in Dauenhauer, Dauenhauer, and Black, *Russians in Tlingit America*, 261, 267.

p. 139   "All the spirits . . ." Patriotic song in Andrew Johnson interview, "Battle of 1804: Part Two," in Dauenhauer, Dauenhauer, and Black, *Russians in Tlingit America*, p. 268.

p. 139   "Gathering together . . ." Letter from Baranov to Kulikalov, April 29, 1805, in Tikhmenev, *History of Russian America*, 2:142.

p. 140   "We carried our . . ." Lisyansky, *Voyage Round the World*, 157.

p. 140   "Presently we saw . . ." Lisyansky, *Voyage Round the World*, 157.

p. 140   "I ordered . . ." Lisyansky, *Voyage Round the World*, 157.

p. 140   "Our bombs . . ." Letter from Baranov to Kulikalov, April 29, 1805, in Tikhmenev, *History of Russian America*, 2:142.

p. 141   "When the Russians . . ." Quotes from Alex Andrews interview, "The Battle at Indian River," in Dauenhauer, Dauenhauer, and Black, *Russians in Tlingit America*, 341, and Andrew Johnson interview, "Battle of 1804: Part Two," in Dauenhauer, Dauenhauer, and Black, *Russians in Tlingit America*, 259.

p. 142   "The dead bodies . . ." Andrew Johnson interview, "Battle of 1804: Part Two," in Dauenhauer, Dauenhauer, and Black, *Russians in Tlingit America*, 260.

p. 142   "Afterwards, they ran . . ." Alex Andrews interview, "The Battle at Indian River," in Dauenhauer, Dauenhauer, and Black, *Russians in Tlingit America*, 342.

p. 142   "We made a mistake . . ." Letter from Baranov to Kulikalov, April 29, 1805, in Tikhmenev, *History of Russian America*, 2:142.

p. 142   On Baranov's charge and quotes, see Lisyansky, *Voyage Round the World*, 157–58.

p. 143   "If I had not . . ." Lisyansky, *Voyage Round the World*, 158.

p. 144   "I know that . . ." Khlebnikov, *Baranov*, 48.

p. 144   "Mr. Baranov . . ." Quotes from Lisyansky, *Voyage Round the World*, 158, 164.

p. 145   "He informed me . . ." Quotes from Lisyansky, *Voyage Round the World*, 159.

p. 145   "The *Neva* could not . . ." Lisyansky, *Voyage Round the World*, 154.

p. 146   "The Russian fleet . . ." Andrew Johnson interview, "Battle of 1804: Part Two," in Dauenhauer, Dauenhauer, and Black, *Russians in Tlingit America*, 257.

p. 146   "It was constructed . . ." Lisyansky, *Voyage Round the World*, 159, 163.

p. 146   "There is only darkness . . ." Quote from Hope, "Kiks.ádi Survival March of 1804," 54.

p. 147   "This had the desired . . ." Lisyansky, *Voyage Round the World*, 159.

p. 147   "We kept a good . . ." Lisyansky, *Voyage Round the World*, 159

p. 148   "Finally, the chief . . ." Eyewitness account, Yury Lisyansky, "Battle of 1804," in Dauenhauer, Dauenhauer, and Black, *Russians in Tlingit America*, 233.

p. 148   On death toll estimates, see Grinev, *Tlingit Indians in Russian America*, 137–38, and Barratt, "Battle of Sitka," 117–18.

p. 148   "Early in the morning . . ." Lisyansky, *Voyage Round the World*, 162.

p. 149   On Finding the Sapling Fort (sidebar), Gannon, "Archeologists Identify Famed Fort Where Indigenous Tlingits Fought the Russians"; Griffin, "Historical and Archeological Investigations at Shis'gi Noow "; Hunt, "Sitka National Historical Park"; Urban and Carter, "Geophysical Survey Locates an Elusive Tlingit Fort."

Chapter 10: Survival March

p. 151   On the decision to evacuate fort and quotes from Hope, "Kiks.ádi Survival March of 1804," 55, 57–58.

p. 152   "We sent an inquiry . . ." Lisyansky, *Voyage Round the World*, 161.

p. 153   "It was an extremely . . ." Hope, "Kiks.ádi Survival March of 1804," 59.

p. 154   "The natives . . ." Lisyansky, *Voyage Round the World*, 162.

p. 154   "It appears that . . ." Lisyansky, *Voyage Round the World*, 162.

p. 155   On the Tlingit rear guard, see Fred Hope interview, December 17, 1998.

p. 156   "The rear-guard warriors . . ." Hope, "Kiks.ádi Survival March of 1804," 69.

p. 156   On Lisyansky's inspection and quotes, see Lisyansky, *Voyage Round the World*, 162.

p. 157   On the abandoned fort, see Barratt, "Battle of Sitka," 146.

p. 157   "they couldn't take sacred objects . . ." Ellen Hope Hays interview, in *Portraits of Leadership*, 8.

p. 157   "What anguish . . ." Lisyansky, *Voyage Round the World*, 162–63.

p. 157   "while they were going . . ." Alex Andrews interview, "The Battle at Indian River," in Dauenhauer, Dauenhauer, and Black, *Russians in Tlingit America*, 342.

p. 157   Mark Jacobs Jr. interview, December 21, 1998, parts 1–2.
         **On the infanticide controversy, there is no consensus among Tlingit culture-keepers. Andrew Johnson said that some children got sick and died on the march; see "Battle of 1804: Part Two," in Dauenhauer, Dauenhauer, and Black, *Russians in Tlingit America*, 262. Herb Hope rejected Lisyansky's claim, saying that "we do not need to quote anything the Russians have to say about the battle"; see Hope, "Kiks.ádi Survival March of 1804," 51. National Park historian George Hall said, "I asked ten elders, who said you would not understand"; see George Hall interview, April 16, 1999, part 1.

p. 158   "The Russians will not . . ." Hope, "Kiks.ádi Survival March of 1804," 68.

p. 158   "It is important . . ." Hope, "Kiks.ádi Survival March of 1804," 68.

p. 159   "We are old . . ." Hope, "Kiks.ádi Survival March of 1804," 69.

p. 160   On Shís'gi Noow, a drawing of the structure, and quotes, see Lisyansky, *Voyage Round the World*, 162–63.

p. 160   On the building of New Archangel, see Lisyansky, *Voyage Round the World*, 218.

p. 160 ·   "With respect to . . ." Quotes from Lisyansky, *Voyage Round the World*, 164–65.

p. 160   On the killings of Alutiit, see Barratt, "Battle of Sitka," 147.

p. 162   "Always remember . . ." Hope, "Kiks.ádi Survival March of 1804," 53, 74.

p. 165   On recreating the Survival March (sidebar), Fred Hope interview, December 17, 1998; Hope, "Kiks.ádi Survival March of 1804."

Chapter 11: Season of the Moon

p. 169   On Baranov's envoy to K'alyáan and quotes, see Hope, "Kiks.ádi Survival March of 1804," 75–78.

p. 170   "The Tlingit were forced . . ." Quotes from Letter from Baranov to Kulikalov, April 29, 1805, in Tikhmenev, *History of Russian America*, 2:142–43.

p. 170   Verst is an old Russian unit of distance, slightly longer than a kilometer.

p. 171   "The mountains surrounding us . . ." Quotes from Lisyansky, *Voyage Round the World*, 170–71, and Yury Lisyansky eyewitness account, "Battle of 1804," in Dauenhauer, Dauenhauer, and Black, *Russians in Tlingit America*, 235.

p. 171   "As soon as we . . ." Yury Lisyansky eyewitness account, "Battle of 1804," in Dauenhauer, Dauenhauer, and Black, *Russians in Tlingit America*, 236.

p. 172   "It appeared they still . . ." Lisyansky, *Voyage Round the World*, 170–71, 220.

p. 172   "they were getting ready . . ." Sally Hopkins interview, "The Battle of Sitka," in Dauenhauer, Dauenhauer, and Black, *Russians in Tlingit America*, 366.

p. 173   "Survival is not enough . . ." Cited by Hope, "Kiks.ádi Survival March of 1804," 58.

p. 173   "Stay away . . ." Hope, "Kiks.ádi Survival March of 1804," 75.

p. 173   On tactics in Tlingit economic war, see Grinev, *Tlingit Indians in Russian America*, 141.

p. 174   On John D'Wolf, see Howe, "Voyage of Nor'west John," and Shorey, "Brief History of the Vessel JUNO."

p. 175   "He ladled vodka . . ." Howe, "Voyage of Nor'west John."

p. 175   "From the kind treatment . . ." D'Wolf, *Voyage to the North Pacific*, 22.

p. 176   "If I had not . . ." Letter from Baranov to Board of Directors, February 15, 1806, in Tikhmenev, *History of Russian America*, 2:174.

p. 176   "The offer was . . ." D'Wolf, *Voyage to the North Pacific*, 32.

p. 176   On D'Wolf's excursion to Chaatlk'aanoow and quotes, see D'Wolf, *Voyage to the North Pacific*, 42–49.

p. 177   "commandant of the fortress." Neither D'Wolf nor von Langsdorff identify the commandant by name, but given his status as war chief, it is likely that this person was K'alyáan.

p. 178   "They wanted to . . ." Sally Hopkins interview, "The Battle of Sitka," in Dauenhauer, Dauenhauer, and Black, *Russians in Tlingit America*, 366.

p. 178   "Do you have . . ." Alex Andrews interview, "The Battle at Indian River," in Dauenhauer, Dauenhauer, and Black, *Russians in Tlingit America*, 344.

p. 178   "Our interpreter returned . . ." Lisyansky, *Voyage Round the World*, 221.

p. 178   "The Russians came back . . ." Sally Hopkins interview, "The Battle of Sitka," in Dauenhauer, Dauenhauer, and Black, *Russians in Tlingit America*, 366.

p. 179   "The embassy stopped . . ." Lisyansky, *Voyage Round the World*, 222.

p. 179   "It is payment . . ." Sally Hopkins interview, "The Battle of Sitka," in Dauenhauer, Dauenhauer, and Black, *Russians in Tlingit America*, 369.

p. 180   Lisyansky was a witness to K'alyáan's arrival and provided the quotes: see Lisyansky, *Voyage Round the World*, 230–31.

p. 180   "promised in the future . . ." Lisyansky, *Voyage Round the World*, 230.

p. 180   Quotes from Baranov-K'alyáan negotiations in Andrew Johnson interview, "Battle of 1804: Part Four," in Dauenhauer, Dauenhauer, and Black, *Russians in Tlingit America*, 269–70.

p. 181   "From now on . . ." Quote from Mark Jacobs Jr. interview, December 21, 1998, parts 1–2.

p. 181   "It took more guts . . ." Herb Hope interview, in *Portraits of Leadership*, 8.

p. 181   "Before taking leave . . ." Lisyansky, *Voyage Round the World*, 245–46.

p. 181   "On August 4 . . ." Lisyansky, *Voyage Round the World*, 316–17.

p. 182   "As to the *Neva* . . ." Lisyansky, *Voyage Round the World*, 317–18.

p. 182   On the attack on New Russia and Rezanov quotes, see de Laguna, *Under Mount Saint Elias*, 174–75; Letter (secret) from Rezanov to Board of Directors, February 15, 1806, in Tikhmenev, *History of Russian America*, 2:174; Letter from Ivan Repin to Baranov, September 24, 1805, in Dauenhauer, Dauenhauer, and Black, *Russians in Tlingit America*, 387–88; and Grinev, *Tlingit Indians in Russian America*, 139–44.

p. 183   "The old man . . ." Davydov quote from Letter from Rezanov to Board of Directors, February 15, 1806, in Tikhmenev, *History of Russian America*, 2:187.

p. 183   "The Englishman Barber . . ." Tikhmenev, *History of Russian America*, 1:100.

p. 184   On Tlingit hostility to New Archangel, see de Laguna, *Under Mount Saint Elias*, 175, and Tikhmenev, *History of Russian America*, 1:99.

p. 184   "I have been assured . . ." Rezanov quote in von Langsdorff, *Voyages and Travels in Parts of the World*, 10.

p. 185   On Appropriation and Repatriation (sidebar), Lisyansky, *Voyage Round the World*. 241; Kaufman, "Oh What Potlatch"; O'Malley, "Cape Fox Artifacts Home at Last"; Bolen, "Restoring Balance"; David Jensen interview, August 17, 2013; Preucel and Williams, "Centennial Potlatch."

Chapter 12: At the Edge of Empire

p. 189   Background on the Saint Nikolai, see Owens, *Wreck of the* Sv. Nikolai, 28–29.

p. 189   On the *Saint Nikolai*'s voyage and wreck, see Timofei Tarakanov narrative (1810), in Owens, *Wreck of the* Sv. Nikolai, 41–43.

p. 191   "We must be ready . . ." Timofei Tarakanov narrative (1810), in Owens, *Wreck of the* Sv. Nikolai, 44.

p. 191   "We place ourselves . . ." Timofei Tarakanov narrative (1810), in Owens, *Wreck of the* Sv. Nikolai, 46.

p. 191   "During the night . . ." Timofei Tarakanov narrative (1810), in Owens, *Wreck of the* Sv. Nikolai, 47.

p. 192   "We knew this . . ." Timofei Tarakanov narrative (1810), in Owens, *Wreck of the* Sv. Nikolai, 54–55.

p. 192   Quotes from Anna and Captain Bulygin, Timofei Tarakanov narrative (1810), in Owens, *Wreck of the* Sv. Nikolai, 59–60.

p. 193   "At long last . . ." Timofei Tarakanov narrative (1810), in Owens, *Wreck of the* Sv. Nikolai, 64.

p. 194   On the Kashaya Pomo people, see Oswalt, *Kashaya Texts*, 8.

p. 194   "If the long-range plans of Peter the Great . . ." Rezanov quote in Tikhmenev, *History of Russian America*, 1:100.

p. 195   "There remains one . . ." Rezanov quote in Watrous, "Ivan Kuskov and the Founding of Fort Ross," 8.

p. 196   "You are strictly . . ." Letter from Baranov to Kuskov, October 14, 1808, in Rogers, *Russian California*, 59.

p. 196   On relations with Kashaya, see Watrous, "Ivan Kuskov and the Founding of Fort Ross," 10.

p. 196   On the Russian-Kashaya treaty, see Spencer-Hancock and Pritchard, "Notes on the 1817 Treaty," 307–8.

p. 197   "Your excellency's letter . . ." Letter from Kuskov to Governor Arrillaga, June 20, 1814, in Rogers, *Russian California*, 62.

p. 198   On decline of Fort Ross, see Watrous, "Ivan Kuskov and the Founding of Fort Ross," 12.

p. 198   Background on the *Atahualpa* and Captain Bennett's encounter with Kaumuali'i, see Joesting, *Kauai*, 74–75.

p. 199   On Georg Anton Schäffer, see Pierce, *Russia's Hawaiian Adventure*, 5–6.

p. 200   "If he does not . . ." Baranov quote in Joesting, *Kauai*, 79.

p. 200   On the suspicions and ill will of British and Americans and Schäffer's exile on Oahu, see Pierce, *Russia's Hawaiian Adventure*, 8–9.

p. 201   "I will rely . . ." Baranov quote in Joesting, *Kauai*, 80.

p. 201   Treaty signing and flag raising ceremony, Mills, *Hawaii's Russian Adventure*, 112.

p. 202   "No power in . . ." Schäffer quote in Pierce, "G. A. Schäffer," 410.

p. 203   "It is their intention . . ." Corney quote in Mills, *Hawaii's Russian Adventure*, 24.

p. 205   On the fort in Kaua'i (sidebar), Hiraishi, "Lawmakers may urge the state to rename Russian Fort on Kaua'i to Pā'ula'ula"; "A Kauai park with ties to Russia is stirring up an international name dilemma."

p. 205   On the fort in California (sidebar), "Kashia Coastal Reserve"; Rosato, "700 Acres of Sonoma County Land to be Returned to Native American Tribe"; Krol, "How This Tribe Got Their Coastal California Lands Returned."

Chapter 13: On the Brink of Extinction

p. 207   On decline of sea otter harvests, see Ravalli, *Sea Otters*, 136–37.

p. 208   "The females love . . ." Davydov, *Two Voyages to Russian America*, 218.

p. 208   Estimates of the sea otter harvest, Ross, *Pioneering Conservation in Alaska*, 15–17; Love, *Sea Otters*, 44–45. Estimate of fur seal decline, Ross, *Pioneering Conservation in Alaska*, 30. Estimate of the harvest for fox, beaver, walrus, Bockstoce, *Furs and Frontiers in the Far North*, 110–11.

p. 210   On collective and individual property rights and household relations, see Oberg, *Social Economy of the Tlingit Indians*, chap. 6; Ostenstad, "Impact of Fur Trade on the Tlingit during the Late 18th and 19th Centuries," chap. 4.

p. 211   "one chieftan's son . . ." Grinev, *Tlingit Indians*, 214.

p. 211   On the fur trade and sociopolitical change, see Ostenstad, "Impact of Fur Trade on the Tlingit during the Late 18th and 19th Centuries," chaps. 5, 6.

p. 211   On Tlingit transition to the cash economy, see Ostenstad, "Impact of Fur Trade on the Tlingit during the Late 18th and 19th Centuries," 61.

p. 212   "They do not . . ." Shelikhov quote in *Russian Penetration of the North Pacific Ocean*, ed. Dmitryshin, Crownhart-Vaughn, and Vaughn, 318.

p. 212   On Portlock's encounter and quotes, see Portlock, *Voyage Round the World*, 271–72.

p. 213   "Saiginakh rememebered . . ." Saiginakh quote in Boyd, "Smallpox in Pacific Northwest," 11–12.

p. 213   "the Tlingit are toughened . . ." Blaschke quote in Kan, *Memory Eternal*, 563n15.

p. 213   On traditional Tlingit remedies, see Emmons and de Laguna, *Tlingit Indians*, 361–62.

p. 214   "The illness was . . ." Saiginakh quote by Boyd, "Smallpox in the Pacific Northwest," 12.

p. 214   Estimates of the smallpox epidemic on the Tlingit, Kan, *Memory Eternal*, 96.

p. 215   "I commend . . ." Shelikhov quote in Tikhmenev, *History of Russian America*, 1:36.

p. 215   "I am concerned . . ." Letter from Arkhimandarit Ioasaf to Shelikhov, May 18, 1795, in *Russian Penetration of the North Pacific Ocean*, ed. Dmitryshin, Crownhart-Vaughn, and Vaughn, 470–71.

p. 216   "I have seen nothing . . ." Letter from Arkhimandarit Ioasaf to Shelikhov, May 18, 1795, Tikhmenev, *History of Russian America*, 2:77.

p. 216   "when the Father Priest . . ." Letter from Baranov to Shelikhov, May 20, 1795, Tikhmenev, *History of Russian America*, 2:68.

p. 216   On Shaman apprenticeship and regalia, see Beck, *Shamans and Kutashkas*, 7–9.

p. 218   "The intelligent conversations . . ." Veniaminov quotes in Nichols and Croskey, "Conditions of the Orthodox Church in Russian America," 46–47.

p. 219   "In contrast to . . ." Kan, *Memory Eternal*, 254.

p. 219   On the decline of shamanism, see Kan, *Memory Eternal*, 274.

p. 221   On Louis Shotridge (sidebar), Preucel, "Shotridge in Philadelphia"; Williams, "Louis Shotridge."

Chapter 14: Once and Future Rivals

p. 223   Catherine the Great quotes in Bolokhovitinov, *Beginnings of Russian-American Relations*, 46.

p. 223   "I am only now . . ." Egorov, "How Catherine II Nearly Sent Troops to Suppress the American Revolution."

p. 224   "We are not . . ." Washington quotes in Bolokhovitinov, *Beginnings of Russian-American Relations*, 10, 18.

p. 224   On Russian opinion of America and quotes, see Bolokhovitinov, *Beginnings of Russian-American Relations*, 40–46.

p. 225   "I am so glad . . ." Saul, *Distant Friends*, 53–54.

p. 225   "the Emperor . . ." Hecht, *John Quincy Adams*, 186.

p. 225   "the dawn of . . ." All quotes from Ledyard, *Memoirs of the Life and Travels of John Ledyard*, chap. 6.

p. 226   "distinguished by . . ." Quote from Morison, *Maritime History of Massachusetts*, 43.

p. 227   On the voyage of the *Columbia*, see Morison, *Maritime History of Massachusetts*, 46–47. The voyage introduced the United States to celebrity Hawaiian Chief Atoo. The *Columbia* made history again on its second voyage as the namesake for the Columbia River in Oregon.

p. 227   "My ardent hopes . . ." Ledyard, *Memoirs of the Life and Travels of John Ledyard*, 364. Ledyard's overland trek was encouraged by Thomas Jefferson and partially financed by the Marquis de Lafayette.

p. 228   "I have told the Americans . . ." Letter from Baranov to Larionov, July 24, 1800, in Tikhmenev, *History of Russian America*, 2:113.

p. 228   "We are traders . . ." Quoted by Baranov in Letter from Baranov to Larionov, July 24, 1800, in Tikhmenev, *History of Russian America*, 2:113.

p. 228   "Chief Tykin . . ." Letter from Kuskov to Baranov, July 2, 1802, in Tikhmenev, *History of Russian America*, 2:139–40.

p. 228   "The Tlingit are armed . . ." Letter from Rezanov to company directors, November 6, 1805, in Tikhmenev, *History of Russian America*, 2:156.

p. 229   Quoted exchange between the tsar and Dashkov, Bolokhovitinov, *Beginnings of Russian-American Relations*, 199, 255.

p. 229   "When we have . . ." Letter from Rezanov to company directors, February 15, 1806, in Tikhmenev, *History of Russian America*, 2:183.

p. 230   "to pursue the course . . ." Quote in Norton, "Pacific in the War of 1812," 7.

p. 230   On Russian-American cooperation, see Bolokhovitinov, *Beginnings of Russian-American Relations*, 271.

p. 232   "with a proposition . . ." Letter from John Jacob Astor to Thomas Jefferson, March 14 1812, National Archives, Founders Online, https://founders .archives.gov/documents/Jefferson/03-04-02-0443.

p. 232   On Astor-Baranov relations and quotes, see Bolokhovitinov, *Beginnings of Russian-American Relations*, 260–61.

p. 233   "Russia is the only power . . ." Madison quote in Bolokhovitinov, *Beginnings of Russian-American Relations*, 312.

p. 233　"The entire northwest coast . . ." Decree is quoted in Irby, "Russian Ukases and the Monroe Doctrine," 13. The Italian mile is equivalent to 1,620 yards, slightly shorter than an English mile.

p. 233　Quotes from Sturgis and Ingersoll in Nakajima, "Monroe Doctrine and Russia," 449–50.

p. 234　"What right has Russia . . ." Adams quote in Nakajima, "Monroe Doctrine and Russia," 450.

p. 234　"The occasion is proper . . ." Quote from President Monroe's State of the Union address to Congress, December 1823, https://millercenter.or/the-presidency/presidential-speeches/december-2-1823-seventh- annual-message-monroe-doctrine. https://millercenter.org/the-presidency/presidential-speeches/december-2-1823-seventh-annual-message-monroe-doctrine.

p. 234　"this apparently extravagant . . ." Canning quote in Nakajima, "Monroe Doctrine and Russia," 447.

p. 234　Quotes in Nakajima, "Monroe Doctrine and Russia," 456–57.

p. 237　On the Alaska Native Brotherhood and Sisterhood (sidebar), "Alaskan Native Brotherhood: History"; "Elizabeth Peratrovich: A Recollection of Civil Rights Leader"; Drucker, *Native Brotherhoods*; Kiffer, "William Paul was the 'Father of Native Land Claims'"; Metcalfe, *Dangerous Idea*.

Chapter 15: Heirs of K'alyáan

p. 239　"Allow me the temerity . . ." Letter from Baranov to the Emperor, August 24, 1805, in Tikhmenev, *History of Russian America*, 2:144.

p. 239　"Pray that God . . ." Quote in Owens, *Empire Maker*, 263.

p. 240　On Baranov's family, see Owens, *Empire Maker*, 265–66.

p. 241　"He was godfather . . ." Khlebnikov, *Baranov*, 99.

p. 241　"Tlingit said goodbye . . ." Khlebnikov, *Baranov*, 99.

p. 241　On the fate of Baranov's chain mail, see Dauenhauer, Dauenhauer, and Black, *Russians in Tlingit America*, 399–400.

p. 241　On the Baranov Peace Hat, see Owens, *Empire Maker*, 268.

p. 242　"The following day . . ." Khlebnikov, *Baranov*, 100.

p. 242　"The famed Chief K'alyáan . . ." Khlebnikov, *Baranov*, 99.

p. 242　Description of K'alyáan from painting by Mikhail Tikhanov in Dauenhauer, Dauenhauer, and Black, *Russians in Tlingit America*, Color Plate 9. Aboard the *Kamchatka* was Mikhail Tikhanov, a former serf whose artistic talents won him emancipation. Tikhanov sketched drawings of the elderly Baranov and the New Archangel colony.

p. 243　"If you have come to kill me . . ." K'alyáan quote in Grinev, *Tlingit Indians in Russian America*, 152.

p. 243　"We received a full dress . . ." Golovnin, "Visit to Sitka and Meeting with K'alyáan" (1818), in Dauenhauer, Dauenhauer, and Black, *Russians in Tlingit America*, 319, and Grinev, *Tlingit Indians in Russian America*, 221.

p. 243 On K'alyáan's death, see Al Perkins interview, February 23, 1999, and Alex Andrews interview, "The Battle at Indian River," in Dauenhauer, Dauenhauer, and Black, *Russians in Tlingit America*, 345.

p. 244 "K'alyáan waited until . . ." Sally Hopkins interview, SITK 25380, Sitka National Historical Park, Record Collection, series V, box 082, file unit 077, Voices: Sally Hopkins and Mrs. Charley Benson, Peter Nielson, translator.

p. 245 On 1855 revolt, see Grinev, *Tlingit Indians in Russian America*, 187–89.

p. 246 "His Majesty the Emperor . . ." Quote from treaty in Gibson, "Sale of Russian America to the United States," 15.

p. 247 On flag exchange ceremony, see Black, *Russians in America*, 284–86.

p. 247 "Ill-feelings exist . . ." Davis quote in Kan, *Memory Eternal*, 185.

p. 247 "Dissatisfaction with the sale . . ." Quote in "Alaska Native Land Claims," chap. 10.

p. 247 "the inhabitants of the territory . . ." Quote from the treaty in Kan, *Memory Eternal*, 177 (emphasis added).

p. 248 Quotes by Hope in "Kiks.ádi Survival March of 1804," 79.

p. 251 On the Raven helmet (sidebar), Johnson, in Dauenhauer, *Russians in Tlingit America*, 158; Andrews, in Dauenhauer, *Russians in Tlingit America*, 345–46; Dauenhauer, *Russians in Tlingit America*, 397–98; Henrikson, "Tlingit Warriors and Their Armor," in *Russians in Tlingit America*, 395.

Epilogue: Reconciling the Past

p. 253 "It seemed like . . ." Fred Hope interview, December 17, 1998.

p. 253 "What we are doing . . ." Gamble quote in Miller, "Coming Together."

p. 254 "The way our ancestors . . ." Quote in Dauenhauer, Dauenhauer, and Black, *Russians in Tlingit America*, 319, and Grinev, *Tlingit Indians in Russian America*, xlv.

p. 254 "The only way this event . . ." Gamble quote in Miller, "Coming Together."

p. 254 "Some people are under . . ." Gamble quote in Miller, "Coming Together."

p. 255 "Pain is like a knot . . ." Nora Dauenhauer quote in Dauenhauer, Dauenhauer, and Black, *Russians in Tlingit America*, 319, and Grinev, *Tlingit Indians in Russian America*, xlv.

p. 255 "the wolf screen . . ." Anaaxoots quote in Dauenhauer, Dauenhauer, and Black, *Russians in Tlingit America*, 319, and Grinev, *Tlingit Indians in Russian America*, xlv.

p. 255 "will be valuable . . ." Stephen Johnson quote in Miller, "Coming Together."

p. 255 On the reconciliation ceremony and Irina Afrosina, see Dauenhauer, Dauenhauer, and Black, *Russians in Tlingit America*, 319, and Grinev, *Tlingit Indians in Russian America*, xlvi.

p. 256 "I would like to pay tribute . . ." Afrosina quote translated in *Sitka Daily Sentinel*, October 4, 2004, 2.

p. 256 On the placement of the marker for the Russian sailors and Aleut hunters, see *Sitka Daily Sentinel*, October 5, 2004, 6.

Bibliography

Interviews and Oral Narratives: Tlingit Culture-Keepers

Andrews, Alex. Kaagwaantaan, Eagle Nest House. Interview, Sitka, 1960. In *Russians in Tlingit America: The Battles of Sitka, 1802 and 1804*, edited by Nora Marks Dauenhauer, Richard Dauenhauer, and Lydia Black. Seattle: University of Washington Press, 2005.

Brady, William "Bill" Murphy. Kiks.ádi. Interview. In *Portraits of Leadership: Chief Katlian*. Teaching Guide: Center for Alaskan Native Studies, 1989.

Brady, Louise. Kiks.ádi, Point House. Interview, December 22, 1999. Sitka National Historical Park Project Jukebox. https://jukebox.uaf.edu/interviews/3313.

Hall, George. National Park Historian. Interview, April 16, 1999, part 1. Sitka National Historical Park Project Jukebox. https://jukebox.uaf.edu/interviews/3309.

Hays, Ellen Hope. Kiks.adi. Interview, December 7, 1998, interview 1, part 1. Sitka National Historical Park Project Jukebox. https://jukebox.uaf.edu/interviews/3301.

———. Interview. In *Portraits of Leadership: Chief Katlian*. Teaching Guide: Center for Alaskan Native Studies, 1989.

Hope, Fred. Kiks.ádi, Point House. Interview, December 17, 1998. Sitka National Historical Park Project Jukebox. https://jukebox.uaf.edu/interviews/3305.

———. "The Kiks.ádi Survival March of 1804." In *Will the Time Ever Come? A Tlingit Source Book*, by Andrew Hope III and Thomas Thornton, 48–79. Fairbanks: University of Alaska Press, 2000.

———. Interview. In *Portraits of Leadership: Chief Katlian*. Teaching Guide: Center for Alaskan Native Studies, 1989.

Hopkins, Sally. Kiks.ádi, Clay House. Interview, Sitka, 1958. *Russians in Tlingit America: The Battles of Sitka, 1802 and 1804*, edited by Nora Marks Dauenhauer, Richard Dauenhauer, and Lydia Black. Seattle: University of Washington Press, 2005.

Jacobs, Harold. *Resilience: War on Tradition, Commemorating the "Last Potlatch."* Exhibit, Alaska State Museum, Juneau, 2022.

Jacobs Jr., Mark. Dakl'aweidí, Killer Whale House. Interview, December 21, 1998, parts 1–2. Sitka National Historical Park Project Jukebox. https://jukebox.uaf.edu/interviews/3315

Jensen, David. L'eeneidí. Interview, August 7, 2013. "Tlingit House Screen Returns to Dog Salmon Clan." https://www.krbd.org/2013/08/07/tlingit-house-screen -returns-to-dog-salmon-clan/.

Johnson, Andrew. Kiks.ádi, Point House. Interviews, 1979. In *Russians in Tlingit America: The Battles of Sitka, 1802 and 1804*, edited by Nora Marks Dauenhauer, Richard Dauenhauer, and Lydia Black. Seattle: University of Washington Press, 2005.

Joseph, Tommy. Kaagwaantaan clan. Interview, August 23, 2022, with authors at Sitka National Historical Park.

———. "Constructing Tlingit Armor: Tommy Joseph at TEDxSitka." YouTube, August 20, 2013. https://www.youtube.com/watch?v=ErDsz3g3zAg.

Perkins, Al. Kiks.ádi clan. Interview, February 23, 1999. Sitka National Historical Park Project Jukebox. https://jukebox.uaf.edu/interviews/3302.

Ramos, George, L'uknax̱.ádi clan. Interview, September 18, 1999, part 2. Sitka National Historical Park Project Jukebox. https://jukebox.uaf.edu/interviews/780.

———. Sharing Knowledge: Alaska Native Collections. Smithsonian Institution. http://https//alaska.si.edu/record.asp?id=261.

White, Charles. L'uknax̱.ádi, Taginaa Hit Taan House. Interview, 1962. In *Haa Shuká, Our Ancestors*, edited by Nora Marks Dauenhauer and Richard Dauenhauer, 499–501. Seattle: University of Washington Press, 1987.

White, Jennie. Shangukeidi, Thunderbird House. Interview, 1984. In *Haa Shuká, Our Ancestors*, edited by Nora Marks Dauenhauer and Richard Dauenhauer, 502–4. Seattle: University of Washington Press, 1987.

Interviews, Oral Narratives, Published Compilations: Tlingit Culture-Keepers

Dauenhauer, Nora Marks, and Richard Dauenhauer, eds. *HaHaa Tuwunáagu Yís, Healing Our Spirit: Tlingit Oratory*. Seattle: University of Washington Press, 1987.

Dauenhauer, Nora Marks, Richard Dauenhauer, and Lydia Black, eds. *Russians in Tlingit America: The Battles of Sitka, 1802 and 1804*. Seattle: University of Washington Press, 2005.

Dauenhauer, Nora Marks, and Richard Dauenhauer, eds. *Ha Shuká, Our Ancestors: Tlingit Oral Narratives*. Seattle: University of Washington Press, 1987.

Hope III, Andrew, and Thomas Thornton. *Will the Time Ever Come? A Tlingit Source Book* Fairbanks: University of Alaska Press, 2000.

Kan, Sergei, ed. *Sharing Our Knowledge: The Tlingit and Their Coastal Neighbors*. Lincoln: University of Nebraska Press, 2015.

Portraits of Leadership: Chief Katlian. Teaching Guide: Center for Alaskan Native Studies, 1989.

Swanton, John Reed. *Tlingit Myths and Texts, Recorded by John R. Swanton*. Washington, DC: Smithsonian Institution Bureau of American Ethnology, 1909.

Travelogues, Letters, Documents: Russian, European, and American Accounts

Barrington, Daines. *Miscellanies*. London: Nichols and White, 1781

Davydov, G. I. *Two Voyages to Russian America, 1802–1807*. Kingston, Ontario: Limestone Press, 1977.

Dixon, George, and Captain Portlock. *Voyage around the World in the Years 1785–1788.* London: 1789.

Dmitryshin, Basil, E. A. P. Crownhart-Vaughn, and T. Vaughn, eds. *Russian Penetration of the North Pacific Ocean, 1700–1797: To Siberia and Russian America.* Vol. 2. Portland: Oregon Historical Society Press, 1988.

D'Wolf, John. *A Voyage to the North Pacific.* Fairfield, CT: Ye Galleon Press, 1968.

Golovnin, V. M. "Visit to Sitka and Meeting with K'alyáan." In *Russians in Tlingit America: The Battles of Sitka, 1802 and 1804*, edited by Nora Marks Dauenhauer, Richard Dauenhauer, and Lydia Black, 317–22. Seattle: University of Washington Press, 2005.

Holmberg, Heinrich Johan. *Holmberg's Ethnographic Sketches.* Fairbanks: University of Alaska Press, 1985.

Khlebnikov, K. T. *Baranov: Chief Manager of the Russian Colonies in America.* Kingston, Ontario: Limestone Press, 1973.

Kruzenshtern, Ivan. *Voyage Round the World in the Years 1803, 1804, 1805 and 1806, by Order of His Imperial Majesty Alexander I, On Board the* Nadeshda *and the* Neva. London: C. Roworth for J. Murray, 1813.

von Langsdorff, G. H. *Voyages and Travels in Parts of the World.* Part 2. London: Henry Colburn, 1814.

La Pérouse, Jean-Francois. *A Voyage Round the World in the Years 1785, 1786, 1787, and 1788.* London: G. G. and J. Robinson, 1799.

Ledyard, John. *Memoirs of the Life and Travels of John Ledyard from His Journal and Correspondence.* Edited by Jared Sparks. London: Henry Colburn, 1828.

Lisyansky, Yury. *Voyage Round the World in the Years 1803, 1804, 1805 and 1806, Performed by Order of His Majesty Alexander I, in the Ship* Neva. London: Booth and Longman, 1814.

Marchand, Etienne. *A Voyage Round the World Performed in the Years 1790–1792.* London: Longman and Rees, 1801.

Portlock, Nathaniel. *A Voyage Round the World, but More Particularly to the North-West Coast of America.* London: Stockdale and Goulding, 1789.

Shelikhov, G. I. *A Voyage to America, 1783–1786.* Kingston, Ontario: Limestone Press, 1981.

Shelikhov, Grigory. *The Voyage of Gregory Shelikhof from His Journal.* London: Collections in Various Departments of Literature, 1795.

Steller, Georg. *Journal of a Voyage with Bering, 1741–1742.* Stanford, CA: Stanford University Press, 1988.

Tikhmenev, P. A. *A History of the Russian-American Company.* Vol. 1. Kingston, Ontario: Limestone Press, 1978.

Tikhmenev, P. A. *A History of the Russian-American Company: Documents.* Vol. 2. Kingston, Ontario: Limestone Press, 1979.

Secondary Sources

"A Kauai park with ties to Russia is stirring up an international name dilemma," *Hawaii News Now*, January 19, 2019, https://www.hawaiinewsnow.com/2019/01/20/kauai-park-with-ties-russia-is-stirring-up-an-international-name-dilemma/.

"Afognak Alutiiq People: Our History and Culture." Afognak Native Corporation,
    July 2008. https://web.archive.org/web/20131113111647/https://www.afognak.com
    /media/Afognak%20Alu tiiq%20History%20Benefits%2007-22-08_letter.pdf.
https://web.archive.org/web/20131113111647/https://www.afognak.com/media
    /Afognak%20Alutiiq%20History%20Benefits%2007-22-08_letter.pdf.
"Alaska Native Brotherhood: History." https://www.anbansgc.org/about-us/history/.
"Alaska Native Land Claims." http://www.alaskool.org/projects/ancsa/landclaims
    /landclaims_unit3_ch10.htm.
"Archaeologists Piece Together How Crew Survived 1813 Shipwreck in Alaska."
    National Science Foundation, September 8, 2015. https://www.nsf.gov/news/news
    _summ.jsp?org=NSF&cntn_id=136012&preview=false.
Barratt, Glynn. "The Battle of Sitka, 1804: A Kind of Victory." Unpublished
    manuscript. Alaska State Library, Historical Collections, Glynn Barratt Collection
    (Fond 1414), MS242.
Beck, Mary. *Potlatch: Native Ceremony and Myth on the Northwest Coast*. Portland, OR:
    Alaska Northwest Books, 1993.
——. *Shamans and Kutashkas*. Portland, OR: Alaska Northwest Books, 1991.
Black, Dawn, and Alexander Petrov. *Natalya Shelikhova: Russian Oligarch of Alaska
    Commerce*. Fairbanks: University of Alaska Press, 2010.
Black, Lydia. *Russians in America, 1732–1867*. Fairbanks: University of Alaska Press,
    2004.
——. "Warriors of Kodiak: Military Traditions of Kodiak Islanders." *Arctic
    Anthropology* 41, no. 2 (2004): 140–52.
Bockstoce, John. *Furs and Frontiers in the Far North*. New Haven, CT: Yale University
    Press, 2009.
Bolen, Anne. "Restoring Balance: A Two-Decade Effort Shepherds Dozens of Tlingit
    Objects Home." *American Indian Magazine* 21, no. 4 (Winter 2020): 8-17.
Bolokhovitinov, Nikolai. *The Beginnings of Russian-American Relations, 1775–1815*.
    Cambridge, MA: Harvard University Press, 1975.
Bolton, Aaron. "Why a Wrangell Boarding School Plan Stirs Bad Memories." KTOO
    News, July 13, 2016. https://www.ktoo.org/2016/07/13/why-a-wrangell-boarding
    -school-plan-stirs-bad-memories-and-opportunity/.
Boyd, Robert. "Smallpox in the Pacific Northwest: The First Epidemic." *Anthropology
    Faculty Publications and Presentations*, no. 141 (Spring 1994). https://pdxscholar
    .library.pdx.edu/cgi/viewcontent.cgi?article=1142&context=anth_fac.
Chevigny, Hector. *Lord of Alaska: Baranov and the Alaskan Adventure*. Portland, OR:
    Binfords and Mort, 1971.
Deur, Douglas et al. *Yakutat Tlingit: An Ethnographic Overview and Assessment*.
    Washington, DC: National Park Service, 2015.
Divin, Vasilii. *The Great Russian Navigator: A. I. Chirikov*. Fairbanks: University of
    Alaska Press, 1993.
Donald, Leland. *Aboriginal Slavery on the Northwest Coast of North America*. Berkeley:
    University of California Press, 1997.

Drucker, Philip. *The Native Brotherhoods: Modern Intertribal Organizations on the Northwest Coast.* Washington, DC: Government Printing Office, 1958. http://www.alaskool.org/projects/native_gov/documents/anb/anb_2.htm.

Dunham, Mike. "Archaeologists Believe They've Found Artifacts from Alaska's 'Cursed' Warship, the *Neva.*" *Anchorage Daily News,* January 14, 2016. https://www.adn.com/culture/article/hunt-alaska-s-cursed-warship/2016/01/15/.

Egorov, Boris. "How Catherine II Nearly Sent Troops to Suppress the American Revolution." *Russia Beyond,* February 6, 2023. https://www.rbth.com/history/335859-catherine-ii-american-revolution.

"Elizabeth Peratrovich: A Recollection of Civil Rights Leader, 1911–1958." http://www.alaskool.org/projects/native_gov/recollections/peratrovich/Elizabeth_1.htm.

Emmons, George. "Native Account of the Meeting between La Perouse and the Tlingit." *American Anthropologist* 13, no. 2 (1911): 294–98.

Emmons, George, and Frederica de Laguna, eds. *The Tlingit Indians.* Seattle: University of Washington Press, 1991.

Enders, John. "Archaeologists May Have Found Site of Alaska Massacre." *Seattle Times,* August 16, 1992. https://archive.seattletimes.com/archive/?date=19920816&slug=1507631.

Fisher, Raymond. *Russian Fur Trade: 1550–1700.* Berkeley: University of California Press, 1943.

Frost, Owen. *Bering: The Russian Discovery of America.* New Haven, CT: Yale University Press, 2003.

———. "Vitus Bering Resurrected: Recent Forensic Analysis and the Documentary Record." *Pacific Northwest Quarterly* 84, no. 3 (1993): 91–97.

Gannon, Megan. "Archeologists Identify Famed Fort Where Indigenous Tlingits Fought the Russians." *Smithsonian Magazine,* January 25, 2021.

Gibson, James. *Feeding the Russian Fur Trade.* Madison: University of Wisconsin Press, 1969.

———. *Otter Skins, Boston Ships, and China Goods.* Seattle: University of Washington Press, 1992.

———. "The Sale of Russian America to the United States." *Acta Slavica Iaponica,* no. 1 (1983): 15–37.

Golder, Frank. *Bering's Voyages: An Account of the Efforts of the Russians to Determine the Relation of Asia and America.* New York: American Geographical Society, 1922.

Griffin, Kristen. "Historical and Archeological Investigations at Shis'gi Noow , the 1804 Fort Site." In *Russians in Tlingit America: The Battles of Sitka, 1802 and 1804,* edited by Nora Marks Dauenhauer, Richard Dauenhauer, and Lydia Black, 291–94. Seattle: University of Washington Press, 2005.

Grinev, Andrei. *Russian Colonization of Alaska.* Lincoln: University of Nebraska Press, 2018.

———. *The Tlingit Indians in Russian America, 1741–186.* Lincoln: University of Nebraska Press, 2005.

Haakanson, Sven, and Amy Steffian. "The Impact of the Rasmuson Art Acquisition Fund on Alaskan Museums." In *Living Alaska: A Decade of Collecting Contemporary Art for Alaska Museums.* Anchorage: Anchorage Museum at Rasmuson Center, 2015.

Hämäläinen, Pekka. *Indigenous Continent: The Epic Contest for North America*. New York: Liveright, 2022.

Hannon, Brian. "Alaskan City Relocates Russian Colonist Statue to a Museum." *Washington Post*, July 15, 2020.

Hecht, Mary. *John Quincy Adams: A Personal History of an Independent Man*. New York: Macmillan, 1967.

Henrikson, Steve. "Armored Warriors of the Northern Northwest Coast." Lecture at Sealaska Heritage Institute, April 13, 2020. https://www.youtube.com /watch?v=eoqS3lg0H4A&t=19s.

———. "Tlingit Warriors and Their Armor." In *Russians in Tlingit America: The Battles of Sitka, 1802 and 1804*, edited by Nora Marks Dauenhauer, Richard Dauenhauer, and Lydia Black, 389–95. Seattle: University of Washington Press, 2005.

Hiraishi, Ku'uwehi, "Lawmakers may urge the state to rename Russian Fort on Kaua'i to Pā'ula'ula", Hawai'i Public Radio, April 13, 2022, https://www.hawaiipublic radio.org/local-news/2022-04-13/lawmakers-may-urge-the-state-to-rename -russian-fort-elizabeth-on-kauai-to-paulaula.

Howe, George. "The Voyage of Nor'west John." *American Heritage* 10, no. 3 (1959). https://www.americanheritage.com/voyage-norwest-john.

Hunt Jr., William. "Sitka National Historical Park: The Archeology of the Fort Unit." *Midwest Archeological Center: Occasional Studies*: 1-299 1, no. 35 (2010).

———. "Tlingit Archeology, Legends, and Oral History at Sitka National Historical Park." National Park Service, July 17, 2018. https://www.nps.gov/articles/aps-v10 -i1-c10.htm.

Irby, Nichols. "The Russian Ukase and the Monroe Doctrine: A Re-evaluation." *Pacific Historical Review* 36, no. 1 (February 1967): 13-26.

"James Hanna (trader)." Wikipedia. https://en.wikipedia.org/wiki/James_Hanna_(trader).

Joesting, Edward. *Kauai: The Separate Kingdom*. Honolulu: University of Hawaii Press, 1984.

Kan, Sergei. *Memory Eternal: Tlingit Culture and Orthodox Christianity through Two Centuries*. Seattle: University of Washington Press, 1999.

Kan, Sergei. "The 19th-Century Tlingit Potlatch: A New Perspective." *American Ethnologist* 13, no. 2 (May 1986): 191–212.

"Kashia Coastal Reserve." https://www.tpl.org/our-work/kashia-coastal-reserve.

Kaufman, Jason Edward. "Oh What Potlatch: Harriman Plunder Returned to Alaska after a Century." *Art Newspaper*, August 31, 2001.

Kiffer, Dave. "William Paul was the 'Father of Native Land Claims.'" *SitNews*, (Ketchikan, AK), February 16, 2009. http://www.sitnews.us/Kiffer/William LewisPaul/021609_william_paul.html.

Kiffer, Dave. "Navy Bombed Angoon 125 Years Ago." *SitNews*, (Ketchikan, AK), October 29, 2007. http://www.sitnews.us/Kiffer/Angoon/102907_angoon _bombed.html.

Knecht, Rick, Sven Haakanson, and Shawn Dickson. "Awa'uq: Discovery and Evacuation of an 18th Century Alutiiq Refuge Rock in the Kodiak Archipelago." *Ethnographical Series* 20 (January 2002): 177–91.

Krause, Aurel. *The Tlingit Indians: Observations of an Indigenous People of Southeast Alaska, 1881–1882*. Fairbanks, AK: Epicenter Press, 2013.

Krol, Debra Ustacia. "How this Tribe Got their Coastal California Lands Returned." *Yes!* (Spring 2018). https://www.yesmagazine.org/issue/decolonize/2018/04/02 /how-this-tribe-got-their-coastal-california-lands-returned

Landfield, Jeff, Paxson Woebler, and Lee Baxter, "Sah Quah." *Alaska Landmine*, August 8, 2022. https://alaskalandmine.com/landmines/sah-quah/.

de Laguna, Frederica. *Under Mount Saint Elias: The History and Culture of the Yakutat Tlingit*. Vol. 1. Washington, DC: Smithsonian Institution Press, 1972.

Lind, Natasha Okhotina. "The Archaeologists and Vitus Bering's Grave: A Study in Source Manipulation." *Historisk Tidsscrift* 118, no. 2 (2018): 297–328. https ://tidsskrift.dk/historisktidsskrift/article/view/115501.

Love, John. *Sea Otters*. Golden, CO: Fulcrum Publishing, 1992.

Massie, Robert K. *Peter the Great: His Life and World*. New York: Random House, 1980.

Matthews, Owen. *Glorious Misadventures: Nikolai Rezanov and the Dream of Russian America*. New York: Bloomsbury, 2013.

McMahan, David, and Daniel Thompson. "Final Report: American-Russian Investigation of the NEVA Wreck and Survivor Camp: Final Report: 200th Anniversary Expedition, Sitka, Alaska." National Science Foundation, January 24, 2020. http://mcmahanconsulting.com/assets/docs/NEVA-Final-Draft-2-3-20 -low-res.3395013.pdf.

McMahan, David, "200-Year-Old Russian Wreck Found on Kruzof Island Near Sitka." *Juneau Empire*, February 23, 2017.

Metcalfe, Peter. *A Dangerous Idea: The Alaskan Native Brotherhood and the Struggle for Indigenous Rights*. Fairbanks: University of Alaska Press, 2014.

Miller, Andrew. "Coming Together: Battle of 1804 Commemorated." *Sitka Daily Sentinel*, October 1, 2004.

Mills, Peter. *Hawaii's Russian Adventure: A New Look at Old History*. Honolulu: University of Hawaii Press, 2002.

Mitchell, Donald. "Predatory Warfare, Social Status, and the North Pacific Slave Trade." *Ethnology* 23, no. 1 (January 1984): 39–48.

Morison, Samuel. *The Maritime History of Massachusetts, 1783–1860*. Boston: Northeastern University Press, 1979. Reprint ed.

Morris, Pat. "Sacred Carving Returned to Tribe." Mail Archive, September 12, 1999. https://www.mail-archive.com/nativenews@mlists.net/msg04262.html.

Nakajima, Hiroo. "Monroe Doctrine and Russia." *Diplomatic History* 31, no. 3 (June 2007): 439-463.

Nichols, Robert, and Robert Croskey, trans. "The Conditions of the Orthodox Church in Russian America: Innokentii Veniaminov's History of the Orthodox Church in Russian Alaska." *Pacific Northwest Quarterly* 63, no. 2 (April 1972): 41-54.

"Northern Sea Otter." Marine Mammal Commission. https://www.mmc.gov/priority -topics/species-of-concern/northern-sea-otters/.

Norton, Louis Arthur. "The Pacific in the War of 1812: Pelts, Ploys, and Plunder." *Coriolus: Interdisciplinary Journal of Maritime Studies* 3, no. 1 (2012): 1-20.

Oberg, Kalervo. *The Social Economy of the Tlingit Indians*. Seattle: University of Washington Press, 1973.

O'Malley, Julia. "Cape Fox Artifacts Home at Last." *NewsSmith*, September 9, 2001. https://www.smith.edu/newssmith/NSFall01/artifacts.html.

Ostenstad, William. "The Impact of the Fur Trade on the Tlingit during the Late 18th and 19th Centuries." Master's thesis, University of Manitoba, 1976.

Oswalt, Robert. *Kashaya Texts*. Berkeley: University of California Press, 1964.

Owens, Kenneth. *Empire Maker: Alexander Baranov and Russian Colonial Expansion into Alaska and Northern California*. Seattle: University of Washington Press, 2015.

———. *The Wreck of the Sv. Nikolai*. Lincoln: University of Nebraska Press, 2001.

Pierce, Richard. "G. A. Schäffer: Russsia's Man in Hawaii." *Pacific History Journal* 32, no. 4 (1963): 397–405.

———. *Russia's Hawaiian Adventure, 1815–1817*. Berkeley: University of California Press, 1965.

Preston, Christopher. "The Far-Reaching Influence of Alaska's Sea Otters." BBC, March 1, 2023. https://www.bbc.com/future/article/20230228-how-alaskas-sea-otters-came-back.

Preucel, Robert. "Shotridge in Philadelphia." In *Sharing Our Knowledge: The Tlingit and Their Coastal Neighbors*, edited by Sergei Kan, 41–62. Lincoln: University of Nebraska Press, 2015.

Preucel, Robert, and Lucy F. Williams. "The Centennial Potlatch." *Expedition Magazine: Penn Museum* 47, no. 2 (2005): 10–15.

Pullar, Gordon, Richard Knecht, and Sven Haakanson. "Archaeology and the Sugpiaq Renaissance on Kodiak Island." *Études Inuit Studies* 37, no. 1 (2013): 79–94.

Ravalli, Richard. *Sea Otters: A History*. Lincoln: University of Nebraska Press, 2018.

Rogers, Jeffrey Lee. *Russian California: Hidden Stories from Fort Ross and Beyond*. San Francisco: California State Parks Foundation, 2012.

Rokfar, Teri. "Managing and Harvesting Mountain Goats for Traditional Purposes by Indigenous User Groups." *Biennial Symposium of the Northern Wild Sheep and Goat Council* 19 (2014): 37–41. http://media.nwsgc.org/proceedings/NWSGC-2014/037_Rofkar_2014.pdf.

Rosato Jr., Joe. "700 Acres of Sonoma County Land to be Returned to Native American Tribe." *NBC Bay Area*, October 20, 2015. https://www.nbcbayarea.com/news/local/700-acres-of-sonoma-county-to-be-returned- to-native-american-tribe/110702/.

Rose, Katherine. "Sitka's Baranov Statue Will Come Down but It's Not Going Far." KTOO News, July 16, 2020. https://www.ktoo.org/2020/07/16/sitkas-baranov-statue-will-come-down-but-its-not-going-far/.

Rose, Katherine, and Erin McKinstry. "Sitkans Gather to Demand Relocation of Controversial Baranov Statue." KTOO News, June 25, 2020. https://www.ktoo.org/2020/06/25/sitkans-gather-to-demand-the-relocation-of-controversial-baranov-statue/.

Rosen, Yereth. "Archaeologists Say They've Found the Campsite Used by Survivors of Legendary 'Doomed' Ship." *Anchorage Daily News*, March 4, 2017.

Ross, Ken. *Pioneering Conservation in Alaska*. Boulder: University of Colorado Press, 2006.

"Russian Doctor Presents Bust of Bering to Alaska." *Jerusalem Post*, August 24, 2010. https://www.jpost.com/Breaking-News/Russian-doctor-presents-bust-of-Bering-to-Alaska.

Saul, Norman. *Distant Friends: The United States and Russia, 1763–1867*. Lawrence: University of Kansas Press, 1991.

Schmidt-Chya, Dehrich. "When the Russians Arrived." In *Imaken Ima'ut—From the Future to the Present: Seventy-Five Hundred Years of Kodiak Alutiiq/Sugpiaq History*, 74–102. Kodiak, AK: Alutiiq Museum and Archaeological Repository.

"Sea Otters and Kelp Forests." Alaska Wildlife Alliance, October 23, 2018. https://www.akwildlife.org/animal-profiles/otters.

"Shelling of the Alaskan Native American Village of Angoon, October 1882." *USN: Naval History and Heritage Command*, October 30, 2017. https://media.defense.gov/2021/Dec/15/2002909572/-1/-1/0/1882_ANGOON_ATTACK_HEALY.PDF

Shorey, Tobin. "Brief History of the Vessel JUNO, 1799–1811." Alaska Historical Society, May 2015. https://alaskahistoricalsociety.org/a-brief-history-of-the-vessel-juno-1799-1811/.

Spencer-Hancock, Diane, and William Pritchard. "Notes on the 1817 Treaty between the Russian American Company and the Kashaya Pomo Indians." *California History* 59, no. 4 (1981): 306-313.

Thornton, Thomas. "Know Your Place: The Organization of Tlingit Geographic Knowledge." *Ethnology* 36, no. 4 (Autumn 1997): 290, 295–307.

Urban, Thomas, and Brinnen Carter. "Geophysical Survey Locates an Elusive Tlingit Fort in South-East Alaska." *Antiquity: A Review of World Archaeology* 95, no. 379 (2021): 1–8.

Vancouver, George. *A Voyage of Discovery of the North Pacific and Round the World*. London: G. G. and Robinson, 1798.

Watrous, Stephen. "Ivan Kuskov and the Founding of Fort Ross." Fort Ross Conservancy. https://www.fortross.org/lib/40/ivan-kuskov-and-the-founding-of-fort-ross.pdf.

Williams, Lucy Fowler. "Louis Shotridge, Preserver of Tlingit History and Culture." In *Sharing Our Knowledge: The Tlingit and their Coastal Neighbors*, edited by Sergei Kan, 63–78. Lincoln: University of Nebraska Press, 2015.

Index

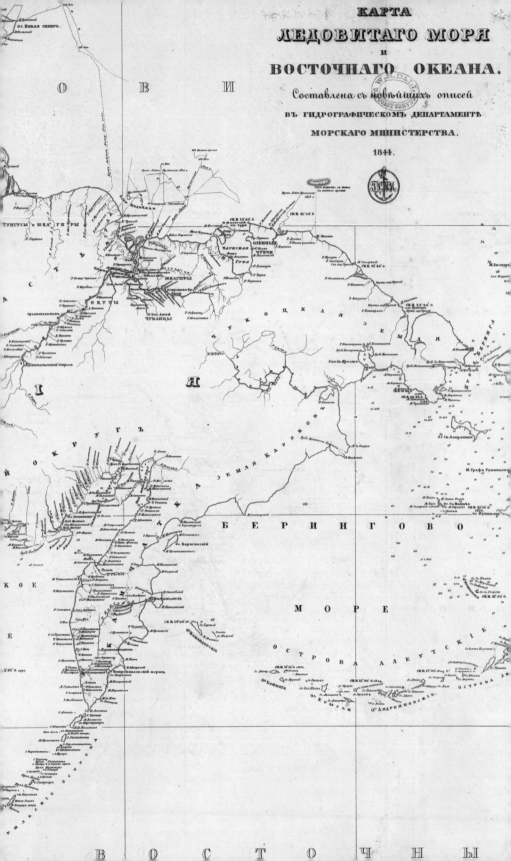